# A BRIDGE ACROSS THE OCEAN

LUCA
CASTAGNA

# A BRIDGE ACROSS THE OCEAN

THE UNITED STATES AND
THE HOLY SEE BETWEEN THE
TWO WORLD WARS

FOREWORD BY
GERALD P. FOGARTY, SJ

AFTERWORD BY
LUIGI ROSSI

The Catholic University of America Press
Washington, D.C.

Originally published in Italian as *Un ponte oltre l'oceano:*
*Assetti politici e strategie diplomatiche tra Stati Uniti e Santa*
*Sede nella prima metà del Novecento (1914–1940)*
© Società editrice il Mulino, Bologna, 2011.
Copyright © 2014
The Catholic University of America Press
All rights reserved
The paper used in this publication meets the minimum requirements of American National Standards for Information Science—Permanence of Paper for Printed Library Materials,
ANSI Z39.48-1984.

Library of Congress Cataloging-in-Publication Data
Castagna, Luca.
[Ponte oltre l'oceano. English]
A bridge across the ocean : the United States and the Holy See between the two World Wars / Luca Castagna.
pages cm
Includes bibliographical references and index.
ISBN 978-0-8132-2587-6 (cloth)
1. United States—Foreign relations—Catholic Church.
2. Catholic Church—Foreign relations—United States.
3. United States—Foreign relations—20th century.   I. Title.
BX1406.3.C37713 2014
327.456'3407309042—dc23      2014005420

To my wife, Rossella

CONTENTS

Foreword by Gerald P. Fogarty, SJ   ix

Preface   xiii

Abbreviations   xvii

1 Divergent Powers   1

2 Incompatible Universalisms   30

3 Troubled Times   59

4 The Interlocutory Stage   85

5 Toward Rapprochement: The 1930s   113

6 A Shared Mission   150

Afterword by Luigi Rossi   167

Bibliography and Sources   171

Index of Names   187

# FOREWORD

Luca Castagna has made a significant contribution to the history of Vatican diplomacy and, in particular, to the history of the Holy See's relations with the United States. He has skillfully navigated the often tortuous paths of the relations between American Catholics and their fellow citizens and between the American Church, American society, and the Vatican. At the beginning of the twentieth century, the American Church was under suspicion in Rome. In January 1899 Leo XIII had condemned "religious Americanism," a movement more French than American, that sprang from the French translation of the biography of Father Isaac Hecker, founder of the Paulists, a society of priests who sought to reach out to Protestant America. But Hecker was not a theologian, and some of his writings were easily misinterpreted. He emphasized human activity, for example, and praised "natural virtues." To the pope, this implied semi-Pelagianism. Hecker also noted the necessity of adapting instruction for conversion of people of different Christian backgrounds; for example, Anglicans were very different from Baptists. For the pope, this implied watering down doctrine to gain converts and recognizing that at least partial Christian truth existed outside the Catholic Church. Obstructing a positive evaluation of American Catholicism in 1899 was the U.S. victory over Spain in August 1898. The religiously pluralistic republic across the Atlantic was emerging as a world power. By 1919, the United States was the key power in ending World War I, and Vatican officials expressed their alarm.

Castagna has painted a vivid portrait of all these movements as he traces the "thawing" of the relations between Washington and the Vatican from World War I to the opening days of World War II. Archbishop Giovanni Bonzano, the apostolic delegate to the United States hierarchy, sought both to have Cardinal James Gibbons, archbishop of Baltimore, intervene with Democratic president Woodrow Wilson about Pope Benedict XV's peace initiatives and to develop his own contacts with the Catholic press to promote American neutrality. Gibbons, however, had failed to prevent Wilson from recognizing either of the warring parties in Mexico and feared lowering the prestige of the Church in an effort to convince the president to maintain neutrality in the war. Bonzano was critical of the cardinal's fears, but probably failed to understand that Wilson, former president of Princeton University and governor of New Jersey, was anti-Catholic and hostile toward "hyphenated Americans." The president was therefore all too ready to believe what the Italian ambassador to the United States, acting on behalf of the Italian foreign minister, said about why the pope was excluded from participation in any future peace conference by a clause in the Treaty of London in 1915. The Italians feared the pope would place the Roman question on the agenda, an issue that was hardly on the American radar scope.[1]

Versailles was Wilson's big moment, and he even condescended to work in a visit to the pope, but his—and the United States' triumph was short lived. The U.S. Senate refused to approve a treaty by which the United States would join the League of Nations, and the government moved more and more toward isolationism. After a long illness, Wilson died shortly after leaving office. From 1922 to 1932, the presidency was under Republican Party control. At the same time, there was an increase in anti-Catholicism in the form of the second Ku Klux Klan, formed in 1915, to oppose blacks, Catholics, and Jews. Although the Klan's power began to dissipate by the end of the twenties, the mentality of keeping the United States free from foreign influence, such as that of the pope, played a major role in the defeat of Democrat Alfred E. Smith, governor of New York, and the first Catholic to run for president. Herbert Hoover, the Republican victor, had repudiated religious bigotry during the campaign, but Archbishop Pietro Fumasoni-Biondi, the apostolic delegate, reported to the Vatican that Republican officials distributed anti-Catholic literature. The delegate advised Pius XI to await Hoover's inauguration in March before congratulating him on his election—early in 1933, the Twentieth Amendment to the U.S. Constitution moved the date of the

---

1. "Italy, conventionally called 'Liberal Italy' from 1861 to 1922, insisted Rome's status had been settled after the conquest of 1870. The prisoner popes, however, never acquiesced to the loss of temporal power. Christ's Vicar broadcast dramatic lamentations about this 'Roman question,' the abnormal status of the pope as a prisoner of Liberal Italy without a temporal sovereignty to guarantee his spiritual autonomy"; see Peter D'Agostino, *Rome in America: Transnational Catholic Ideology from the Risorgimento to Facism* (Chapel Hill: University of North Carolina Press, 2004), 1.

presidential inauguration to January 20. Chafing from Smith's defeat, Catholics clearly felt like second-class citizens.

In the meantime, the Church in the world and in the United States was undergoing dramatic change. In 1929 Cardinal Pietro Gasparri and Mussolini signed the Lateran Pacts, ending the Roman question and establishing the Vatican City State to guarantee papal freedom from Italian state interference. The pacts themselves drew little attention in the United States, except to arouse some anti-Catholicism now that the pope had temporal authority. But the changes ushered in by the end of the Roman question would have profound repercussions for the American Church and nation. With the treaties signed, Gasparri resigned his office and was replaced by Eugenio Pacelli, former nuncio to Bavaria and then to the Weimar Republic. Pacelli found already employed in the secretary of state a monsignor from Boston, Francis Spellman. In the fall of 1932 Spellman became the auxiliary bishop of Boston, whose ordinary, Cardinal William O'Connell, intensely disliked his subordinate. But Spellman was entrusted with the task of making contact with whoever won the presidential election of 1932. The election of Franklin D. Roosevelt signaled a new turn in relations between the White House and Catholics in general, including the Holy See.

By the election of 1932, the world was almost four years into the Great Depression. In 1931 Pius XI issued *Quadragesimo Anno,* an encyclical recommending government action to end the crisis. During his campaign, Roosevelt quoted the encyclical. As Castagna ably narrates, leaders of Catholic social justice, under the umbrella of the National Catholic Welfare Conference, the organization of bishops formed after World War I to coordinate Catholic efforts on a national basis, soon embraced Roosevelt's New Deal. There were, of course, dissenters like the "Radio Priest" Charles Coughlin, who from his Detroit suburban parish accused Roosevelt of moving toward socialism. But the contrast with previous administrations was palpable. Archbishop Amleto Cicognani, appointed apostolic delegate in 1933, described for Pacelli his warm reception by Roosevelt in the White House. Shortly thereafter, Roosevelt received an honorary doctorate from the Catholic University of America. Even the president's decision to establish diplomatic relations with the Soviet Union did not endanger the warm relations—in fact on this issue the Holy See proved to be more open than the American bishops. But the highlight of the relations between Washington and the Vatican occurred in November 1936. In October, Pacelli became the highest ranking Catholic prelate to visit the United States. On a chartered plane, he flew across the country to California. Then, immediately after Roosevelt's election to a second term, Pacelli received an invitation to join the president for lunch at Roosevelt's mother's house, Hyde Park, north of New York City. The meeting had been arranged through Spellman with the aid of Joseph Kennedy, a prominent businessman, later ambassador to the United Kingdom, and father of President John F. Kennedy. From external evidence, the president and cardinal discussed some form of diplomatic relations.

Pacelli was ecstatic about his visit to the United States. Yet all was not well in Europe. In January 1937 he met with a group of prominent German bishops and drafted an encyclical against National Socialism, *Mit brennender Sorge,* issued by Pius XI in March. Despite the Holy See's reservations about the United States in 1899, the far-away republic was one of the few places where the Church was flourishing. Pacelli soon had occasion to express his affection for the United States. In February 1939 Pius XI died. A few weeks later, Pacelli was elected to succeed him and took the name Pius XII. In the audience for the coronation were Joseph Kennedy and his family, including the future president. It was the first time the United States sent a representation for a papal coronation. In April 1939 the new pope appointed Spellman archbishop of New York. Within a year, Spellman had worked out a compromise on diplomatic relations with Roosevelt. Since congress was still hostile toward such relations, Roosevelt agreed to appoint a "personal representative" to the pope. Although there were still protests, his appointment of Myron C. Taylor, an executive of the U.S. Steel Corporation and an Episcopalian, helped mitigate the opposition. The establishment of full diplomatic relations between the Holy See and the United States would have to wait until 1984. But the period Castagna covers amply traces the "thaw" between the two entities.

Castagna's work is richly documented not only from the Vatican but also the U.S. and Italian government archives. He has enhanced these sources with newspapers and journals in both the United States and Italy. His bibliography of published secondary literature is exhaustive, and his book must now be added to that list.

Gerald P. Fogarty, SJ<br>
University of Virginia

## PREFACE

From 1937 President Franklin Delano Roosevelt intensified his efforts to overcome the resistance of the most hard-headed isolationists in the Congress. He proceeded with the caution of one who was wholly aware of the reactions of American public opinion to a decision as unpopular as entry into a new war alongside the unstable European countries, but also with the firmness and charisma that had always distinguished him. And so it was that he was able to escape from the quicksands of appeasement and put the huge military, economic, technological, and diplomatic potential of America at the service of democracy and anti-Nazism. It was of course a slow and gradual, though unremitting, process, moved by the conviction that passive acceptance of the war, and its aftermath, into which the Old Continent had plummeted once again, would have notable repercussions on U.S. security and that, in order to prevent the victory of the totalitarian powers, they would again have to take on the responsibility of the civilizing mission they had too hurriedly abandoned after Versailles.

From the progressive revision of neutralist legislation to the adoption of a plan of rearmament and military and economic support first to Great Britain, then to the Soviet Union, the American buildup to the war called for decisions that were at times courageous and revolutionary. Among these, the decision to reestablish diplomatic contact with the Holy See must certainly be included. It was made official on December 23, 1939, in Roosevelt's Christmas message to Pius XII, who had become pope only a few months earlier.

As Gaetano Salvemini commented, "it was impossible not to admire President Roosevelt's wisdom in nominating Taylor, which enabled him to kill several birds with one stone"; in fact, he "had chosen the right time and manner to carry out his plan, pleasing both the Pope and Mussolini, and causing only slight upset to American public opinion."[1] Though

---

1. Gaetano Salvemini, *L'Italia vista dall'America* (Milan: Feltrinelli, 1969), 262.

Roosevelt was praised by the Catholic Church authorities and, early on at least, unopposed by the Italian government, the sending of Myron Charles Taylor to the Vatican as his personal representative—with the rank though not the name of ambassador—and his activity assisted by the secretary to the American embassy Harold H. Tittmann, caused no slight protest on the part of certain representatives of several Protestant sects, private American citizens, and even the Fascist authorities.

Any relationship with the pope was considered taboo which, especially since the closing down of the American mission in the Papal States in 1867, had never failed to rekindle demonstrations against Catholicism and the pope, almost always involving all levels of American society, causing an unavoidable reduction of diplomatic contact between the end of the nineteenth century and the early decades of the following century.

The conservative involution that characterized the second half of Pius IX's pontificate, combined with his refusal to accept Italian unity, provided the U.S. Senate with a pretext to interrupt the dialogue with the Vatican, considered by many in the United States to be the anachronistic symbol of obscurantism and the ancien régime. The "Vatican Question," for the most part ignored by successive Republican and Democratic administrations, came to the fore again in all its complexity during the First World War. This complexity was due, first to the imperfect relations between the Roman curia and the American Catholic Church, who had found the Vatican's accusations of heterodoxy hard to swallow; but above all to the attitude of Woodrow Wilson, whose prejudice against Catholicism, an organic part of the ideology of the WASP (white, Anglo-Saxon, Protestant) tradition, expressed itself in a systematic refusal to comply with Benedict XV's peace initiatives and efforts at collaboration. Ignoring the possible similarities between the pope's "Note" to the heads of peoples at war and Wilson's own Fourteen Points was a clear affirmation of the basic incompatibility between Wilson's plan to rebuild the international system and that of the pope, whose objectives were in fact just as unrealistic.

The sudden wave of nationalism that characterized American society in the decade following the Great War and which saw in the fresh outbreak of anti-Catholic nativism one of the most violent and politically widespread manifestations, contributed to the rejection of any prospect of approaching the Holy See. Immersed in the problem of conversion and therefore in the so-called postwar normalcy, all three Republican administrations of the twenties basically showed that they were unwilling to deal with such an issue; neither, on the other hand, did Pope Ratti seem to have any particular intention to mobilize Vatican diplomacy and the American ecclesiastical hierarchy to this end, and he chose to follow the "concordatarian" policy that, among other things, led to the much-wished-for reconciliation with the Kingdom of Italy in 1929.

A radical change in Washington's relations with the Vatican had to await the arrival of Franklin Delano Roosevelt. Or rather, it was the convergence of the inspiring aims of the New Deal and the Catholic Church's social doctrine, as well as the readiness with which the president and certain prominent new leaders of the American Church set up a relationship of mutual collaboration that laid the foundations, first for the rehabilitation of Catholicism in the national sociopolitical context, and later for the lifting of a long diplomatic blackout. What speeded up the thaw between the two greatest "moral forces" of the world was the undoubted contribution of Nazi-Fascist escalation and the increasing, unrelenting hardening of Pius XI's and Roosevelt's attitude to the German and Italian regimes. This did not come to a head until the end of 1939, when the war had already begun to sow death and destruction, after a long pause, beginning with Cardinal Eugenio Pacelli's visit to the United States (October–November 1936) and followed, in sudden bursts and just as sudden slowdowns for three years, which were the most convulsive and dramatic of twentieth-century history.

Since there is no comprehensive study of the subject, this book attempts a reconstruction of relations between the United States of America and the Vatican in the twenty years between the wars, and describes the main events of the period up to the outbreak of the Second World War, contextualizing the development of events within the disturbing international scenario of the twenties and thirties. It aims to show that the temporary rapprochement of late 1939, largely facilitated by overcoming the political and cultural barriers that had prevented the complete integration of Catholicism into American society and, as a result, had helped to increase the unending resistance to accepting the Vatican as an interlocutor on the same level as other international actors, had an essentially pragmatic connotation with the objective of curbing the development of Nazi-Fascism.

With this aim in mind, and starting from the methodological and interpretive orientations suggested by the existing literature, the book uses a combination of primary sources of diverse provenance, mostly used for the first time, found in the Vatican Secret Archives, in the Franklin Delano Roosevelt Presidential Library, the U.S. National Archives, the Archives of the Italian Ministry of Foreign Affairs, and the Alderman Library of the University of Virginia.

Finally, I wish to express the great debt I owe to those who have contributed to the preparation and writing of this book. Deeply felt thanks go to Luigi Rossi, my irreplaceable teacher and guide, who has so patiently followed every step of my research and given me so much advice and precise methodological suggestions. Alfonso Conte has never failed to give me affectionate words of encouragement. Roberto Parrella and Carmine Pinto have made valuable comments, while Gerald P. Fogarty's seminars during my weeks at the University of Virginia pointed to aspects and problems that encouraged further investigation. Roy Boardman is the invaluable and untiring translator of the English edition of this book. Thanks are also due to the staff of the archives and libraries I have consulted. I have had the benefit of the courtesy and professional skills of Jane Stoeffler, Maria Mazzenga, and John Shepherd of the American Catholic History Research Center of the Catholic University of America, and Bob Clark of the Franklin Delano Roosevelt Presidential Library. More than a simple thank you goes to my parents and my brother. This book is dedicated to my wife, Rossella.

Luca Castagna<br>
University of Salerno<br>
March 2014

# ABBREVIATIONS

| | |
|---|---|
| a. | *anno* |
| ACUA | Archives of the Catholic University of America |
| ACV | Archivio della Congregazione per i Vescovi |
| ADSS | *Actes et documents du Saint-Siège relatifs à la Seconde Guerre mondiale* |
| AES | *Affari Ecclesiastici Straordinari* |
| ANCWC | Archives of the National Catholic Welfare Conference |
| AP1 | *Affari Politici, 1919–1930* |
| AP2 | *Affari Politici, 1931–1945* |
| APOG | Archivio Politico Ordinario e di Gabinetto |
| ASMAE | Archivio Storico Diplomatico del Ministero degli Affari Esteri |
| ASV | Archivio Segreto Vaticano |
| b. | *busta* |
| CI-E | *Conflitto Italo-Etiopico* |
| DASU | Delegazione Apostolica degli Stati Uniti d'America |
| DC | Diplomatic Correspondence |
| doc. | document |
| DS | Department of State |
| f. | *foglio* |
| FDRPL | Franklin Delano Roosevelt Presidential Library |
| fold. | folder |
| FRUS | *Papers Relating to the Foreign Relations of the United States* |

# ABBREVIATIONS

| | |
|---|---|
| LP | Lansing Papers |
| NARA | National Archives and Records Administration |
| OF | Official Files |
| OGS | Office of the General Secretary |
| pos. | position |
| PPF | President's Personal Files |
| prot. | protocol |
| PSF | President's Secretary's Files |
| r. | recto |
| rep. | report |
| RG 59 | Record Group 59 |
| RP | John A. Ryan Papers |
| SE | Stati Ecclesiastici |
| SS | Segreteria di Stato |
| Sub. | Subseries |
| v. | verso |

# A BRIDGE ACROSS THE OCEAN

# 1

# DIVERGENT POWERS

### POLITICAL AND DIPLOMATIC BACKGROUND

Congress will probably never send a minister to his Holiness, who can do them no service, upon condition of receiving a Catholic legate or nuncio in return; or, in other words, an ecclesiastical tyrant, which, it is to be hoped, the United States will be too wise ever to admit in their territories.[1]

These were the words of John Adams writing on August 4, 1779, to the Continental Congress in Philadelphia. Free of all protocol formality, they did not derive from diplomatic clashes or impoliteness between the Union and the Papal States; rather they reflected and in some ways consecrated a culture impregnated with antipapism that was already deeply rooted in North America before the birth of the United States.

In the opinion of the "Founding Fathers," the great democracy that was about to see the light on the other side of the Atlantic should not for any reason at all have a connection with the Apostolic See, which "stank of outdated authoritarianism and obscurantism."[2] Hence the assertions of Adams, which were destined to become a pillar of United States antipapism, reflecting as they did the spirit of freedom and Puritan aversion to Catholicism. In essence, they laid

---

1. Charles F. Adams, *The Works of John Adams, Second President of the United States* (Charleston, S.C.: Bibliolife, 2008), 7.109–10.
2. Massimo Franco, *Imperi Paralleli: Vaticano e Stati Uniti: Due secoli di alleanza e conflitto 1788–2005* (Milan: Mondadori, 2005), 20.

the foundations of what would become the later relations between Washington and the Vatican: relations that for almost two centuries had been marked by incomprehension and at times by outright hostility, during which the attitude expressed by Adams at the end of the eighteenth century continued to make itself felt.

When in 1788 Pius VI sent emissaries to Paris to negotiate with the ambassador of the newborn republic of North America, Benjamin Franklin, on the possibility of nominating a bishop of the new state, President Washington's response was that the American Revolution, among other things, had brought with it freedom of religious expression and that for this very reason the pope would not find any veto on the part of the government. And so John Carroll was nominated to be the first Catholic bishop of America.[3] The see chosen was Baltimore, the only city where there existed a numerous, compact Catholic community that promised to become an ideal place from which Catholicism would expand into other areas of the Union. The "lay" *nulla osta* which led to the institution of the first diocese was, in any case—at least in intention—a simple and innocuous gesture of goodwill toward the Vatican; it was not a sign that the U.S. establishment intended to give formal recognition to the Holy See, nor was it a demonstration of any particular interest in attributing some kind of diplomatic status to papal representatives.

And yet, toward the end of the eighteenth century, significant progress was made in that direction. The tendency of the first federal governments to safeguard the commercial interests of the United States, in fact, encouraged compliance with the requests for more-or-less institutionalized contact put forward by the Holy See. This was, paradoxically, why John Adams, who a few years before had been a hardened opponent of setting up relations with the Roman "tyrant," in 1797 sent to the Vatican the first consular representative, Giovanni Sartori, one of the eleven consuls called to represent the interests of the United States to the Holy See until 1867, three years

---

3. See Milton Lomask, *John Carroll, Bishop and Patriot*, 4th ed. (New York: Vision Books, 1962).

before the fall of the Papal States.[4] Although they were not ambassadors, the papal government granted them unusual privileges and favors, including that of being admitted to all formal ceremonies on the same terms as the diplomats representing other countries.[5] In this way, the papal court attempted to take further steps toward full recognition and it was for this reason that in 1826 a consul, Count Ferdinando Lucchesi Palli di Campofranco, was sent to New York together with as many as twenty-one vice-consuls.

The responsibilities of the consular office in Rome were not confined to overseeing trade and the safety of United States citizens abroad; its real objective was to monitor, from an ideal position, the signs of revolution that were spreading throughout Europe in the nineteenth century. As can be seen from a report sent by Sartori's successor, Felix Cicognani, to Washington in 1831, which refers to the presence of Austrian troops in the Papal States and to Gregory XVI's plan to flee to Spain, Rome was an invaluable center for gathering information; and the legation to the Supreme Pontiff guaranteed a "listening point," not only into the Holy See, but into the whole of the Old Continent, becoming a kind of diplomatic "crossroads" where strategies and trends of most of the European chanceries met and were discussed.[6]

The initial liberal character that Pius IX gave to his papacy was greeted with great enthusiasm in the United States; in spite of the fact that a radical antipapal attitude persisted in Protestant public

---

4. The American consuls to the Papal States were, in order of succession: Giovanni Sartori, Felix Cicognani, George W. Greene, Nicholas Brown, William C. Sanders, Daniel LeRoy, Horatio de V. Glentworth, William Dean Howells (accepted but did not take up the post), W. J. Stillman, Edwin C. Cushman, and David Armstrong, the first to serve in the Kingdom of Italy. See Francis L. Stock, "The United States at the Court of Pius IX," *Catholic Historical Review* 7 (1923): 103.

5. This was reported on February 20, 1838, by one of the United States consuls in Rome, Green, to U.S. Secretary of State John Forsyth. Quoted in Francis L. Stock, *Consular Relations between the United States and the Papal States: Instructions and Dispatches*, (Washington, D.C.: American Catholic Historical Association, 1945), 2.60.

6. Felix Cicognani to Martin Van Buren, Rome, February 21, 1831, quoted in Stock, *Consular Relations*, 33.

opinion, the figure of Giovanni Maria Mastai Ferretti seemed, in fact, to break away from the conservatism of previous popes and induced the United States to take more seriously the possibility of creating a closer relationship with the Holy See.

About one year after his election on June 1, 1847, Pius IX had expressed to the U.S. consul Nicolas Brown a desire to establish diplomatic relations between the two governments. The message was referred by Secretary of State James Buchanan to President Polk who, in a brief part of his speech to Congress in December 1847, was favorable to such a hypothesis.[7] This resulted in the status of the United States official being raised from that of consul to that of chargé d'affaires, a wise step forward which, though on the one hand clearly showed the Polk administration's openness to the "Vatican question," on the other ended up by igniting a heated debate in political circles. On March 21, 1848, in fact, the U.S. Senate discussed a proposal to include in the federal budget funds to finance the new appointee by the president to the papal court: this was the secretary of the U.S. Legation to Paris, Jacob L. Martin. There were basically two arguments in favor of raising the level of the mission in Rome. Underlining the fact that the pope gave his support to European insurrections, Senator Lewis Cass even expressed himself in favor of sending an ambassador. "He has given the first blow to despotism and taken the first step towards freedom," said Cass of the work of Pius IX; it was certainly true that "European diplomacy will have plenty to do at his Court and his most able representatives will be there," and he concluded by advising that "our government too should be represented."[8]

The other main argument in favor of the initiation of formal relations, put forward by Senator John Dix of New York, concerned the question of commercial benefits. Many politicians, including those who agreed with the administration on the setting up of a post, held

---

7. See James F. Connelly, *The Visit of Archbishop Gaetano Bedin to the United States, June 1853–February 1854* (Rome: Pontificia Università Gregoriana Editrice, 1960), 77–78.

8. Cass's contribution to the debate is reported by Jim Nicholson, *USA e Santa Sede: La lunga strada*, 2nd ed. (Rome: Trenta Giorni Edizioni, 2004), 17.

that the Papal States were of no interest at all from the business point of view. Dix, however, showed his belief in the new approach of Pius IX by declaring that he knew of "no State of the same size as that of the Papal States that could hope in greater prosperity."[9]

Surprisingly, matters of a religious nature played a totally marginal role in the discussion of 1848. In response to those who, like Senator Andrew Butler, maintained that the mission assigned to Martin would end up by favoring the Catholic Church in the United States, Lewis Cass underlined the fact that Washington was sending its representative to the pope as sovereign and that this had nothing to do with his role as head of the Roman Catholic Church. This was a fundamental distinction designed to nip in the bud the reactions of the diffident and hostile Protestant public; not only Martin, but all his successors, received from the Department of State the exhortation always to keep in mind, in all circumstances, that this must be made clear to the papal government in order to avoid any misunderstanding. The emissaries of the federal government also should not interfere in any way with ecclesiastical matters, even if they were in some way connected with the United States.[10]

When in January 1849 Lewis Cass Jr. succeeded Jacob Martin, the political scenario in Rome and the whole of Italy was profoundly changed. The stirrings of insurrection that had begun the previous year, in fact, spread rapidly and involved the capital of the Papal States. The republican revolutionaries compelled Pius IX to leave the capital and take refuge in Gaeta, where he was at the time of Lewis Cass Jr.'s arrival. The pope had been thought of as a reformer in the United States, but this belief was fading, giving way to the reappearance of skepticism and the old prejudices that had been only partly removed during those months of slight easing of tension. Pius IX's firm opposition to the Roman Republic—to whose leaders the American experience of freedom and independence constituted

---

9. Ibid., 18.
10. See Carlo De Lucia, "Si svolse in italiano il primo colloquio tra un Papa e un diplomatico americano," *L'Osservatore Romano,* April 9–10, 1984, p. 6.

an admirable exemplary "lesson" of democratic heroism[11]—was confirmation of how the pope's early liberal leanings were illusory. The U.S. government, in fact, was loath to offer collaboration to one who defended his throne against the revolution, while assuming an attitude of complete neutrality.[12]

Archbishop Gaetano Bedini's visit to the United States confirmed that mutual understanding was only in its early stages and that the revolutionary events of the mid-nineteenth century had been a tough testing ground for the uncertain equilibrium achieved by sending Martin to Rome. Charged in 1853 by Pius IX to verify the state of the process of evangelization in North America, the prelate was met by hostility. Apart from anything else, his life story seemed tailored to provoke antipapist hatred. Having escaped from Rome after the proclamation of the Republic, Bedini had been one of the protagonists of the negotiations with the Austrian authorities to put down the insurrection and reestablish the temporal power of the pope. The *New York Observer* went as far as to portray him as a "bloody butcher," and the pontifical diplomat was the object of vehement contestation by Italian refugees and the Protestant press. His arrival in Cincinnati, a stronghold of the American German community, was greeted by public burnings of the effigy of the pope and by an intense newspaper campaign announcing an imminent papist conspiracy to demolish the foundations of republican freedom.

11. For a more detailed account, see Giovanna Angelini, Arturo Colombo, and V. Paolo Gastaldi, *La galassia repubblicana: Voci di minoranza nel pensiero politico italiano* (Milan: Franco Angeli, 1998), 103–18; Maurizio Ridolfi, "La Démocratie en Amérique di Tocqueville e la sua ricezione nell'Italia del Risorgimento," in *Gli Stati Uniti e l'Unità d'Italia*, ed. Daniele Fiorentino and Matteo Sanfilippo (Rome: Gangemi, 2004), 138–39. More specifically, on South Italy, see Luca Castagna, "Il modello statunitense nel dibattito tra i democratici meridionali: Il caso de Il Popolo d'Italia, 1864–65," *Nuova Antologia* 2262 (2012): 306–23.

12. See Daniele Fiorentino, "Il governo degli Stati Uniti e la Repubblica romana del 1849," in *Gli Americani e la Repubblica romana del 1849*, ed. Sara Antonelli and Giuseppe Monsagrati (Rome: Gangemi, 2000), 89–130. For a comparison between the attitudes of Washington and London to the Holy See during the period 1848–49, see Giuseppe Monsagrati, "Alle prese con la democrazia, Gran Bretagna e U.S.A. di fronte alla Repubblica romana," *Rassegna Storica del Risorgimento* 86 (1999): 287–306.

His presence therefore became an embarrassment to government authorities. While, on the one hand, the Pierce administration had no intention of losing the opportunities that the pontifical presence gave them in trade and a way of keeping updated on European revolutions, on the other hand account had to be taken of the threatening reactions and resistance that relations with the Church of Rome provoked in public opinion. This is why Bedini was considered a "distinguished visitor": an important guest, but with no particular immunity; above all, this was intended as a clear message to Pius IX that the time for diplomatic relations was not yet ripe.[13]

In spite of the fact that, in 1854, Congress had raised the rank of the Rome representative to that of resident minister, the U.S. mission seemed less and less inviting and prestigious. Unused to the meticulous and at times stifling Vatican protocol, on arrival from Washington the American diplomats had to be submitted to thorough checks of their administration and were concerned about the way in which any open approach to the pope might reflect on internal reactions. Furthermore, the compensation was considered too low given the fact that the federal government was unable to justify high remuneration for a mission said to be "illegitimate" by the greater part of the population. Consequently, all four resident ministers in Rome from 1858 to 1863 resigned almost immediately after nomination.[14]

The fifth and last U.S. representative to the Papal States was Rufus King, an eminent exponent of the Republican Party and editor from Milwaukee. His mission lasted about three years, from 1863 to 1867, a period that was thick with problems in the United States due to the Civil War, and also for the Vatican, which was dealing with

13. Bedini's visit is reconstructed in detail by Connelly, *The Visit of Archbishop Bedini*, 78.

14. John Stockton was nominated resident minister in June 1858 and remained in Rome until March 1861; Rufus King, who succeeded him, turned down the office and was replaced by Alexander W. Randall, who served from August 1861 to the following August; Richard M. Blatchford was in the post from August 1862 to May 1863, leaving it to Rufus King until the summer of 1867 when the mission was terminated. See. U.S. Department of State, *Principal Officers of the Department of State and United States Chiefs of Mission, 1778–1986* (Washington, D.C.: U.S. Government Printing Office, 1986), 58.

growing opposition to the temporal power of the pope on the part of the liberal elites of the newly born Kingdom of Italy. Given such a delicate situation, the imperceptible steps forward being made earlier were more or less thwarted.

The post–Civil War period marked the historical watershed in relations between Washington and the Holy See. The papal court, already accused of having supported the Confederate cause, attracted even more hatred from abolitionist Protestant public opinion for having enlisted into the pontifical army, as a zouave soldier, John Surratt, a U.S. citizen accused, together with John Wilkes Booth and others, of the assassination of President Lincoln. To demonstrate goodwill, the Vatican retained Surratt until he could be handed over to the U.S. authorities. Although there was no extradition treaty between the two countries, King wrote to Secretary of State Seward that the sudden capture had been made "with the single purpose of showing the ready disposition of the Papal authorities to comply with the anticipated request of the American government."[15] The attitude of the Papal States fully reflected the friendly relationship laboriously built up over those years between U.S. representatives and the Holy See and, furthermore, made it clear that the pontiff intended to maintain good relationships with Washington. Pius IX, however, had inherited the consequences of Vatican politics during the years of the Civil War. Also, the United States began to be convinced that, after the proclamation of the Kingdom of Italy, the end of the papacy was near.[16]

Between the end of 1866 and the beginning of the next year, there were rumors of an imminent suspension of relations with the Papal States, which had become a troublesome ally both internally and internationally. The pretext to proceed to the effective closure of the mission to Rome was a rumor relating to the presumed "ex-

15. Rufus King to William Seward, Rome, March 1, 1867, FRUS, DC, 1867, Part 1: 704.
16. On the Surratt issue, see Alessandro Mancini Barbieri, "Nuove ricerche sulla presenza straniera nell'esercito pontificio, 1850–1870," *Rassegna Storica del Risorgimento* 63 (1986): 161–86.

pulsion" of the American Protestant Church from the Vatican. Ever since the institution of the first legation to Rome, the pontifical authorities had permitted the celebration of Protestant religious services, first at the home of the American representative and then, as the congregation grew in number, at an apartment provided by the U.S. government. As was reported in the *New York Times*, the Roman curia had decided to break that tacit compromise and not to block the ceremonies.[17] The episode, skillfully set up by those who wished to break off relations with the pope, ended up by accelerating the decision of Congress, and on February 28, 1867, they stated "that no money hereby or otherwise appropriated shall be paid for the support of an American legation at Rome, from and after the thirtieth day of June." Cutting the funding of the pontifical mission did not formally interrupt diplomatic relations, but prevented the concrete possibility of developing them.[18] Rufus King received the communication as late as March 11.[19] Even after this date, the diplomat was given no indication of how to justify his imminent departure from the Vatican. On April 20, William Seward simply wrote: "You will be at liberty to consult your own feelings and interest, either to remain at Rome without compensation or provisions for your expenses, or to resign, or to leave Rome without resigning."[20] Wrong-footed by his government's decision, King left the Pontifical State, repeating what he had asserted the previous February: that is, his conviction that "the United States has no need to resort to subterfuge," so "there can be no necessity of founding upon a false pretext."[21] Admonishing his administration for not dealing with the situation with due clarity, he was of the opinion that the closure of the mission in Rome would turn out to be counterproductive in such complex international cir-

---

17. On this issue, see Rufus King to William Seward, Rome, February 18, 1867, FRUS, DC, 1867, Part 1: 700–703.

18. See Ennio Di Nolfo, *Vaticano e Stati Uniti 1939–1952: Dalle carte di Myron C. Taylor* (Milan: Franco Angeli, 1978), 20.

19. William Seward to Rufus King, Washington, D.C., March 11, 1867, FRUS, DC, 1867, Part 1: 706.

20. William Seward to Rufus King, Washington, D.C., April 20, 1867, ibid.

21. Rufus King to William Seward, Rome, May 7, 1867, ibid.

cumstances because it would deprive Washington of that window on European affairs that had until then been looked on favorably in spite of the deep anti-Catholic feelings among the American people.

As brutal in its timing as it was lacking in formality, the Senate's action deeply offended Pius IX.[22] The progressive fall in trade with Lazio, which in 1867 was the only part of the Italian peninsula still in the hands of the pontiff, and the matters concerning the presumed prohibition of Protestant practices in the Vatican, were undoubtedly only a pretext to bring about the results desired by those who attributed to the Holy See "the character of undue privilege and support of a confession, a Catholic confession, among the many existing in American society."[23] Indeed, it was the events related to the process of Italian unification and, in particular, the strenuous opposition of Pius IX to the aspirations of the newborn Kingdom of Italy that determined the sudden suspension of relations by the United States. In effect, as the earthly role of the papacy gradually became more and more limited and open to discussion politically, the U.S. senators became aware of the "purely religious, or predominantly religious, nature of the pontifical mission in the world." That was, maintains the historian Ennio Di Nolfo, "in the eyes of American legislators, the very nature of the relations that they wished to have with this institution changed."[24]

Whatever the prevalent reason, the decision of 1867 was the umpteenth, and perhaps the most striking demonstration of deeply rooted antipapist prejudice in U.S. society. In fact, it introduced a very long period of diplomatic blackout due to last seventy-three years. The cut in the funding of the mission to Rome decided by Congress was never seriously taken into consideration. While Republican administrations, almost uninterruptedly in power during the fifty years following the Civil War, simply ignored the Vatican

22. "I am given to understand," said King, "that the Pope himself feels hurt by this hasty and apparently groundless action of Congress, and thinks it an unkind and ungenerous return for the good will he has manifested towards the American government and people"; ibid.
23. Di Nolfo, *Vaticano e Stati Uniti*, 21.
24. Ibid., 22.

question in order not to fall out with the Protestant electorate, with the victory of the Democrats in the 1912 elections anti-Catholicism found in Woodrow Wilson one of its chief supporters. "Singularly ill-disposed towards non-Anglo Saxons in general and the pope in particular,"[25] Wilson had shown his contempt of Catholic immigrants as early as 1902, when he wrote:"now there came multitudes of men of the lowest class from the south of Italy and men of the meaner sort out from Hungary and Poland, men out of the ranks where there was neither skill nor energy not any initiative of quick intelligence,... as if the countries of the south of Europe were disburdening themselves of the more sordid and hapless elements."[26]

Wilson's attitude toward Catholics was already formed long before he entered the White House, and it was confirmed during the Mexican Revolution of 1915. On that occasion, the president, ignoring the requests for neutrality from the ecclesiastical hierarchy, gave support to the government of Venustiano Carranza, who continued to persecute the Catholic Church.[27] During the First World War, the clash between Benedict XV and Wilson became more or less total since the latter considered pontifical diplomacy an inappropriate interference by a spiritual leader.[28] As a result, he opposed both all participation on the part of the Holy See to the Versailles Peace Conference and Vatican efforts to arbitrate between belligerent countries. The Vatican, on its side, being supported by the majority of local Catholics, contested the Anglophile line followed by Washington, harshly criticizing it arms supply to the Triple Entente.[29]

---

25. Gerald P. Fogarty, "Roosevelt and the American Catholic Hierarchy," in *FDR, The Vatican, and the Roman Catholic Church in America, 1933–1945*, ed. David B. Woolner and Richard G. Kurial, (New York: Palgrave Macmillan, 2003), 12.

26. Woodrow Wilson, *A History of the American People* (Charleston, S.C.: Bibliolife, 2009), 5.212.

27. See Louis M. Teitelbaum, *Woodrow Wilson and the Mexican Revolution, 1913–1916* (New York: Exposition Press, 1967); and John T. Ellis, *The Life of James Cardinal Gibbons* (Milwaukee, Wis.: Bruce Publishing Company, 1952), 2.516–19.

28. On this subject, see Peter D'Agostino, *Rome in America: Transnational Catholic Ideology from the Risorgimento to Fascism* (Chapel Hill: University of North Carolina Press, 2004), 111.

29. On this topic, see Luigi Bruti Liberati, "Santa Sede e Stati Uniti negli anni

Even the attempts made by Vatican Secretary of State Pietro Gasparri to negotiate with Germany for a compromise solution to avert the imminent collapse of diplomatic relations with the United States after the sinking of the *Lusitania* were considered inopportune by Wilson and the liberal press. Considering the pope's initiatives an undue intrusion into the internal affairs of the country, the president showed himself to be well disposed "to accepting the arguments of the Italian government according to which the policy of Benedict XV was motivated only by a desire to protect the Catholic population of the Central Powers,"[30] in particular the Austro-Hungarian Empire.

### RISK OF SCHISM

With Italy's entry into the war together with the Entente and the signing of the Treaty of London, Vatican diplomacy saw its hopes of success for the Central Powers diminish and, for this reason, began to do its best to ensure that the United States, the non-European nation with the largest number of Catholics, would give support to Benedict XV's demands. To this end, once the truth of the content of an interview given by the pope himself in June 1915 to the newspaper *La Liberté* had been denied, Cardinal Pietro Gasparri launched an international "awareness-raising" campaign by issuing a circular addressed to all the apostolic nunciatures. One of the recipients of this communication was Giovanni Bonzano, who was not a diplomatic representative but the apostolic delegate to the United States of America. The first part of the circular announced the increasing difficulty, following Italy's entry into the war, of the Holy See's communicating both with the states in war who were "enemies" of the Kingdom of Italy, and with neutral states.[31] While considering the

---

della grande guerra," in *Benedetto XV e la pace, 1918,* ed. Giorgio Rumi (Brescia: Morcelliana, 1990), 129–50.

30. Gerald P. Fogarty, "La Chiesa negli Stati Uniti nella Grande Guerra e a Versailles," in *La Conferenza di pace di Parigi fra ieri e domani (1919–1920)*, ed. Antonio Scottà (Soveria Mannelli: Rubbettino, 2003), 215.

31. On the subject of Vatican protests about freedom of communication dur-

guarantees received in the previous March on the free circulation of coded messages from "neutral" ambassadors to the Vatican[32] a clear demonstration of "maximum goodwill"[33] on the part of the Salandra government, Gasparri took note of the continuation of the difficulty of communicating, and wondered "what would happen if, when the crisis came, the Salandra Ministry were to be succeeded by a radical Ministry."[34] It was "therefore clear that the situation created at the Holy See by the events of 1870" had become "essentially risky and uncertain because dependent on the changing circumstances of men and events."[35] And yet, in spite of Benedict XV's being repeatedly accused of wishing to resort to foreign powers in order to regain that which unified Italy had taken away, Vatican independence remained a distant mirage: a very difficult goal to reach but which, even so, should not be the cause of international public opinion's disinterest in the fate of the pope. Gasparri, in fact, bitterly pointed out about the long circular: "but if the Holy Father, for reasons it is easy to understand, does not call on foreign armies to restore his temporal throne, this does not mean that the governments of Catholic States, or those which have Catholics among their subjects, have no right to be preoccupied by the abnormal situation of the Holy See; not at all—it is their duty to be concerned."[36] According to the information received, therefore, Bonzano should have discussed these issues both with the Italian diplomats in Washington and with the Department of State, so involving U.S. representatives in Rome and consequently the Italian Ministry of Foreign Affairs.

---

ing the war, see Minute of the Royal Ambassador in Madrid to the Spanish government, Madrid, June 24, 1915, ASMAE, APOG, b. 177.

32. Sidney Sonnino to Vittorio E. Orlando (personal), Rome, March 30, 1915, ibid.

33. Pietro Gasparri to Giovanni Bonzano, Vatican, August 4, 1915, ASV, DASU, V, pos. 68, f. 3r.

34. Ibid., f. 4r. Apart from the future of Salandra's government, Gasparri's preoccupations had their origin in the decision of the diplomatic representatives of Austria, Bavaria, and Prussia to leave Rome immediately after Italy's declaration of war on May 23, 1915.

35. Ibid. 36. Ibid.

Unable to rely on official diplomatic channels, the apostolic delegate and James Gibbons, the only American cardinal from 1887 to 1911, were the only authoritative interlocutors the Vatican possessed who could bring about the wishes of Gasparri and Benedict XV. And yet, when the war broke out, relations between the American Church and the Holy See were anything but peaceful; the old disputes that had emerged during the last twenty years of the nineteenth century, never resolved either by Leo XIII or even by his successor Pius X, continued to persist.

As James Hennesey notes in his powerful history of Catholicism in the United States, the prelates, especially the younger ones, were so anxious to integrate that they ended up rejecting Roman centralism, seeing its unwillingness to renew and rigid formalism as the weak points in the Catholic Church. These were deficiencies on which Puritan rhetoric had always based the presumed "anti-American" character of Catholicism itself. Rome, on its side, was suspicious of the "specificity" of the United States; it was feared that the need to show themselves to be attached to their homeland not only helped better integration into the national sociocultural fabric, but that it even concealed heterodoxy and hidden agendas intent on perverting Catholicism, just as had happened long before with Protestant Reformation.[37]

The Third Plenary Council of U.S. bishops, which took place in Baltimore in 1884, was a crucial event for relations between the American Church and the Holy See. From the council there emerged two extremely significant points which, in substance, confirmed the image of the American Church given by reports sent to Rome over the years by various prefects of the Congregation for Propagation of the Faith. Above all, that Vatican interference in the internal affairs of the American episcopate could not easily be reconciled with the traditional collegial Church status and its independent vocation. Hence the almost unanimous rejection both of the idea of sending an apostolic delegate

---

37. See James Hennesey, *American Catholics: A History of the Roman Catholic Community in the United States* (New York: Oxford University Press, 1981), 184–203.

to Washington to represent the pope, and even that the council should be presided over by the delegate initially chosen by the Vatican, the Augustinian bishop Luigi Sepiacci, who was replaced by James Gibbons, in the meantime nominated archbishop of Baltimore.[38] Secondly, it is to be noted that, at the very end of the council, the internal splits in the episcopate began to widen. In fact, with a hierarchy made up above all of Irish, Germans, and French, and a mixed population of immigrants of various nationalities, the American Church did not show itself able to adopt a unified political or cultural line. This lack of "national homogeneity," observes Ornella Confessore, aggravated the difficulties of Catholic communities, "even if they were minorities, immersed in a continually hostile and aggressive society," and threatened to disarticulate it.[39]

The product of a pluralistic reality into which it attempted to fully integrate, the American Catholic Church was divided politically into conservatives and liberals; geographically, between small dioceses in the West and large urban sees on the Atlantic Coast; and finally, ethnolinguistically, with conflict between the English-speaking clergy on one side and the German- and the French-speaking bishops on the other. The latter, having a more European and traditional conception of Catholicism, were not very willing to accept the model of the young, dynamic American society; while the Irish, especially, wished to qualify the Church's actions by means of support from the politics of reform in the name of social justice and state education. Within a few years of the Council of Baltimore, the irreconcilability of the two positions further complicated matters, so much so that historians have been induced to identify, within the American Catholic world, the existence of conservative and liberal "parties."[40]

---

38. See Fogarty, "The Bishops versus Religious Orders: The Suppressed Decrees of the Third Plenary Council of Baltimore," *The Jurist* 33 (1973): 384–98.

39. Ornella Confessore, *L'americanismo cattolico in Italia* (Rome: Edizioni Studium, 1984), 17.

40. For a detailed picture, see Gerald P. Fogarty, "American Conciliar Legislation, Hierarchical Structure and Priest-Bishop Tension," *The Jurist* 32 (1972): 400–409.

Strong in their control both of the Catholic University of America, and of the American College in Rome, the progressive wing of the episcopate, led by the archbishop of Baltimore James Gibbons; by bishops John Ireland of St. Paul and John Keane of Richmond; and by Denis O'Connell, rector of the American College in Rome, promoted as much the collaboration of the civil authorities (legitimizing the right of the state to put public schools side by side with parochial schools) as support for the working class's labor union demands, so demonstrating a new awareness of the increasingly complex social issues relating to the industrial development of the country.[41] Diversely, and especially through the influence of the Jesuit journal *La Civiltà Cattolica*, the German and conservative faction would not accept a socially committed model of Catholicism.[42]

The institution of the Apostolic Delegation to Washington in January 1893 seemed to be a choice that was favorable to the progressive bishops. Wishing to stem the conflicts within the hierarchy, Leo XIII entrusted the delicate position of delegate to Francesco Satolli, who had been archbishop of Lepanto. The pope's aim was certainly not to set up diplomatic negotiations with a government presided over by the Democrat Grover Cleveland, but to try to mend the hoary fracture in the American Church without giving the impression of wishing to interfere too much in its internal affairs.[43] Although faced with the indifference of the U.S. government, Satolli's initial success reassured the pope of the rightness of his choice. And yet the enthusiastic at-

41. On the positions of the "liberal" faction of the American hierarchy and the work of its main exponents, see James Moynihan, *The Life of Archbishop John Ireland* (New York: Harper & Brothers, 1953); Francis McNamara, *The American College in Rome, 1855–1955* (Rochester, N.Y.: Christopher Press, 1956), 278–85; and Patrick H. Ahern, *The Catholic University of America, 1887–1896: The Rectorship of John J. Keane* (Washington, D.C.: The Catholic University of America Press, 1949).

42. See Colman J. Barry, *The Catholic Church and German-Americans* (Milwaukee, Wis.: Bruce Publishing Company, 1953), 62–64, 28–96; Frank Trommler and Elliott Shore, *German-American Encounter: Conflict and Cooperation between Two Cultures* (New York: Berghahn Books, 2001), 49–60.

43. See Robert J. Wister, *The Establishment of the Apostolic Delegation in the United States of America: The Satolli Mission* (Rome: Università Gregoriana Editrice, 1980).

titude of the liberal prelates toward the delegate was paradoxical: it resulted in a "Pyrrhic victory"[44] according to Gerald Fogarty, which repudiated Rome's proposals of autonomy in the way that it would have fatally permitted the Vatican authorities themselves to have more say in determining the American Church's line of conduct.

Leo XIII's initial welcoming of Catholic Americanism soon gave way to a decisively more cautious approach during the 1890s. The possibility of "Americanism" attracting Catholics of the Old Continent, so losing its purely national connotation, was something that worried even the Holy See.[45] Following the translation of Ireland's speeches published in France in 1894 by the Paris publisher Lecoffe, many Catholic supporters of the Third Republic had begun to look more deeply into the writings of Isaac Hecker which had appeared in *Catholic World*[46] and the positions of James Gibbons and John Ireland in the school controversy.[47]

The outcome of the Spanish-American War of 1898 also contributed to determining the Vatican's reaction to Catholic Americanism. "What Spain would think of Leo XIII if at this moment of her humiliation he were to pay compliments to her conquerors": so wrote the rector of the American College in Rome Denis O'Connell to Father Walter Elliott, author of *The Life of Father Hecker*, in December 1898.[48]

---

44. Gerald P. Fogarty, *The Vatican and the American Hierarchy from 1870 to 1965* (Stuttgart: Hiersemann, 1982), 114.

45. See Lillian P. Wallace, *Leo XIII and the Rise of Socialism* (Durham, N.C.: Duke University Press, 1966).

46. See David J. O'Brien, *Isaac Hecker: An American Catholic* (Mahwah, N.J.: Paulist Press, 1992), 21-339.

47. Thomas E. Wangler, "John Ireland and the Origins of Liberal Catholicism in the United States," *Catholic Historical Review* 56 (1971): 617-29. See also Daniel F. Reilly, *The School Controversy, 1891-1893* (Washington, D.C.: The Catholic University of America Press, 1944), 75-86, and Marvin R. O'Connell, *John Ireland and the American Catholic Church* (St. Paul: Minnesota Historical Society Press, 1988), 317-47.

48. Denis O'Connell to Walter Elliott, Paris, December 10, 1898, quoted in Fogarty, *The Vatican and the Americanist Crisis*, 287; and Thomas T. McAvoy, *The Great Crisis in American Catholic History: 1895-1900* (Chicago: Regnery Press, 1957), 273.

As was shown by the emphasis given by the liberal and Democratic press, the war had taken on the meaning of a real ideological and cultural conflict between the "old" and the "new" worlds, and its outcome seemed to consecrate the political model and economic dynamism of the United States. Furthermore, the inability of John Ireland to mediate with President McKinley was confirmation of how harmful it was to the Holy See not to have any official diplomatic channels with the White House.[49]

Leo XIII reacted officially on January 22, 1899, with the apostolic letter *Testem Benevolentiae,* where he asserted that, as they were structured in the North American Republic, relations between Church and State could in no way be considered an example to be emulated. Basically, he made a distinction between "political" Americanism and "religious" Americanism: while the former was to be respected in that it had been produced by sudden historical events in the United States, the latter entertained real suspicions "that there are some among the American clergy who conceive of and desire a Church in America different from that which is the rest of the world."[50]

The specter of a schism was therefore to be shooed off by reaffirming once again the unity and indivisibility both of the doctrine and the institutional structure of the Church of Rome. Within the context of the final phase of his papacy, the condemnation of Americanism clearly reflected Leo XIII's conservative involution.[51]

The extent to which both the Vatican and most of Europe were ill prepared to accept the model of the United States was made even more evident at the beginning of the twentieth century, and especially after Giuseppe Melchiorre Sarto was made pope and took the name of Pius X. One of the reasons for his encyclical condemning modernism, the *Pascendi Dominici Gregis* (1907), was the conviction

---

49. On the reactions of the American Catholic press to the 1898 war, see Luigi Rossi, *L'indipendenza negata: Il Manifest Destiny di Cuba nel 1898* (Salerno: Edizioni del Paguro, 2000), 74–81.

50. This translation is that in John T. Ellis, *Documents of American Catholic History* (Chicago: Regnery Press, 1966), 2.538–47.

51. On this point, see Margaret M. Reher, "Leo XIII and Americanism," *Theological Studies* 34 (1973): 679–89.

that there was a strong link between this and Americanism.⁵² The superimposition of these two phenomena had considerable repercussions on the American Church. Released from the control of the Congregation for Propagation of the Faith in June 1908 by the *Sapienti Consilio* apostolic constitution, the Holy See, in fact no longer considered it a mission and it therefore passed under the jurisdiction of the Congregation for Extraordinary Ecclesiastical Affairs. However, it was not really a "promotion," neither was it a mere recognition of sufficient maturity; on the contrary, the reactionary intention of the curia of Pius X was to gain greater control of the episcopate by replacing "liberal" exponents with more easily manageable, deeply conservative ones who were willing to support the "romanization" strategy of the upper hierarchy and the doctrinal homologation that was the new pope's aim.⁵³

However, the conservative line of Pius X was disavowed by his successor. As Philippe Chenaux notes, in fact, the election of Benedict XV "was not the best guarantee of the continuity of Vatican policy during the War which had just broken out."⁵⁴ In the view of some of the old American liberals, the election of Giacomo Della Chiesa was a sign of hope for a return to the more open approach of Leo XIII.

One of the new pope's first decisions was to replace the secretary of state Merry del Val with Pietro Gasaparri, a move which was, both symbolically and in substance, emblematic of the new direction that Giacomo Della Chiesa intended to take in a historical set of circumstances heavily marked by the bloody war that had just broken out. But, as Gerald Fogarty maintains, there was also an intention to break with the recent past, which had not had the hoped-for effect of improving relations both with the government and with the

---

52. Michael V. Gannon, "Before and after Modernism: The Intellectual Isolation of the American Priest," in *The Catholic Priest in the United States: Historical Investigations,* ed. John T. Ellis (Collegeville, Minn.: St John's University Press, 1971), 338–39.

53. See John T. Ellis, *American Catholicism* (Chicago: University of Chicago Press, 1957), 122–31.

54. Philippe Chenaux, *Pio XII: Diplomatico e pastore* (Cinisello Balsamo: Edizioni San Paolo, 2004), 77.

members of the American hierarchy, who would have been able to influence it.

Apart from the hostility of the Wilson administration, Benedict XV had only the help of the elderly cardinal Gibbons and of the apostolic delegate Bonzano for communications with the White House; most of the local episcopate either lacked direct contact with the federal establishment or, as in the case of O'Connell, was openly against any intention of U.S. involvement in the strategy adopted by the "new" Roman curia. Furthermore, the complex wartime equilibrium influenced assignment into vacant positions in the Church hierarchy, so further complicating the possibility of nominating those whom the Holy See considered appropriate for its diplomatic objectives. This is seen in the case of George Mundelein. Chosen in 1915 for the archdiocese of Buffalo, this prelate of German origin, despite his having a decisively critical attitude to the forthcoming invasion of Belgium by the Second Reich, was in the end sent to Chicago at the request of the British Foreign Office, who wished to avoid having a "German" in a diocese bordering francophone, pro-French Canada during the hostilities.[55]

From the time of his nomination as archbishop of Baltimore in 1872, Gibbons set up cordial, though often heated, relations with many U.S. presidents, but things went differently with Wilson. At the beginning of his first mandate in 1913, the cardinal was seventy-eight and "seemed to have lost a large part of his ability to deal with politicians."[56] His marked vanity, which John Tracy Ellis underlines in his biography of the cardinal, induced him to make frequent reference to his sporadic meetings with the president at the White House, with the inevitable result of earning the dislike of Wilson and his entourage who tended anyway to be hostile to the Catholic Church.[57]

---

55. On the question of Mundelein and Buffalo, see James P. Gaffey, *Francis Clement Kelley and the American Catholic Dream* (Bensenville, Ill.: Heritage Foundation, 1980), 1151–55; and Thomas E. Hachey, "British War Propaganda and American Catholics," in *The Catholic Historical Review* 61 (1975): 58.

56. Fogarty, "La Chiesa negli Stati Uniti," 214.

57. See Ellis, *The Life*, 231–32.

While the position of the cardinal of Baltimore was undoubtedly not the best, Bonzano's was no better. The apostolic delegate had been completely taken up with the internal issues of the episcopate, so remaining at the edges of the almost-nonexistent relations that a small group of prelates had with the federal establishment.

Given these circumstances, it is not surprising that any work of mediation by these two archbishops during the crucial phases of the war was in vain. During the three years 1916–18, in fact, in spite of the Holy See having increasingly more patently disavowed its initial pro-German position, aiming instead at an improvement in relations with the Entente and above all with the United States, Wilson became the main opponent of Vatican participation in the peace talks.

### PARTIAL NEUTRALITIES

During his years spent in the service of Vatican diplomacy, first as secretary to the nunciature in Madrid and then as the minute-writer and deputy secretary of state, Giacomo Della Chiesa had learned to appreciate Leo XIII's policy of openness, and he fully shared in its aim to guarantee the Church's greater participation in international events. He criticized, on the other hand, not only the conservative line taken by his predecessor Pius X and by Cardinal Merry del Val, but also its exclusively pastoral character. Hence the conviction that, given the increasing conflicts between European countries, by resolving the Roman question, the Holy See could have become the promoter of an extensive diplomatic initiative and be able to give voice to the need to keep the peace, the lack of which was attributed to the persistence of the "abnormal" condition the pope had been forced to find himself in since 1870.[58] Nominated secretary of state in October 1914, Cardinal Pietro Gasparri was, on the other hand, a relentless sustainer of the realpolitik. Though not exactly morally neutral, his attitude of scrupulous impartiality implied the Holy See's

---

58. On these aspects, see Mauro Letterio, ed., *Benedetto XV: Profeta di pace in un mondo in crisi* (Bologna: Minerva, 2008).

need to maintain great reserve in pointing to responsibilities and the accusation of "crimes" committed by the countries at war. Such a choice was, therefore, the necessary precondition to achieving the mediation policy that was the aim of the pope himself.[59]

The extremely noncommittal appeals for peace launched by Benedict XV in the early stages of the war combined with his frequent references to the Roman question induced the powers of the Entente to believe that the pope intended to support the cause of the central European monarchies.[60]

Given the almost nonexistent diplomatic relations with France and Great Britain, and, likewise, the pope's unwillingness to dialogue with liberal Italy, it would have been easier for Benedict to negotiate with Berlin and Vienna. Furthermore, his not having publicly condemned Germany's act of aggression and having limited himself to underlining the inhuman character of the war was interpreted as a sure sign that the real objective of the Church was to preserve the territorial integrity of Germany and of the Austro-Hungarian Empire, who were potentially more willing to comply with the requests of the Vatican.[61]

The Entente's fears of a rising conservative trend in Europe, which Benedict XV could use in order to "return to being the keystone of international order for post-war construction," were by no means unfounded.[62] Neither was the diplomatic initiative of the Holy See, Germany, and Austria from November 1914 to January 1915.

59. On Gasparri, see above Giovanni Spadolini, ed., *Il Cardinale Gasparri e la questione romana: Con brani delle Memorie inedite* (Florence: Le Monnier, 1972).

60. See John F. Pollard, *The Unknown Pope: Benedict XV and the Pursuit of Peace* (New York: Geoffrey Chapman, 1999); and Antonio Scottà, ed., *Benedetto XV, La Chiesa, La Grande Guerra, la pace, 1914–1922* (Rome: Edizioni di Storia e Letteratura, 2009).

61. Apart from the classic studies by Luigi Salvatorelli, *La politica della Santa Sede dopo la Guerra* (Milan: Istituto per gli Studi di Politica Internazionale, 1937), 41–54, and by Italo Garzia, *La questione romana durante la prima guerra mondiale* (Naples: ESI, 1981), 16–18, see also Walter A. Renzi, *In the Shadow of the Sword: Italy's Neutrality and Entrance into the Great War, 1914–1915* (New York: Peter Lang, 1987), 154–58.

62. Chenaux, *Pio XII*, 79.

Among the various possible solutions to the Roman question that emerged during the war, the one that had great resonance was the plan set out in October 1914 by the German Catholic leader Matthias Erzberger, supported by ex-chancellor Bernhard von Bulow. This plan aimed to avert Italy's intervention against the Central Powers by ceding Trentino to the pope, who would then concede it to the King of Italy in exchange for the sovereignty over part of the city of Rome. However, the "Herzberger hypothesis," put forward during the very early stages of the war, took for granted the success of German military plans and, for this reason, failed to take into account the unexpected changes that came about during the first winter of the battles. Also, it was based on Italy's neutrality and on the conviction that the neutralist position would prevail over the heated political debate on whether or not to enter the war. But it only resulted in rekindling the liberal leaders' hostility toward the Holy See, so speeding up the process of Italy's joining the Entente.[63]

In spite of Benedict XV's hurried statement, on the occasion of the consistory of January 22, 1915, that "to involve the pontifical authorities in the contentions of those at war would certainly be neither convenient nor useful,"[64] secret negotiations between Italy, France, Great Britain, and Russia noticeably increased. When Sonnino came to know of the Herzberger plan, he advised Italian embassies to maintain a position of absolute intransigence in order to block any Catholic attempt to win assent to the Church's plan to solve the Roman question.[65]

Benedict XV's reaction to Article 15 of the Treaty of London was as impulsive as it was counterproductive in the sense that it ended up by bearing out the hypothesis of a "pan-Germanic plot" spon-

63. See Francesco Margiotta Broglio, "Marzo 1917: Uno Stato per il papa," *I Classici di Limes: Quando il papa pensa il mondo* 1 (2009): 109–12.
64. The text of this address is to be found in *L'Osservatore Romano*, January 23, 1915.
65. On the Pact of London and related repercussions on Vatican strategy, see John F. Pollard, "Il Vaticano e la politica estera italiana," in *La politica estera italiana, 1860–1985*, ed. Richard J. B. Bosworth and Sergio Romano (Bologna: Il Mulino, 1991), 197–230.

sored by the Holy See. As the historian Philippe Chenaux maintains, "Benedict's statements tended, perhaps, to be over-generalized."⁶⁶ So much so that Thomas Nelson Page, U.S. ambassador to Italy, was induced to communicate to Secretary of State Robert Lansing that the pope's attitude showed the Holy See's wish to take sides against the Entente.⁶⁷

By saying that the Holy See expected "the best solution to come not from foreign armies, but from the triumph of a feeling for justice," the Vatican secretary of state prepared the ground for the Vatican's new line during the war.⁶⁸ It led to the increasing cooling of relations with the Central Powers and, at the same time, relaxed relations with the Entente; as far as a solution to the "Roman question" was concerned, however, the Holy See aimed to involve neutral countries.

In reply to the request for clarification on the matter of Benedict XV's attitude from the ministers of Great Britain and Belgium posted at the Holy See, the secretary of state prepared two documents: a letter dated July 1, 1915, addressed to the British plenipotentiary Howard, who "tried hard to clear up any misunderstanding about the Vatican's position with regard to the maritime block imposed by the Central Powers";⁶⁹ and a memorandum sent on July 7 to the Belgian van Heuvel that condemned even more explicitly the German violation of the neutrality of Belgium "as being contrary to international law."⁷⁰ Contextually, the cardinals of the Congregation for Extraordinary Ecclesiastical Affairs told the German authorities that they were not a little puzzled about certain other plans to solve the Roman question. This is shown, for example, by the caution with

66. Chenaux, *Pio XII,* 79.

67. See Dragan R. Zivojinovic, *The United States and the Vatican Policies, 1914–1918* (Boulder: Colorado Associated University Press, 1978), 31.

68. *Il Corriere d'Italia,* June 28, 1915, quoted in Margiotta Broglio, "Marzo 1917," 112.

69. Pietro Gasparri to Henry Howard, Vatican, July 1, 1915, ASV, War 1914–1918, vol. 67.

70. Pietro Gasparri to Jules van Heuvel (memorandum), Vatican, July 7, 1915, ibid.

which Eugenio Pacelli received the suggestion made by the Bavarian minister von Ritter to solve the problem of Rome by means of a press campaign. This kind of action, wrote Pacelli on September 1, "must be taken by the neutral countries more than in the countries at war."[71] As a result, the Holy See began to watch the United States of America with greater attention. Being sure to have the support of an non-European emerging power with about sixteen million Catholics would, at least as far as the Vatican was concerned, strengthen the position of Benedict XV, whose possibility of taking an active part in the peace process had been greatly reduced by the identification of the presumed impartiality of the Holy See in the cause of the Central Powers. The turbulent historical events of relations with North America and, not least, with Wilson's administration, further complicated the pontiff's plans.

The breakout of the war had revealed America's inability to "translate its strength and economic supremacy into an effective political and diplomatic influence." The choice to remain neutral, however, permitted it to "confirm once again their diversity, and the[ir] ethical and political superiority."[72] But neutrality did not mean isolationism. A man of great ideals who was trying to introduce a new code of values into international relations, Wilson was at the same time a figure who was well-suited to the image of America at that time; deeply aware of material interests, his ideas reflected the turmoil and the expansionist plans of the U.S. economy.[73]

Washington did not hesitate to protest against the naval blockade instituted by London and refused to accept both the British argument that its navy was following procedures that had been adopted by the United States themselves during the Civil War, and the

---

71. Eugenio Pacelli to Otto von Ritter, Vatican, September 1, 1915, ASV, AES (1903-1922), Bavaria, pos. 21, quoted in Chenaux, *Pio XII,* 89.

72. Mario Del Pero, *Libertà e impero: Gli Stati Uniti e il mondo, 1776–2006* (Rome: Laterza, 2008), 197.

73. On the first phase of United States neutrality, see Patrick Devlin, *Too Proud to Fight: Woodrow Wilson's Neutrality* (New York: Oxford University Press, 1975); and Arthur S. Link, *Wilson: The Struggle for Neutrality, 1914–1915* (Princeton, N.J.: Princeton University Press, 1960).

idea that the new trading methods and the new war strategies made is necessary to change some of the rules governing navigation.[74] Generally speaking, however, Wilson replied with moderation and in fact accepted the behavior of the English. Apart from still not having sufficient ways of putting on pressure, the president had to take account of public opinion at home, which was contrary to overaggressive methods that would threaten involving the country directly in the war. Much of the political and economic establishment was strongly oriented in favor of Great Britain in the name of "a common denominator, cultural, political and linguistic, of their close commercial and financial links and an aversion to authoritative German militarism."[75]

At the elections in November 1916, Wilson was reconfirmed as president, though by a small majority of votes. Most of the electorate appreciated the way he had kept the country out of the war and therefore expected him to continue along the same path and strengthen programs of internal reform which, after the enthusiasm of the Progressive Era, had been considerably held up.[76] But, shaken by the submarine battles, the president was beginning to entertain the conviction that prolonged nonintervention in international affairs would be impractical and counterproductive.

The United States' involvement, indirect though it was, in the war, intensified to the point of definitively losing its impartial character. Washington became a real "arsenal" of the Entente countries, and large quantities of ammunition, provisions, and raw materials were sent to them. Germany, as well, was considered by the administration and by Anglophile public opinion to be the essence of imperialism and the Second Reich's militarism, the negation of American

74. See Jonathan Glover, *Humanity: A Moral History of the Twentieth Century* (New Haven, Conn.: Yale University Press, 1999), 64–67.

75. Del Pero, *Libertà e impero*, 197. In this regard, see also John W. Coogan, *The End of Neutrality: The United States, Britain and Maritime Rights, 1899–1915* (Ithaca, N.Y.: Cornell University Press, 1981).

76. The second presidency of Wilson is examined in detail by Kendrick A. Clements, *The Presidency of Woodrow Wilson* (Lawrence: University Press of Kansas, 1992), 115–42.

liberalism; therefore, the defeat of Germany was the necessary precondition to the consolidation of U.S. prosperity.[77]

However, not all the population of the United States shared in supporting the cause of the Entente. Accepted by the great majority, and influenced by Britain's propaganda campaign that presented the war as a kind of Manichaean contraposition of Anglo-Saxon democracy and Austro-German autocracy, it generated different reactions from the peoples of various nationalities and cultures that made up American society. On the other hand, in a nation of immigrants from every part of Europe, divergences and splits of this kind were inevitable during a war that involved almost the whole of the Old Continent. While the Jewish and Swedish communities, hostile for different reasons to Russia, were in favor of the initial neutrality, the Germans, who were more numerous and better integrated, took up a position in favor of their homeland and supported the Central Powers. The Irish-Americans, particularly influential on the East Coast and with an historical aversion to Great Britain, went so far as to be critical of the Wilson administration at the very time that he chose to support the Entente.[78]

It seems, then, that the war ended up by causing a crisis in the fragile balance of U.S. multiethnic society by reigniting and actually increasing the age-old antagonisms between groups of diverse European extraction who had quite recently immigrated into the United States. Invited to show their loyalty to their adopted country, they responded, sometimes vehemently, by showing an inveterate faith in their countries of origin. Washington's Anglophone line caused a hardening of their positions as the support of the Anglo-Franco-Russian cause let go of its initial and, for the most part, shared posi-

---

77. On the indirect involvement of the United States in the war, see Ross Gregory, *The Origins of American Intervention in the First World War* (New York: Norton & Co., 1971), 26–76; and Frederick S. Calhoun, *Uses of Force and Wilsonian Foreign Policy* (Kent, Ohio: Kent State University Press, 1993), 11–34.

78. See Alexander DeConde, *Ethnicity, Race and American Foreign Policy: A History* (Boston: Northeastern University Press, 1992), 82–88; and Tony Smith, *Foreign Attachments: The Power of Ethnic Groups in the Making of American Foreign Policy* (Cambridge, Mass.: Harvard University Press, 2000), 35–46.

tion of neutrality and threatened, in the immediate future or only partially, to damage the interests of some, Germany and Ireland, in particular.[79]

Cutting across the already irreconcilable "national" demands, the religious element made the picture even more complicated. For Catholicism, above all, the war was an important testing ground. Ever since the origins of the North American republic, the Catholic Church had been considered by the Protestant majority as the utmost expression of European obscurantism, and therefore contrary to the liberal democratic principles of the Founding Fathers. In spite of their having consolidated their presence in the wake of the migrations of the late nineteenth and early twentieth centuries, the Catholic community had met with numerous obstacles in its attempts to fully integrate into American society. Regarded as an "extraneous," "alien," and even "anti-American" body, even as they significantly increased in number, they were systematically marginalized and excluded from the main political, economic, and social dynamics of the country.[80] What, in all probability, discredited the image of the Church of Rome more than anything else was the figure and historic role of the pope; that is, the fact that the head of a religious order, at the same time as holding spiritual power over its believers, had also, until 1870, exercised temporal power over a statelike institution as its absolute monarch and that, having lost that power, claimed its legitimacy.

The very existence of a Roman question was therefore inconceivable in American eyes, for in the North American republic each religious doctrine had contributed to the consolidation of democratic institutions.[81] Consequently, the attempts made by Benedict XV

79. Dean R. Esslinger, "American German and Irish Attitudes toward Neutrality, 1914–1917: A Study of Catholic Minorities," *Catholic Historical Review* 53 (July 1967): 194–216.

80. See Matteo Sanfilippo, *L'affermazione del cattolicesimo nel Nord America: Elite, emigranti e Chiesa cattolica negli Stati Uniti e nel Canada, 1750–1920* (Viterbo: Sette Città, 2003).

81. See Giorgio Spini, "I rapporti politici tra Italia e Stati Uniti," in *Italia e Stati Uniti nell'età del Risorgimento e della Guerra Civile*, ed. Agostino Lombardo (Florence: La Nuova Italia, 1969), 121–87. See also Giovanni Pizzorusso, "I cattolici

to recruit American Catholics in order to raise the problem of the juridical status of the Vatican in peace negotiations turned out to be counterproductive.

Whose "cause" would the Catholics have supported? That of the United States, where they had fled to escape poverty and European persecution? That of their country of birth? Or would they have disregarded national interests in support of the Holy See? Given that Benedict XV had shown that he wished to preserve the integrity of the Central Powers on whose survival depended the possibility of reestablishing the papacy's temporal authority over Europe, the Wilson administration became convinced that dissent toward the pro-British line of the government on the part of Catholics, especially Italian, Irish, and German Catholics, had in a certain sense been "instigated" by Vatican policy.[82]

By anticipating a trend that was to become stronger in the twenties, the "Great War" therefore had a double negative effect: it not only distanced Catholics from other American citizens, but also helped to a further deterioration of the difficult relations between Washington and the Holy See.[83]

---

nordamericani e la sovranità temporale dei romani pontefici," in Fiorentino and Sanfilippo, eds., *Gli Stati uniti e l'Unità d'Italia*, 113–24.

82. On German and Irish Catholics, see Philip Gleason, *The Conservative Reformers: German-American Catholics and the Social Order* (Notre Dame, Ind.: University of Notre Dame Press, 1968), 160–71; and Edward Cuddy, "Pro-Germanism and American Catholicism, 1914–1917," *Catholic Historical Review* 54, no. 3 (October 1968): 427–54. On Italian Catholics, see Chrisopher M. Sterba, *Good Americans: Italian and Jewish Immigrants during the First World War* (New York: Oxford University Press, 2003), 86–104, 133–52.

83. See D'Agostino, *Rome in America*, 104.

# 2

# INCOMPATIBLE UNIVERSALISMS

## WILSON, BONZANO, AND GIBBONS: AN UNSUCCESSFUL DIALOGUE

Woodrow Wilson had never attempted to conceal his sometimes extreme anti-Catholicism. Indeed, it seems that from the time of his first meeting with James Gibbons in Washington in 1913, he addressed the cardinal as "Signor" and did not even ask him to sit down.[1]

However, the attitude of the United States president toward the Holy See was not the only reason for the failure of Benedict XV's attempt to relax the great tension with the United States. It is true that Wilsonian antipapism is rooted in the history and culture of the country, just as it was not unusual that Giovanni Bonzano and James Gibbons should prove to be incapable of dealing with the government, given that no one had managed to do any better since the mid-nineteenth century. The reasons for the obstinacy and disagreements that were destined to increase in the final phases of First World War and even to harden in the decade that followed seem, rather, to derive from a mingling of many diverse elements, among which was the heated nationalism that characterized the United States in the war years and which, in the eyes of the conservative instincts of the nativists, can be summed up in their attitude regarding those immi-

---

1. Ellis, *The Life*, 516–19.

grants "who have poured the poison of disloyalty into the very arteries of national life."[2]

During the years preceding America's entry into the First World War, these accusations were addressed mainly to the German-Americans who, more than any other ethnic group, defended the cause of their country of origin. What notably contributed to fanning the unusual fervor with which native Americans attacked Prussian militarism and the positions of the German community was the messianic zeal of the Progressive era. In fact, when the original enthusiasm for internal reforms gradually died out, progressivism was seen at this singular historical juncture as being the ideological reservoir that could be drawn on to prepare the nation for a war that was to be presented as a crusade for democracy against the militarist authoritarianism of the Central Powers. Anti-German attitudes, then, had already become the main subject of debate in the United States during the transitional two years of 1915–16, and stirred up the most deeply rooted nativists.

In John Higham's view, "the breakup of Protestant xenophobia reflected a shift of attention from the pope to the more substantial and exciting menace of the Kaiser," and anti-Catholicism and anti-German attitudes ended up by reinforcing each other. The two movements grew hand in hand, first because of the Holy See's initial tendency to support the positions of Berlin, and second in the light of the considerable discrepancy between the episcopate's line of conduct and that of the Catholic press in response to the cooling of relations between the Vatican and the Central Powers. This was a factor that, combined with the multiethnic makeup of the American Church, mitigated against a well-defined Catholic attitude toward the war, and which inevitably reduced the room for maneuver and the likelihood of success of the dialogue between Bonzano, Gibbons, and the Wilson administration.

When, in January 1916, the Holy See came to know of Article 15 of the Treaty of London, the Apostolic Delegation in Washington,

---

2. John Higham, *Strangers in the Land: Patterns on American Nativism, 1860–1925* (New Brunswick, N.J.: Rutgers University Press, 2004), 200.

who the previous summer had been informed by a circular from Gasparri, received new instructions. In his telegram of January 17, the Vatican secretary of state called the Vatican's exclusion from an eventual peace conference unjust and offensive "both because the Holy See is the highest moral authority in the world, and because it cannot pronounce itself really neutral, but impartial, in the present war because many of those fighting in the war are its children and subjects, and therefore it cannot identify with other strictly neutral powers."[3]

On the basis of such an "exceptional" international status, Bonzano was urged to ensure that the "American Press should properly inform and interest public opinion on these various questions."[4] Presumably the final objective was to get the government to deal with and resolve the Roman question by means of an awareness-raising campaign by the media.

In response to the provocative article "Rome on the Potomac" that appeared in the magazine *Outlook* before the outbreak of the war,[5] the American Catholic press came to the assistance of Benedict XV's diplomatic initiatives by backing both his right to mediate in international affairs and the urgent need for a redefinition of the Vatican's status.

Among the various editors that Giovanni Bonzano was able to check out in this phase, Nicholas Gonner—former honorary president of the German Catholic Central Verein, member of the executive council of the American Federation of Catholic Societies, and editor of the *Catholic Tribune* in Dubuque, Iowa—was without doubt the most amenable to the directives from the Apostolic Delegation. Having decided to put his experience and knowledge of public opinion at the service of the Church, Gonner had responded to Bonzano's request "to insist upon the necessity of being free and independent for the

3. Pietro Gasparri to Giovanni Bonzano, Vatican, January 17, 1916, ASV, DASU, V, pos. 68, f. 5.
4. Ibid.
5. "Rome on the Potomac: What the Papal Hierarchy Is Doing at the American Capital," *Outlook*, February 11, 1913, pp. 10–12, quoted in D'Agostino, *Rome in America*, 113.

government of the universal church" by systematically reporting the reason for the pope's condition becoming "so deploringly disagreeable."[6] He and other Catholic editors took an editorial line that Gonner himself feared might become "over-zealous and perhaps overstep the boundary line of a cautious defense by too much impetuosity."[7] Bonzano "deeply approved,"[8] especially after the Dubuque publisher expressed the wish that President Wilson would recognize the pope and the Holy See "as factors for real neutrality and real peace for the world."[9] In this way, the *Catholic Tribune* became a means by which the Apostolic Delegation gauged the positions of Catholic newspapers and magazines. Gonner's articles on the Roman question and the peace negotiations were sent by Bonzano to Richard Tierney, editor of the equally combative Jesuit magazine *America*, with the aim of issuing as strong an article as possible developing ideas regarding the position of the Holy Father,[10] and to the bishop of Salt Lake City, Joseph Glass. Both men were urged to communicate the content to the editor of the Los Angeles *Tidings*, which until then had been skeptical about Gonner's invectives really obtaining the favor of the Vatican authorities.[11]

Although effective in conditioning the opinions of the press, the propaganda entrusted by the Holy See to Giovanni Bonzano had a significant impact only on Catholics but did not succeed in tempering antipapist invectives in liberal and Protestant circles where it ended up by creating even more intolerance; neither did it give any

6. Giovanni Bonzano to Nicholas Gonner, Washington, D.C., January 23, 1913, and Nicholas Gonner to Giovanni Bonzano, Dubuque, May 7, 1913, ASV, DASU, 9 (dioceses), Dubuque, pos. 66, ff. 7, 11.

7. Nicholas Gonner to Giovanni Bonzano, Dubuque, January 14, 1916, ibid., 5, pos. 68, ff. 10–12.

8. Giovanni Bonzano to Nicholas Gonner, Washington, D.C., January 23, 1916, ibid., f. 13.

9. Nicholas Gonner to Giovanni Bonzano, Dubuque, January 23, 1916, ibid., f. 9.

10. Giovanni Bonzano to Richard Tierney, Washington, D.C., January 21, 1916, ibid., f. 15.

11. Giovanni Bonzano to Joseph Glass, Washington, D.C., January 21, 1916, ibid., f. 14.

incentive to the political establishment to take an interest in the Roman question.

Apart from spreading feelings of hostility to Catholicism, the need to act with great prudence was further dictated by Bonzano's low status as a mere pope's representative among the American ecclesiastical hierarchy, a status that did not allow him to officially report the positions of the Holy See. In fact, the delegate was forced to tell his interlocutors to consider his communications strictly confidential. To use his name in the campaign conducted by the Catholic media would certainly have sparked off a violent reaction in the press. Moreover, the relative young age of the Apostolic Delegation, and the vastness of the United States made it difficult for the delegate to count on the reliability of contacts across the country in its entirety. Relations between the Delegation, the clergy, and civil society were definitely better articulated on the Atlantic coast. Furthermore, the fact that Bonzano had to turn to the bishop of Salt Lake City about questions relating to a Los Angeles newspaper shows how the Apostolic Delegation was unable to effectively exercise its role as mediator between the ecclesiastical hierarchy and the U.S. government. Therefore, until America's entry into the war, Bonzano operated in the wings, by means of the newspaper headlines, trying in this way to influence public opinion. Consequently, the task of interfacing with the White House in search of consensus and support for the claims of Benedict XV was required only of Gibbons, whose attempts were largely ineffective.

In accord with the positions of the Holy See, most members of the American episcopate maintained the neutrality wished by the Wilson administration, avoiding any leaning toward the Central Powers. And yet, largely because of the indiscretion of James Gibbons's revelations to journalists about his visits to the White House, all attempts at mediation not only failed to meet with the president's approval, but ended up by being exploited by the anti-Catholic dailies. Mediation failed to such an extent that the members of the Entente feared much more what Peter D'Agostino called the "disruptive potential" of the Catholic population than the tepid, badly coordinated intentions of the ecclesiastical hierarchy to get Washington to listen to the pope's cause. One example is the letter sent in April 1916 by the Italian ambassador Vincenzo Macchi di Cellere to Sidney Sonnino, in which the diplomat pointed out that American Catholics were a "very important element which, transferred from the religious to the political field, could give them a voice and perhaps enable them to deal with problems that were of importance to the interior life of the country or which relate to the attitude of the State in its foreign relations."[12] The ambassador continued: they are "already a group which carries such weight that, if moved from one side to the other, could upset the balance"[13] and condition the foreign affairs agenda of the administration.

Though legitimate, the fears of the Italian, French, and British governments turned out to be unfounded in the light of Wilson's actions after his reelection to the presidency in November 1916. In a competition mainly notable for the unknown element of how the German community would vote, Wilson was able to count on the vote of the West, which was won thanks to the reforms of the later part of his first administration, just—as the Italian ambassador in Washington noted—what played a role in no small measure was "the agreement quickly made with the Irish Catholic party to put a stop to the persecution of Catholics encouraged by Carranza in Mexico."[14] But more than anything else, the electoral majority recognized that the president had kept the country out of the war and, giving them back their confidence, wanted the position of neutrality to continue. Wilson, on the contrary, had believed for some time that it was necessary to take a more active part in the crisis, and for the whole of the duration of the electoral campaign avoided having to confirm the choice made in August 1914. The continuation of the war, in fact, had induced him to reflect both on its causes and on the changes

12. Vincenzo Macchi di Cellere to Sidney Sonnino, Washington, D.C., April 18, 1916 (n.1398/179), ASMAE, APOG, b. 190.

13. Ibid.

14. Vincenzo Macchi di Cellere to Sidney Sonnino, Washington, D.C., November 27, 1916, ibid.

to be made to the international system in order to avoid such a catastrophe ever occurring again. In what Frank Ninkovich defined as the "internationalism of the crisis,"[15] there was implicit the deep Wilsonian conviction that, in a world of unavoidable interdependence, the traditional means of self-regulation of relations between states no longer worked and that it was therefore necessary to replace them with a new collective structure: a covenant by which the community of world powers could prevent war and assert authority. However, since he put the emphasis on democracy and on self-determination as the basic principles of the new pact, Wilson's plan anticipated many of the contradictions and ambiguities that were greatly to impede its realization. Its universalistic aim, in fact, was shot through with the idea that it was possible to maintain an equidistance between parties, so bringing about an inevitable intensification of hostility toward all "subjects" who did not conform to the model set by the United States. Hence the impossibility of including in the League of Nations the authoritarian and militarist Central Powers, but also the profound conviction of the incompatibility of the Holy See, a force that symbolized conservatism and on which depended the initial support of the Austro-German cause.

### DIVERGENCES OF OPINION ON PEACE

During the winter of 1916–17 the divergences of opinion between Washington and the Vatican seemed to be decreasing. After Wilson, in the name of the neutral powers, proposed a peace conference on December 18, 1916, Giovanni Bonzano was invited by Gasparri to encourage the president's attempts at mediation. At first suggested by Cardinal Gibbons, the apostolic delegate's initiative met with the favor of both the secretary of state, Robert Lansing, and the White House. At the same time, the Holy See had increased its pressure on

15. Frank Ninkovich, *The Wilsonian Century: U.S. Foreign Policy since 1900* (Chicago: University of Chicago Press, 1999), 48–77; on this issue, see also Federico Romero, "Democrazia ed egemonia: Woodrow Wilson e la concezione Americana dell'ordine internazionale nel Novecento," *Passato e Presente* 21 (2003): 17–34.

William II of Germany to show clear signs of being open to negotiation. The peace campaign of the Central Powers a few days before the United States' proposal was announced did not, in fact, receive the welcome they had hoped for from the Vatican, which maintained an attitude of absolute reserve. Wilson's note to the countries at war, on the other hand, received a much warmer welcome in the Vatican. *L'Osservatore Romano* published the complete text accompanied by a flattering comment,[16] which, as Philippe Chenaux notes, "underlined the opportunity offered by such an initiative."[17]

America's entry into the European war scenario had considerable repercussions on the strategies of the Holy See. Since this event changed the balance in favor of the Entente, it was, more than anything else, a demonstration of the ineffectiveness of the work of mediation carried out by the Apostolic Delegation and the American episcopate. Neither Bonzano nor, above all, Gibbons had succeeded in toning down the antipapist attitudes of Wilson and the American public. The "crusade for democracy" that the United States was preparing did not include any kind of involvement of the pontiff; in fact, he was seen as constituting an obstacle to the pursuit of Wilson's objectives.

Apart from this, the American episcopate's and the Vatican's responses to the declaration of war on April 6 were diametrically opposed. As supporters of the "preparedness campaign," the bishops sent President Wilson a letter in which they declared: "We are all true Americans, ready as our age, our ability, and our condition will permit, to do whatsoever is in us to do, for the preservation, the progress and the triumph of our beloved country."[18] Gibbons himself, convinced that the military experience would help to temper the character of young soldiers, called the members of Congress "instruments of God in guiding us in our civic duties."[19] The silence of the Holy See

---

16. "La nota degli Stati Uniti ai governi belligeranti e ai neutri per affrettare la fine della guerra," *L'Osservatore Romano*, December 24, 1916.

17. Chenaux, *Pio XII*, 95; see also Bruti Liberati, "Santa Sede e Stati Uniti," 136.

18. The full text of this letter is quoted in Hennesey, *American Catholics*, 225.

19. Quoted in Thomas T. McAvoy, *A History of the Catholic Church in the United States* (Notre Dame, Ind.: University of Notre Dame Press, 1969), 364.

with regard to the position taken up by the American hierarchy, on the contrary, gave it to understand that Vatican diplomacy was almost resigned to the impossibility of collaborating with Washington in defining the conditions of an eventual peace negotiation. This can be seen in the almost total absence of communication, from March to July 1917, between the secretary of state, the Apostolic Delegation, and Cardinal Gibbons. This fact, if compared with the frequency of Gasparri's solicitations to his American interlocutors, explains how the Vatican had decided to change the nature of its efforts in mediating for peace.

There no longer existing the indispensible condition of American neutrality and, with it, any reasonable possibility of obtaining protection for the integrity of Austro-German territory at the same time as a solution to the Roman question, the Holy See made a desperate attempt to restore its good name in the eyes of the Entente, basically by trying to save the moral authority of the pope and Vatican impartiality. This was the reason, in May 1917, for the nomination of Eugenio Pacelli as apostolic nuncio to Bavaria, entrusting him with the delicate task of sounding out the real intentions of the Central Powers.[20]

On August 1, 1917, Benedict XV published his Peace Note. His document underlined the priority of the moral force of the law over the war; this, in effect, meant simultaneous reciprocal arms reduction, the institution of international arbitration, freedom of speech, and, above all, freedom of the seas. Regarding the pending questions about territories, especially those between Italy and Austria and between Germany and France, the pope did not hesitate to break away from his predecessors' positions and follow the principle of self-determination of peoples as a basis for a future political reorganization of the continent. His hopes for a positive response from the governments at war, however, were soon to be dashed.[21]

20. See Emma Fattorini, *Germania e Santa Sede: Le nunziature di Pacelli tra la Grande Guerra e la Repubblica di Weimar* (Bologna: il Mulino, 1992), 45–92.

21. On the pontiff's Note of August 1917, see Angelo Martini, "La Nota di Benedetto XV alle potenze belligeranti nell'agosto 1917," in *Benedetto XV, i cat-*

While in Germany the government delayed taking up a position, limiting itself to a generic and uncompromising show of sympathy for the points expressed by the pope, the Vatican secretary of state addressed James Gibbons again. In spite of its previous reservations about the cardinal, the Holy See continued to use him as an intermediary with Wilson even after the United States' entry into the war. There was no alternative, of course. Giovanni Bonzano received the Note on August 10,[22] and it was his task to sort out Gasparri's instructions. "The purpose of communicating these proposals to Your Eminence," wrote the delegate to Gibbons, "is that you may endeavor to exert your influence either directly or indirectly towards favorably disposing the government of the United States."[23]

The cardinal's reaction to this exhortation was to avoid any public expression of the pope's initiative, but he did promise "to use to whatever power I may possess to influence the people and the Government of the United States toward favorable consideration of the proposals";[24] he also said he was convinced "that the President's forthcoming reply to the Holy Father's letter will be expressed in a courteous and benevolent language which will exercise a sobering influence on the Press of this country as well as on the allied Powers."[25]

Evidently the almost total lack of contact in those final months prevented Gibbons from obtaining any detailed knowledge of the government's real positions. Above all, it seems that he knew nothing about Robert Lansing's opinion that the Note "emanates from Austria-Hungary and is probably sanctioned by the German Government."[26] The representatives of the Allied Powers, however, must

---

*tolici e la prima guerra mondiale,* ed. Giuseppe Rossini, 361–86 (Rome: Edizioni Cinque Lune, 1963); and Antonio Scottà, "Benedetto XV, la pace e la Conferenza di Parigi," in Scottà, ed., *La Conferenza di Parigi,* 441–42.

22. Pietro Gasparri to Giovanni Bonzano, Vatican, August 10, 1917, ASV, DASU, 5, pos. 63 b/1, f. 40.

23. Giovanni Bonzano to James Gibbons, Washington, D.C., August 4, 1917, ibid, f. 41.

24. James Gibbons to Giovanni Bonzano, Baltimore, August 17, 1917, ibid, f. 43.

25. Ibid.

26. Robert Lansing to Woodrow Wilson, Washington, D.C., August 13, 1917,

have been better informed. To the Italian ambassador, Macchi di Cellere, for example, Lansing was unable to "disguise his irritation," nor "keep himself from admitting that the Vatican's proposal could not have been made at a less opportune careful moment."[27] A more thorough reading of the pope's proposal led the U.S. secretary of state to the conclusion "that it practically goes no further than the German peace proposal of last December."[28] On the other hand, the fact of being issued at a time when "the military tide of the Central Powers is at the flood" and "the power of the United States is just beginning to be exerted,"[29] showed that the Note was in reality an expression of the "earnest wish to preserve the Austro-Hungarian Empire which has been the main support of the Vatican for half a century, and has been always faithful to the doctrine of temporal power."[30] It was, then, quite clear that the Department of State, unlike what Gibbons and the Holy See believed, had had a negative reaction to the pontifical document. As far as replying to it was concerned, Lansing "evidently obeyed the instruction not to pronounce himself in any way, but to gather the impressions of others";[31] he thought he had gone far enough by saying that "it would, anyway, be puerile to give an immediate reply and that it was better to wait for the Central Powers to express themselves in order to weigh up their reaction."[32] This gave the Italian embassy the impression that "Wilson will reply to the pontiff's Note and the others will reply separately."[33] Moreover,

---

FRUS, LP, vol. 2: 43. The text of the Note was delivered to Lansing on the evening of August 11 by the British ambassador Cecil Spring Rice.

27. Vincenzo Macchi di Cellere to Sidney Sonnino, Washington, D.C., August 14, 1917, ASMAE, APOG, b. 177.

28. Robert Lansing to Woodrow Wilson, Washington, D.C., August 20, 1917, FRUS, LP, vol. 2: 44.

29. Ibid., 45.

30. From Lansing Desk Diary, August 21, 1917, quoted in Zivojinovic, *The United States*, 86.

31. Vincenzo Macchi di Cellere to Sidney Sonnino, Washington, D.C., August 21, 1917, ASMAE, APOG, b. 177.

32. Ibid.

33. Vincenzo di Cellere to Sidney Sonnino, Washington, D.C., August 23, 1917, ibid.

Wilson was precluded from not replying "for valid internal reasons relating to the great power of the Catholic party in the hands of the fanatical and intransigent Irish who were virtually German allies" as well as the fact that "the President himself was the author of an unwished-for peace initiative which had received a more deferential response."[34]

On August 27, without waiting any longer for the Central Powers to make a move, Wilson took up a position in the name of the allied countries and sent an official reply to the Holy See through English diplomatic channels. While recognizing "the dignity and force of humane and generous motives"[35] that inspired it, the president accused the pope's Note of aiming at a substantial reaffirmation of the status quo ante bellum without, however, making reference to the fact that "the intolerable wrongs done by the furious and brutal power of the Imperial German Government ought to be repaired."[36] That would be totally insufficient to guarantee a just and enduring peace, while the war, and that of United States intervention in particular, was "to deliver the free peoples of the world from the menace and the actual power of a vast military establishment controlled by an irresponsible government."[37] The German regime, in effect, could not be considered a credible interlocutor in a future peace treaty, and for this reason, it had to be defeated. To Wilson, Benedict XV's message sounded more like an appeal for an "armistice" than a way of influencing the consciences of European countries and inducing them to combat despotism. By reaffirming the incompatibility of the assumptions behind the pope's initiative and the underlying reasons for the war being fought by the allied governments, the president's words expressed a serious claim for the need to exclude the Holy See from peace negotiations.

Wilson's response to the pope's Note met with great success.

34. Ibid.
35. Robert Lansing to Thomas N. Page, Washington, D.C., August 27, 1917, FRUS, 1917, The World War, Supplement 2, vol. 1: 178.
36. Ibid., 179.
37. Ibid., 178.

Though less explicit in its detail, the allied governments—whom American diplomats had sounded out beforehand[38]—agreed on the fact that the pope's proposal was far too favorable to Germany. In London, Wilson's words were received more enthusiastically than any previous statement;[39] in Paris it was said that the position of the United States reflected faithfully that of all the other allied countries;[40] while the Italian government's response was equally favorable, with the minister of foreign affairs Sonnino and Ambassador Macchi di Cellere being among the first to hope that Wilson would quickly take up a position.[41]

Comments on the Note by the American press were just as negative. In August, the *New York Times* published a series of editorials which, echoing Wilson's words, accused the pope—said to be in agreement with the Central Powers—of having left the real problems of the war totally unsolved, proposing as they did an unacceptable form of armistice which made all the countries at war equally to blame.[42]

Apart from embittering public opinion, which tended already to be anti-Catholic, Benedict XV's initiative put the American ecclesiastical hierarchy in an even more difficult position. Effectively excluded from the discussions that had preceded the decision to promulgate the Note, the episcopate found itself having to deal with the consequences. Even though they had achieved appreciable results, in fact, the bishops had worked to defend Catholic citizens from the accusation of having been disloyal to the country during the war. Aware of how much local public opinion loathed the idea of the pope exercising his leadership in international affairs, they were equally convinced that the best way of softening the tone of the defamatory campaign against the pope was not to contest the official

38. Robert Lansing to Diplomatic Representatives in Allied Countries, Washington, D.C., August 18, 1917, ibid., 165.
39. Thomas N. Page to Robert Lansing, Paris, August 31, 1917, ibid., 182.
40. William Sharp to Robert Lansing, Paris, August 31, 1917, ibid., 182.
41. John Jay to Robert Lansing, Rome, August 21, 1917, ibid., 167; and Vincenzo Macchi di Cellere to Sidney Sonnino, ASMAE, APOG, b. 177.
42. "The Pope's Peace Proposal," *New York Times*, August 15, 1917, p. 8.

## INCOMPATIBLE UNIVERSALISMS

position of the government. This is the direction they had chosen to take up to that point.

But reactions to the publication of the Note were not unanimous. In a speech delivered to the Federation of Catholic Societies, for example, the archbishop of San Francisco, Edward Hanna, asserted that "there can be no permanent peace on earth until rulers hearken to the appeal of the Pope;[43] decisively more cautious, James Gibbons did no more than underline the way the pope was "actuated by lofty, humane, and disinterested motives,"[44] hoping he did not need to make public declarations in favor of Benedict, nor have to take resource to British bishops against the exclusion of the Vatican from the eventual Peace Conference.

According to Peter D'Agostino, Gibbons's caution was the fruit of a realistic evaluation of possible future support for the Note by Wilson and the Department of State;[45] John Tracy Ellis, on the other hand, saw in it a sort of "spite" for his having been excluded from the direct approaches of the apostolic delegate Bonzano to Robert Lansing the previous December.[46] However, there is no evidence that Gibbons's decisions derived from precise instructions from the Holy See. But it is true that the American Catholic press became a protagonist in a very heated cut-and-thrust with those newspapers that had contested the pope's initiative. The severe accusations of the *New York Times*, the *New Republic*, and the *Atlantic Monthly* that the Note concealed Benedict XV's wish to win back temporal power in order to extend the privileges of the Church, were followed from September to November by the equally vehement rejoinders of the *Catholic News*, the Jesuit journal *America*, and the Paulist periodical *Catholic World*.[47]

43. "Says Rulers Must Hearken to Pope," *New York Times*, August 27, 1917, p. 1.
44. "Cardinal Gibbons's View," in *New York Times*, August 16, 1917, p. 2.
45. See D'Agostino, *Rome in America*, 117.
46. See John T. Ellis, "James Gibbons of Baltimore," in Gerald P. Fogarty, ed., *Patterns of Episcopal Leadership* (New York: Macmillan, 1989), 120–23; and also Bruti Liberati, "Santa Sede e Stati Uniti," 138–45.
47. "The Pope's Peace Plea," *Catholic News*, August 18, 1917, p. 4; "The Pope's Peace Note," *America*, October 6, 1917, p. 653; *Catholic World*, November 1917, p. 283,

Nevertheless, Sidney Sonnino's accusations against the Vatican for its presumed responsibility for the defeat of the Italian army at Caporetto (October 24, 1917) contributed to making the argument even more bitter. Immediately confirmed by the *Morning Post* of London, the inferences of the Italian government soon spread to the United States. While an editorial in the *New York Tribune* confirmed the idea that there has been papal involvement, stating that "every clerical influence has been exerted to break down the morale of the Italian soldiers," *America* and the *Catholic News* called these accusations an "outrageous misrepresentation."[48]

As early as August, *L'Avvenire d'Italia*, on the contrary, had commented on the pope's document that "the part that concerns freedom of the seas is expressed in the same words as President Wilson,"[49] while it was not until September that *America*, having read the president's response to the Note, pointed out that "in certain fundamentals Wilson and Benedict XV are in complete harmony."[50] But it was the article by Count Giuseppe Della Torre, published in *Nuova Antologia* a little before the disappointing response of the German government to the Note, that dealt in detail with the compatibility of the pope's text with Wilson's actions.[51] This article, comments Antonio Scottà, "expressed in organic form Benedict XV's political vision not only with regard to the war, but to the whole internal organization of a nation inspired by the democratic system and that of the international community."[52] It was also given to understand that the

---

which quotes the defamatory article by Herbert Croly published in the *Atlantic Monthly*.

48. "The Pope and the War," *Catholic News*, December 1, 1917, p. 4, which makes reference to the *Morning Post* and the *New York Tribune*; "Anti-Catholic Propaganda in the Allied Camp," *America*, December 22, 1917, p. 278. On the presumed involvement of the Vatican in the Battle of Caporetto, see Christopher Seton-Watson, *Italy from Liberalism to Fascism, 1870–1925* (London: Methuen, 1967), 477–97.

49. *L'Avvenire d'Italia*, August 17, 1917.

50. "The President's Reply," *America*, September 8, 1917, p. 552.

51. Giuseppe Dalla Torre, "L'appello di pace del papa e la risposta di Wilson," *Nuova Antologia*, September 1917, pp. 189–90.

52. Scottà, "Benedetto XV, la pace," 443.

Holy See was amazed by the negative response of the United States since the Note, in effect, reaffirmed the same principles laid out by Wilson.

Similarly, it was an error on Gasparri's part to overestimate the basic analogy between the pope's proposal and the position of the United States. The Vatican secretary of state was aware that Washington would not have accepted compromises with Germany, especially regarding the Belgium situation. Unlike Wilson, however, he believed in the possibility of involving the Central Powers in the negotiation process. In a note to the British ambassador to the Holy See, in fact, though admitting that "it would most certainly be in the interests of peace for German's responses to all the points to be explicit," Gasparri maintained that Germany would like to leave "the door open to an exchange of ideas."[53] With regard to disarmament, the institution of an international arbitration and, more generally, the willingness of countries at war to bring the conflict to an end in the interests of a lasting peace, he also cited the examples of England and the United States as proof that "voluntary military service certainly guarantees the contingent necessary for maintaining public order, but cannot provide the huge armies required by modern warfare."[54] This was a subtle attempt to censure excessive Austrian-German militarism, followed, however, by the incautious and totally inappropriate urgency of a request to participate in the peace treaties.[55]

Gasparri's words succeeded only in irritating both Wilson and Lansing; and not only because the cardinal made no reference to the official reply of the U.S. government.[56] In fact, the president rejected the whole idea of his own plan for redesigning the international system being put side-by-side with the pope's Note; he believed that simply stating democratic principles, self-determination, and Bene-

---

53. Francesco Imperiali to Sidney Sonnino, London, September 28, 1917, AS-MAE, APOG. B. 177, which reports the content of Gasparri's note to the British minister Count John. F. C. de Salis.

54. Ibid.

55. Ibid.

56. Vincenzo Macchi di Cellere to Sidney Sonnino, Washington, D.C., October 8, 1917, ibid.

dict XV's claim to be the prime moral force was insufficient to demonstrate the impartiality of the Holy See, and certainly not enough to legitimize the Vatican's request for a solution to the Roman question.

Wilson therefore felt the need to reaffirm the special nature of his thinking: to underline the fact that the methods used until then were functional to the reasons for his country's entering the war; to separate the American crusade for democracy against both Soviet heresy and papal conservatism. He did this on August 8 by announcing his fourteen-points peace program, which condensed all the touchstones of Wilsonian democratic idealism, above all the creation of a great international organization to protect the independence and territorial integrity of every state.

The reactions of the American press to Wilson's new program were by no means homogenous.[57] While the propaganda of liberal circles continued to present the pope's plan as German-oriented, the Catholic press insisted on the similarities between America's Fourteen Points and the pope's Note. For the latter it was an occasion to intensify the polemic against Article 15 of the Pact of London of which, until December, the Soviet revolutionary government had circulated an inaccurate version which, as well as pointing once again to the decision to exclude the Holy See from an eventual peace conference, added that it was the wish of the Triple Entente to prevent Vatican diplomats from mediating in any way.[58]

On January 18, one of the founders of the *Catholic Encyclopedia* and director of the monthly *Messenger*, the Jesuit John Wynne, informed Giovanni Bonzano that he had asked all the Catholic editors east of Pittsburgh to present Wilson's points as being identical to those of Benedict XV. It seemed to him that "the similarity of these two messages should be emphasized in order to offset the manifest propaganda of our Press to construe the Pope's attitude as pro-German and to

---

57. On Europe's reaction to Wilson's Fourteen Points, see Thomas Knock, *To End All Wars: Woodrow Wilson and the Quest for a New World Order* (New York: Oxford University Press, 1991), 180–98.

58. The Soviet version of Article 15 was published in "The Holy Father's Calumniators," *America*, December 8, 1917, p. 217.

blame him for the collapse of the Italian armies."[59] The reply to his appeal, however, came not only from the Atlantic coast. The bishop of St. Cloud (Minnesota), for example, told the apostolic delegate that he had mobilized the faithful and the local press in defense of the pope.[60] Similar responses came from all over the country.

The basic point of Catholic mobilization in America, the amendment of the controversial Article 15 of the Pact of London, became the main concern of Vatican diplomacy in the nine months preceding the Peace Conference. Encouraged by the openness of the new Italian prime minister Vittorio Emanuele Orlando,[61] Gasparri would have liked Gibbons to put direct pressure on Wilson and to use the influence of Catholics in the allied countries. During his first mission to Rome, however, Father Sigorney Fay, the American Red Cross delegate in Italy, pointed out to the Vatican secretary of state and his delegate archbishop Bonaventura Cerretti the problems of dealing directly with the American president, and advised them to contact the British ambassador in Washington. Fay, in fact, had close relations both with the minister of foreign affairs, Lord Balfour, and with the British ambassador to the Holy See, Count de Salis, and knew how the press campaign launched by American Catholics and the pressure exercised by the episcopates of New Zealand, Canada, and Australia had made a deep impression on the government of London to the point of inducing them to consider abolishing Article 15.

Gibbons gauged his movements, therefore, according to Fay's advice. One result was *America*'s publication of "The War Policy of the Pope," an article which, in appearance at least, limited itself to praising the humane efforts of Benedict XV, who was called "a co-sufferer with all the nations in the conflict," but whose real aim was to raise the awareness of the faithful and encourage them to support the pope because "more than ever he needs the support of his loyal

---

59. John Wynne to Giovanni Bonzano, New York, January 18, 1918, ASV, DASU, 5, pos. 63 b/1, f. 65.

60. Joseph Busch to Giovanni Bonzano, St. Cloud, January 20, 1918, ibid., f. 67.

61. See Vittorio E. Orlando, *Miei rapporti di governo con la Santa Sede* (Milan: Garzanti, 1944), 102–3.

children."⁶² This article was enthusiastically received by both Bonzano and Gasparri,⁶³ published one day before Gibbons's meeting on February 24 with the British ambassador to the United States, Lord Rufus Reading, and influenced the meeting's outcome. In fact, the idea of an international front supporting the Holy See's request to take part in peace negotiations so intimidated the British diplomat that he immediately sent a telegram to Balfour with a summary of Gibbons's observations and a request to sound out the allies' opinions on modifying the provisions of the secret Pact of April 1915.

However, both Washington and Rome stood firm. On July 3, 1918, Sidney Sonnino informed the ambassadors in London, Paris, and Washington of the proposal to modify Article 15 discussed by the Belgian cardinal Desirè Mercier and Lord Balfour as suggested by Gasparri. The text of this message, which was unofficially communicated by a Belgian deputy, read: "Aucun non belligerent ne sera admis à la Conférence éventuelle de paix, si ce n'est du consentement des soussignés."⁶⁴ By strengthening the position of all countries not at war, this change introduced not a few elements of ambiguity, but above all it threatened to remove from the Italian government the power of veto on the admission of the Holy See. "It is my opinion," observed Sonnino, "that we cannot in any way consent to the discussion of any review, modification or substitution of the sanctioned provisions;"⁶⁵ and he asked the embassies to "act at once to demolish any further attempt by the Holy See and to keep him precisely informed of any further events."⁶⁶

Above all else, Sonnino feared that Wilson would give way to the British initiative. And he wrote to Macchi di Cellere on August 2 that "I have very confidentially been informed that the Vatican is working to get President Wilson to take the initiative of recommending to

---

62. "The War Policy of the Pope," *America*, February 23, 1918, pp. 487–88.

63. Giovanni Bonzano to James Gibbons, Washington, D.C., February 26, 1918; and Pietro Gasparri to Giovanni Bonzano (cipher), Vatican, April 24, 1918, ASV, DASU, 5, pos. 663 b/1, ff. 79, 74.

64. Sidney Sonnino to the Ambassadors in Paris, London and Washington (telegram n. 1111), Rome, July 3, 1918, ibid.

65. Ibid.

66. Ibid.

your Government the modification of Article 15 of the Convention of London so that all the allied powers agree that no neutral state can be admitted to the Peace Conference without their consent."[67]

The next day, Sonnino warned the ambassador that, in his conversations with the Belgian minister of foreign affairs, Gasparri had made known the intention of the American bishops to meet in order to publically demonstrate against the exclusion of the Holy See from peace negotiations.[68] However, Macchi di Cellere came to the conclusion that Italy had nothing to fear because the American government "is avoiding and will avoid unto the last any declaration and modification, not binding but simply compromising," their being "fully against the tendencies and aspirations of the Vatican."[69] These impressions were supported by the equally reassuring statements of Robert Lansing to the ambassador during a confidential conversation. "We are a republic, and like France, Switzerland and other republics we do not wish to set up relations with the Holy See," whose objectives, the secretary of state confided, "are openly in contrast to the democratic ideals of America."[70]

On the other hand, first in February and then in May, the U. S. government had repeated its wish not to accept compromises either on the question of the breakup of the Austro-Hungarian Empire or on the involvement of the pontifical representatives at the imminent Peace Conference.

Cardinal Gibbons was fully aware of this. When, following the positive outcome of the discussions between Mercier and the British government, the Vatican's secretary of state asked him, through Bonzano, to meet the American president, sure that "a word from Mr. Wilson to the Italian government would solve everything,"[71] the elderly archbishop of Baltimore refused to comply with Gasparri's

67. Sidney Sonnino to Vincenzo Macchi di Cellere (confidential), Rome, August 2, 1918, ibid.
68. Sidney Sonnino to Vincenzo Macchi di Cellere, Rome, August 2, 1918, ibid.
69. Vincenzo Macchi di Cellere to Sidney Sonnino, Washington, D.C., August 24, 1918, ibid.
70. Ibid.
71. Pietro Gasparri to Giovanni Bonzano (cipher), Vatican, July 31, 1918, ASV, DASU, 5, pos. 63 b/1, f. 88.

request, pointing out that, at such a crucial moment in the war, it would be difficult for the United States to take up a position on the internal affairs of their Italian ally. Basically, he "refused to allow himself and the American Church to be drawn into a situation that might increase American anti-Catholic prejudice."[72]

On October 10, 1918, when the defeat of the Central Powers seemed imminent, Gasparri asked Bonzano to arrange a meeting between Gibbons and Wilson to discuss the request for an armistice made by Austria-Hungary.[73] The following day, the secretary of state sent to the Apostolic Delegation the text of an appeal for peace signed by Benedict XV and addressed to the president.[74] Vatican documents give us to understand that, not Gibbons, but Bonzano, presumably delegating his secretary the task of delivering it, transmitted the pope's letter to the White House. This is shown by the fact that, in his reply to Benedict XV of October 17, Wilson courteously thanked "the Archbishop John Bonzano."[75] Regarding Gibbons, the delegate told Gasparri that he had met him on October 14 to discuss his personal mediation as requested. On that occasion, however, the headstrong cardinal had considered the Holy See's step inopportune, and making it understood that he would limit himself to writing to Wilson because he believed that "a visit to the White House would anger the President."[76] For at least another three weeks, Bonzano received no further news and was therefore led to suppose that Gibbons "had received no reply on the matter."[77] This supposition, though it was not clear whether or not Gibbons had written to the president before his official reply, was the pretext used by the delegate to raise

72. Fogarty, "La Chiesa negli Stati Uniti," 220. See also Ellis, *The Life*, 272–78; and Bruti Liberati, "Santa Sede e Stati Uniti," 145.
73. Pietro Gaspari to Giovanni Bonzano (cipher), Vatican, October 10, 1918, ASV, DASU, 5, pos. 63 b/1, f. 91.
74. Pietro Gasparri to Giovanni Bonzano (telegram), with the attached letter from Benedict XV to Woodrow Wilson, Vatican, October 11, 1918, ibid., f. 94.
75. Woodrow Wilson to Giovanni Bonzano, Washington, D.C., October 17, 1918, ibid. f. 96.
76. Giovanni Bonzano to Pietro Gasparri, Washington, D.C., October 28, 1918, ibid., f. 93 rv.
77. Ibid.

the question of his deep reserves about the cardinal's sense of discretion. "Once again," wrote Bonzano, "he must have kept the secret very jealously, given the fact that a Sulpician Father spoke about this task given to His Eminence as being inopportune and dangerous."[78]

Apart from Gibbons's attitude, it was Wilson's reply that caused greater concern. It was, in fact, a short and formal letter, almost a simple act of courtesy, quite inoffensive in the way it carefully avoided dealing with the subjects on which the pope hoped the president would pronounce himself. So much so that Gasparri, in an almost desperate attempt, asked Gibbons, this time without Bonzano's intervention, to launch a further appeal to Wilson pointing out what, in the Vatican's view, were the points on which to base the negotiation once the hostilities were definitively over. Above all, "the allies and Mr. President should agree on the main conditions for peace with Germany in order to avoid further misunderstanding"; and then, "these conditions should be such as not to leave seeds of revenge; and therefore moderate and compatible with the honor of Germany."[79] These words were followed by Gibbons's unsurprising silence, and were not to be repeated at the now imminent Conference of Versailles.

## TOWARD VERSAILLES

Wilson arrived in Europe three months before the opening of the Peace Conference. With the intention of agreeing with the allies on a common strategy to use at the conference, he went first to France, then to England, and finally to Italy. His visit to Italy, scheduled for early January 1919, was seen by the Holy See as yet another opportunity to convince the president to revisit Article 15 of the Pact of London and to discuss a possible solution to the Roman question.

On November 29, 1918, Bishop Patrick Hayes, about to be nominated archbishop of New York, communicated to Bonzano that he

78. Ibid.
79. Pietro Gasparri to James Gibbons, Vatican, October 30, 1918, ibid., pos. 63 b/2, f. 108.

had mobilized some of the most influential figures of the New York area, among whom were the judge of the supreme court, Victor Dowling; deputy Thomas Smith; Morgan O'Brien; Nicholas Brady; John D. Ryane, who has just retired from the position of second assistant secretary of war; and even the elected governor Alfred Smith. All were aware of the importance of a meeting between Wilson and Benedict XV, and assured that "proper representation will be made in the right place."[80] Dowling said that he would send, through the director of the committee for war activities of the Knights of Columbus, William Mulligan, a letter to Colonel Edward House, a trusted adviser to the president; and also Al Smith and the Massachusetts senator David Walsh did everything they could "to make known how important the matter is politically."[81]

When the cardinal of Boston William Henry O'Connell received the compliments of the apostolic delegate for his speech to the League of Catholic Women, he said he was upset by the Vatican's exclusion, remarking how the Associated Press had been "far more intent upon reporting what distinguished prelates have to say in superlative adulation of the President than in anything concerning the Holy See."[82] Alluding to the excessive deference paid to the president, he was almost certainly referring to Gibbons's appeal of November 27. "As an American as well as a Catholic, as one who is bound to you by the bonds of patriotism as I am bound to the Holy Father in the bonds of religion,"[83] the cardinal asked the president to pay a visit to the pope as soon as he arrived in Rome. Such a gesture of openness to the representative of the greatest moral force remaining in the world would, in Gibbons's view, reinforce the image of Wilson, "the one who raised the late war from the plane of national jealousies into the plane of idealism and made it a conflict and a struggle for

---

80. Patrick Hayes to Giovanni Bonzano, New York, November 29, 1918, ibid., f. 118.

81. Ibid.

82. William H. O'Connell to Giovanni Bonzano, Boston, December 3, 1918, ibid., f. 145rv.

83. James Gibbons to Woodrow Wilson (copy), Baltimore, November 27, 1918, ibid., f. 123.

justice."[84] To this request, however, the president gave a noncommittal reply, saying that he would take the suggestion into consideration.[85] This was the umpteenth time that the United States showed that it believed that the role of the pope should be limited to spiritual matters without any claim of a political nature.

However much against his will, Wilson agreed to meet Benedict XV. When his journey to Italy was being planned and the possibility of a visit to the pope was put forward, the president had impulsively refused. The Catholic Church did not figure among the forces he intended to mobilize for his peace plan; if it had, it would have played a marginal role. The difficulty he experienced in relating to the Vatican, on the other hand, had never been only religious. If, as a Presbyterian, he had followed the expansion of Catholicism in America with diffidence, as a political leader he had no intention of "experiencing the competition of democracy maintained by Christian beliefs as had been described in Benedict's peace proposal."[86] Furthermore, as Bonzano said at the beginning of December, the president "had a bad impression when Mr. Davison, President of the American Red Cross, was not conceded an audience with the pope."[87]

It was Joseph Tumulty, his personal adviser, who almost certainly persuaded Wilson to change his mind by suggesting that he should look carefully and pragmatically at the influence the pope could exercise on European people in favor of his ideas,[88] before giving up. The audience, the first ever with an American president, took place in the Vatican on January 9, 1919. There is no official American archival evidence, or documents in the Vatican archives, to show that, contrary to the expectations of the Holy See, this exchange had

84. Ibid.
85. Woodrow Wilson to James Gibbons, Washington, D.C., November 30, 1918, ibid., f. 129.
86. Danilo Veneruso, "La Conferenza di pace di Parigi nel contesto dei tentativi di Wilson e Lenin di costruire aree ad estensione mondiale," in Scottà, ed., *La Conferenza di pace di Parigi,* 59.
87. Giovanni Bonzano to Pietro Gasparri, Washington, D.C., December 6, 1918, ASV, DASU, 5, pos. 63 b/2, f. 126.
88. Joseph Tumulty to Wilson, Washington, D.C., December 18, 1918, FRUS, 1919, The Paris Peace Conference, vol. 1: 150.

no significant content, or that Wilson was unwilling to venture beyond relatively unimportant matters, so avoiding the need to deal with questions relating to the imminent peace negotiations.[89]

Having received yet another refusal from Wilson to back their requests, Vatican diplomats attempted to get introduced into the Paris talks the Roman question, and the American Church played a primary role.

Just before the conference opened on January 17, Gasparri, through Bonzano, asked Cardinals O'Connell and Gibbons to translate into French for the benefit of the archbishop of Malines-Brussels Desirè Mercier, a message of the type: "subscriptions in favor of war orphans going well."[90] According to the codes used by the Holy See to make their wishes known at Versailles, this apparently innocent telegram, Gasparri explained, meant that the Belgian primate should "ask the Peace Congress, in the name of the Cardinals, the Episcopate and the Catholics of America for the territorial sovereignty of the Pope."[91] The hopes that the Belgian archbishop, who enjoyed great prestige among the victors, would be able to move the waters on the question of the Vatican's position in international matters, were dashed, coming up against a wall of disinterest during the conference. On March 25, in fact, Mercier wrote both to Wilson and to Clemenceau asking them to close the negotiations with a religious service in the Cathedral of Notre Dame and to send there all the cardinals of the allied countries. Later, in May, he informed Gasparri of what he had done and attached a reply from the French president, whose support was lukewarm. Mercier also said that he had been informed by Edward House that there was little chance of involving Wilson in a "plan of any religious and Catholic nature."[92] House had

89. "Visit to Pope caused no hostile criticisms; it had no political significance." This was the comment of the American ambassador to Italy, Nelson Page, two days after Wilson's visit to the Vatican. See Nelson Page to Woodrow Wilson, Rome, January 11, 1919, ibid., 154.

90. Pietro Gasparri to Giovanni Bonzano (cipher), Vatican, Janary 17, 1919, ASV, DASU, 5, pos. 63 b/3, f. 148.

91. Ibid.

92. Desirè Mercier to Pietro Gasparri, Malines, May 14, 1919, ASV, AES, War Europe, vol. 15, fasc. 23c.

already told Father Francis C. Kelley of Chicago about his perplexity regarding Wilson's intentions to discuss the Roman question with Mercier as he considered that it was totally extraneous to United States interests.[93]

On February 2, 1920, Gasparri, who had never completely interrupted the negotiation with the Italian prime minister, Francesco Saverio Nitti, exhorted the Apostolic Delegation in Washington to put pressure on Wilson to assume a "more favorable attitude to Italy, highlighting the fact that otherwise Italy's internal peace would be seriously compromised with grave repercussions in the whole of Europe."[94] Bonzano turned, therefore, to those he considered best suited to the purpose: those members of the episcopate who, unlike Gibbons, had better contact with the government. Responses were almost immediate: Archbishop Dennis Dougherty of Philadelphia told Bonzano he had spoken to a close friend in the ministry of justice, Mitchell Palmer; while Patrick Hayes of New York said that he had been present at the nomination ceremony of the new secretary of state, Bainbridge Colby, to explain the problem.[95] However, they must soon have realized that it was not exactly the best of moments to discuss matters with the president.

During these delicate months, Wilson did not consider reviewing his position on the "Adriatic question," neither did he do anything about the territorial aspirations of the Vatican. A few friends in Washington had given Dennis Dougherty to understand that Wilson would be inflexible over Fiume.[96] "Nothing could be done; Wilson is practically powerless, and the others, namely England, France and Italy, know it just as well as we do" was the comment of the archbishop of Chicago, George Mundelein, who suggested that Bonzano

---

93. See Francis C. Kelley, *The Bishop Jots It Down* (New York: Harper, 1939), 266.
94. Pietro Gasparri to Giovanni Bonzano, Vatican, February 23, 1920, ASV, DASU, 5, pos. 101, f. 3.
95. Dennis Dougherty to Giovanni Bonzano, Philadelphia, February 25, 1920, and, in the same date, Patrick Hayes to Giovanni Bonzano, New York, ibid., ff. 6–7, 8–9.
96. Dennis Dougherty to Giovanni Bonzano, Philadelphia, February 27, 1920, ASV, DASU, 5, pos. 101, ff. 10–11.

"remain inactive."[97] The internal state of confusion of the Democratic Party was such, he added, "that no one knows what to do and no one has the courage to take any steps."[98] A few days after receiving this communication from Mundelein, the apostolic delegate received confirmation from Admiral William Benson that Wilson would not like to hear that the Vatican was putting pressure on his staff through the episcopate.[99]

But neither Wilson nor the Democratic Party was to be the Holy See's interlocutors for much longer. Politically weakened by the midterm elections of 1918, the president had by now lost control of the executive. His inflexibility and the zeal, at times exaggerated, with which he had defended the outcome of the Conference of Versailles ended up by reinforcing the vast front of the opposition, ready to exploit the ever-increasing "Europhobia" of public opinion by presenting both the Peace Treaty and the League of Nations as a symbol of the servitude of the country in the interests of unreliable European countries. The defeat of the Democrats at the presidential election of 1920 showed how tired people were of Wilson's high-sounding idealism. James Cox and the candidate to the vice-presidency Franklin Delano Roosevelt intended to repropose Wilson's internationalist plan, but were beaten by a wide margin by the Republican candidate Warren Harding who, instead of proposing heroic sacrifices at home and abroad, promised the nation to heal the wounds caused by the war.

### A MISSED OCCASION?

The end of the war and the outcome of peace negotiations gave the Americans a deep sense of disappointment. The plan to reestablish the international system on a democratic basis, which was Wilson's justification for entering the dispute, was wrecked, showing that however immensely destructive the war had been, it had not suc-

97. George Mundelein to Giovanni Bonzano, Chicago, February 28, 1920, ibid., f. 17r.
98. Ibid., f. 17v.
99. Giovanni Bonzano to Pietro Gasparri, Washington, D.C., March 9, 1920, ibid., ff. 23–28.

ceeded in bringing about a break with the past. Once the phase of patriotic enthusiasm was over, the United States began to reflect on the structural contradictions of Wilsonian universalism, and in particular on the clear discrepancy between victorious-sounding aims and the decidedly modest results of mediation with European allies. Wilsonianism and, with it, the war experience, began to be perceived as a negative parenthesis, a deviation from the normal course of U.S. history.[100]

The three Republican administrations that followed after World War I interpreted their role as a return to prewar "normalcy," and the need to distance themselves from Wilsonism took on a decidedly more temperate and less assertive attitude in world politics.[101]

With the exit of Wilson and the stylistic excesses of Wilsonianism, relationships with the Holy See too brought about a return to prewar normality. Wilson's attitude to the Vatican was in many ways absolutely organic to the ideological canons of the WASP culture, just as his refusal to recognize the pope as having a role to play in mediation in international affairs represented a substantial re-proposal of the policy to freeze all relations with the Holy See in 1867.

And yet, during the war, Wilson pushed all such radical positions beyond their usual limits. Behind his visceral antipapist attitude there was much more both of a personal repulsion to Catholic immigrants, and of criticism of the pro-German line of the Holy See. Basically, there was the idea of total incompatibility between his own radical design of the international system and that of Benedict XV, which was just as universalistic in its vocation. Apart from the correspondences and similarities between his Fourteen Points and the pope's Note, Wilson rejected the whole idea of the Vatican being able to take part in the existential mission with which he believed the United States to be invested.

---

100. For some reflections on the limits of Wilsonian universalism, see, among others, Lloyd Ambrosius, *Wilsonianism: Woodrow Wilson and His Legacy in American Foreign Relations* (New York: Macmillan, 2002), 125–34.

101. Thomas Guinsburg, "The Triumph of Isolationism," in *American Foreign Relations Reconsidered, 1890–1993*, ed. Gordon Martel (London: Routledge, 1994), 90–105.

From this point of view, then, the "Great War" aligned all the traditional reasons for antagonism and incompatibility between the North American Republic and the Holy See, and projected them for the first time since the Italian Risorgimento onto the intricate territory of international relations. In spite of the fact that attempts to influence American politics had been useless, the Vatican drew some important lessons from the inauspicious war experience. First, that they would have to look elsewhere, and above all with greater pragmatism than Benedict XV, in order to resolve the Roman question; and second, that in order to mend the tear with the White House, it was necessary to solder relations with the American ecclesiastical hierarchy which was gradually giving birth to a new leadership that was better integrated into the local political circuit and more willing to fall in with Vatican strategy.

This, then, was the beginning of a decade of transition at the end of which, despite the recurrence of American nativism, the Holy See and the North American Republic would take their first, even if imperceptible, steps toward an improvement in their relations.

# 3

# TROUBLED TIMES

## AFTER THE GREAT WAR:
## RAGING AMERICAN NATIONALISM

Contrary to Wilson's hope, World War I was not the war to end all wars. At Versailles, his attempts to arrive at a compromise enabling the construction of a stable international system regulated by the democratic principles contained in his Fourteen Points of January 1918 were frustrated by the European allies, especially the French, who worked for their respective national interests.

The stubborn, short-sighted attitude of European statesmen made them "continue to believe they ruled the world, but in fact they laboriously plodded along in an attempt to solve the international problems of their continent."[1] Incapable of adapting to the transformations brought about by the Great War, they allowed old antagonisms to cause new rancor, which was to spark off a new catastrophe in the space of a few years.[2]

The combination of international stability, American supremacy, and recovery of credits created close interconnections. Hence Washington's attempts to stimulate European economic recovery on which depended not only the repayment of debts incurred during the war, but also European political stability and the retrenchment of revo-

---

1. Ennio Di Nolfo, *Dagli imperi miliari agli imperi tecnologici. La politica internazionale dal XX secolo a oggi*, 3rd ed. (Rome: Laterza, 2008), 57.
2. On these points, see Anthony P. Adamthwaite, *The Making of the Second World War* (New York: Routledge, 1989), 27–33.

lutionary movements, above all communism. Added to this was the need to avoid any continuation of the excessive loss of balance that came about at Versailles and which, apart from anything else, would have penalized American exports.³ Together with the equally complicated issues of disarmament and war reparations, these were the main issues of postwar American foreign policy: an internationalism variously described by historians as independent, conservative, even normal.⁴ In other words, the U.S. approach was cautious, strictly in harmony with the delicate scenario of the early 1920s, which did not call for any rebuilding of the international system, but for attempts to solve specific problems. This, then, was neither disinterest nor selfish isolationism, but a decision to cooperate based on the conviction that the primacy earned during the war would guarantee the ability to influence the decisions made by other powers.⁵

The protagonists of this policy were the three Republican administrations of 1921–1933, for the Republicans had gained control of the executive branch after eight years of Democratic government. In all probability, any Republican could have won in 1920, but Warren Harding was a particularly strong candidate because he could in no way be identified with any of the large-scale plans to remake America or the world. Unlike the other potential candidates of the Grand Old Party, he had never attempted to revive the Treaty of Versailles or to join the League of Nations. His ideas on many of the controversial issues of the time, usually expressed in speeches overloaded with commonplaces, were vague, so that during the electoral cam-

---

3. See Frank Costigliola, *Awkward Dominion: American Political, Economic and Cultural Relations with Europe, 1919–1933* (Ithaca, N.Y.: Cornell University Press, 1984); and Melvin P. Leffler, *The Elusive Quest: America's Pursuit of European Stability and French Security, 1919–1933* (Chapel Hill: University of North Carolina Press, 1977).

4. These three descriptions are found respectively in Guinsburg, "The Triumph of Isolationism," 90–105; Robert D. Schulzinger, *U.S. Diplomacy since 1900*, 6th ed. (New York: Oxford University Press, 2007); and Ninkovich, *The Wilsonian Century*, 78–105.

5. See Selig Alder, *The Uncertain Giant, 1921–1941: American Foreign Policy between the Wars* (New York: Collier Books, 1965).

paign he did no more than utter a dozen or so statements without ever making his views clear. And yet this was enough to bring him victory in the 1920 presidential elections.[6]

Harding gave the impression of being able to satisfy the needs of American society when, at Boston in May 1920, in a speech before his nomination as a candidate for the presidency, he promised the country a return to "normalcy." By this term, destined to enter American political folklore, he meant the wish to return to an even and peaceful way of living after the fretful parenthesis of the war that had clearly influenced every single aspect of American life and accelerated the profound processes of change which, in large measure, were the legacy of the controversial Progressive Era.

From lifestyles to models of consumption; from the organization of production systems to interethnic, intercultural and interreligious dynamics; from forms of political participation to the very definition of the priorities of both foreign and home affairs, the image of the United States in the postwar decade is one of a country in transition where, side by side with economic growth and the spread of consumer culture after the restraints of reconversion, there emerged an equally spontaneous wave of nationalism.[7]

Anti-alienism, religious fundamentalism, prohibitionism, and libertarianism were all manifestations of the outburst of nativism or, as Mario Del Pero has described it, that "beast patriotism"[8] that characterized early postwar American society. Though its origins were many and heterogeneous, what these reactionary and conformist movements had in common was the unsatisfied need for order and stability. Alarmed by what they saw as the ugly specter of racial degenera-

6. See Wesley M. Bagby, *The Road to Normalcy: The Presidential Campaign and Election of 1920* (Baltimore.: Johns Hopkins University Press, 1962).

7. Among the immense literature on the United States during the 1920s, see especially John H. Hicks, *Republican Ascendancy, 1921–1933* (New York: Read Books, 2008); and David J. Goldberg, *Discontented America: The United States in the 1920s* (Baltimore: Johns Hopkins University Press, 1999), 40–65. The sociocultural factors are dealt with in detail in Lynn Dumenil, *The Modern Temper: American Culture and Society in the 1920s* (New York: Hill & Wang, 1995).

8. Del Pero, *Libertà e impero*, 231.

tion and the decline of the nation, millions of citizens believed that by voting, first for Harding's "normalcy," then for Calvin Coolidge, they would be able to revive the image of social equilibrium that had existed before the Great War. In effect, this was the WASP America that was moving to defend its identity by trying its muscles and reacting emotionally at the same time, clearly anxious to block any sign of change in the national social and political structures. This sparked off a long and bitter cultural conflict between the majority of white Protestants, who thought of themselves as the inheritors of the founding values of the Republic, and of ethnic minorities, who were seen more than ever as "hyphenated" outsiders after the increase in migration between the end of the nineteenth century and the beginning of the twentieth.[9]

During the mobilization campaign of 1916, and more so after the war, the American nativists, goaded on by British propaganda, turned their nationalistic hatred in particular on the communities of naturalized Germans and Irish. Opposed, for different reasons, to the administration's decision to side with the Triple Entente countries, these communities were accused of disloyalty and ingratitude to the United States for backing—sometimes with demonstrations of violence—the interests of their respective nations of origin against those of their adopted country.

After the war, and during the so-called Red Scare of 1919–20, nativism was above all an antidote to political radicalism. In effect, this was a reaction against the penetration of revolutionary ideas into the country, ideas that, in the wake of Bolshevism, threatened to spread in the "Old Continent." Once hostilities were over, immigrants were automatically identified as presumed agents of enemy states. This stereotype, though the fruit of anti-alienist demagogic

---

9. For a long-period overview on this subject, see Michael C. LeMay, *From Open Door to Dutch Door: An Analysis of U.S. Immigration Policy since 1820* (Westport, Conn.: Greenwood Press, 1987), 20–37. On the racism of American intellectuals in the nineteenth and twentieth centuries, see James B. Gilbert, *Work without Salvation: America's Intellectual and Industrial Alienation, 1880–1910* (Baltimore: Johns Hopkins University Press, 1977); and Higham, *Strangers in the Land*, 109–10, 154–57.

simplifications of the time, was inevitably inflated by the substantial involvement of naturalized workers in prevalently industrial strikes, as well as by their membership in subversive organizations such as the pro-Soviet fringe of the American Socialist Party.

However, antiradicalism ceased to be a priority as soon as the great fear of revolution faded. "Once the war and the immediate postwar period passed," observes John Higham, "the two leading nativist traditions of the early twentieth century, Anglo-Saxonism and anti-Catholicism, reoccupied the field."[10] Their aggressive reappearance was a direct consequence of the sudden arrival, between May and September 1920, of a new influx of immigrants at Ellis Island. The pages of the two most influential magazines of the time, the *Literary Digest* and *Current History*, began to fill up with editorials on the devastating effects that the new wave of migration would have on the fragile socioeconomic system of the United States.[11] The very popular *Saturday Evening Post* even reissued passages on the theory of race that Madison Grant had collected in *The Passing of the Great Race*, published in 1916, but which had not until then found a particularly large reading public.[12] In this regard, the restrictive measures taken by Congress—the Emergency Quota Act (1921) and the more drastic National Origins Act (1924)—were the main achievement of the nativist battle. The second of these, above all, in calculating "national quotas," privileged European immigrants from northern Europe to the disadvantage of those from the south and east. Furthermore, a more general analysis of this legislation made it unequivocally explicit that the United States no longer believed either in the country's capacity to absorb different ethnic, cultural, and religious groups or that the historical tendency to interbreeding should be encouraged.[13]

And it went even further. Given the profound changes that

10. Higham, *Strangers in the Land*, 266.
11. "The New Tide of Immigration," *Current History* 12 (1920): 704–5; *The Literary Digest*, June 5, 1920. p. 32.
12. *Saturday Evening Post*, May 7, 1920, p. 20.
13. On the triumph of restrictionism in the 1920s, see Donna R. Gabaccia, *Immigration and American Diversity: A Social and Cultural History* (Malden, Mass.: Blackwell, 2002), 168–99.

American society was experiencing, nativism did not exhaust its ideological and cultural drive with the "Anglo-Saxonism" and other expressions of intolerance, moral conformism, and political conservatism I have described. It was, in fact, through the fresh outbreak of anti-Catholicism, both in its theoretical formulation and in its concrete manifestations, that it fully developed its potential aggressiveness and extremism. After all, hostility to Catholicism had deep roots in the history and culture of the United States.[14]

## "NORMAL" ANTIPAPISM IN THE EARLY 1920S

Considered to be antithetical to the founding values of the Republic, Catholicism became the favorite target of the Protestant public as far back as the early nineteenth century. Though they feared the spread of the cult practices, models of instruction, and political aspirations of the Catholics, they particularly poured invective on the figure and work of the popes.[15]

From 1834 to 1836 the Reverend William C. Brownlee, editor of the *American Protestant Vindicator*, one of the best-known anti-Catholic periodicals of the time, promoted the theory that there existed an international papal conspiracy backed by the European Catholic monarchies that aimed at the destruction of American freedom.[16] Also around the 1830s, similar preoccupations regarding a possible putsch prepared by Pope Gregory XVI were expressed in the writings of Samuel F. B. Morse.[17] Furthermore, a flourishing literary genre be-

14. On this topic, see Robert P. Lockwood, ed., *Anti-Catholicism in American Culture* (Huntington, Ind.: Our Sunday Visitor, 2000).

15. For a detailed analysis of the priorities of American Protestant fundamentalism in the nineteenth century, see Ray A. Billington, *The Protestant Crusade, 1800–1860: A Study of the Origins of American Nativism* (Chicago: Quadrangle Books, 1964).

16. These ideas appear again in William C. Brownlee, *Popery, An Enemy to Civil and Religious Liberty; and Dangerous to Our Republic*, (New York: John S. Gaylor, 1836); and in Brownlee, *Letters in the Roman Catholic Controversy* (New York: Published by the Author, 1834), 325–59.

17. See Samuel F. B. Morse, *Foreign Conspiracy against the Liberties of the United States* (New York: Leavitt, 1835), 42–59.

gan to report episodes of Catholic clergy pedophilia and sexual abuse of cloistered nuns which suggested that high-up Vatican members cohabited with them.[18] A belief just as deeply ingrained and diffused in the United States was that, for Catholics, obedience to the pope came before anything else, like during the Mexican War of 1846–48, when about two hundred soldiers, mostly Irish, of the Union Army, who were often forced to the front line as soon as they arrived on American shores, decided to desert, and with Captain John O'Reilly as their leader, formed the San Patricio Battalion to fight side by side with their religious brothers, the Mexicans.[19]

Italian unity, and especially the intransigence and obstinacy with which Pius IX claimed the temporal power that the events of September 1870 had deprived him of, were only detrimental to the pope's image on the other side of the Atlantic. In political and diplomatic terms, the abrupt freezing of relations with the Holy See before the conquest of Rome by the Kingdom of Italy was the most striking demonstration of how the United States wished to distance itself from the Church of Rome.

Anti-Catholic attitudes, largely shared by both Democrats and Republicans, drew new life from the late nineteenth-century national population increase, this in large measure due to entry into the country of numerous influxes of European immigrants, many of them Catholic. The American Protective Association fought to introduce competence in English for purposes of naturalization and in order to dismiss Catholic teachers from public schools. Its founder, Henry Bowers, repeatedly underlined in the *APA Magazine* the incompatibility of Americanism and Catholicism, while the *North American Review* and the *American Patriot* published various articles by another declared enemy of political Romanism, William J. H.

---

18. See Rebecca Reeds, *Six Months in a Convent* (Boston: Russell & Co., 1835).

19. See especially Ted C. Hinckley, "American Anti-Catholicism during the Mexican War," *Pacific Historical Review* 31, no. 2 (May 1962): 121–37; Richard B. McCormack, "The San Patricio Deserters in the Mexican War," *The Americas* 8 (October 1951): 131–42; and Robert C. Doyle, *The Enemy in Our Hands: America's Treatment of Prisoners of War from the Revolution to the War on Terror* (Lexington: University of Kentucky Press, 2010), 69–88.

Traynor, who stated that the pope's encyclicals attempted to exempt the faithful from respect for the U. S. Constitution.[20]

During the Great War, both at home and on the front, the participation of the American Catholic community was significant.[21] This was not enough, however, to soften the tone of Protestant propaganda.[22] In spite of the fact that the ecclesiastical hierarchy itself had, on more than one occasion, sided with President Wilson's policies, most of public opinion saw in the local Catholic press's solidarity with Benedict XV yet more evidence that it was right to doubt the loyalty and patriotism of the Catholics.[23] This was a problem whose solution was certainly not helped by the Vatican's "ambiguous" attitude toward the Central Powers or, even less, by the pope's claim to have a right to a mediational role in the peace process.

Anti-Catholicism had absolute preeminence in the dreadful postwar nativist wave. Coming to a head in the climate of insecurity and vulnerability produced by the upset of demographic and economic balance following the new influx of immigration, it spread mainly in the South. That is, it flourished in the rural areas and small towns that regarded with growing preoccupation the linguistic, religious, and cultural Babel in the ever-growing metropolis, and it was inevitably accompanied by the coeval revival of Protestant fundamentalism, giving rise to a formidable degree of intolerance.[24]

---

20. See Les Wallace, *The Rhetoric of Anti-Catholicism: The American Protective Association, 1887–1911* (New York: Garland, 1990); and David H. Bennett, *The Party of Fear: From Nativist Movements to the New Right in America* (Chapel Hill: University of North Carolina Press, 1988), 171–77.

21. See Patricia McNeal, "Catholic Conscientious Objection during World War II," *Catholic Historical Review* 61 (1975): 232.

22. A large, well-documented collection of American anti-Catholic literature and journalism of the first twenty years of the twentieth century is to be found in Justin Nordstrom, *Danger on the Doorstep: Anti-Catholicism and American Print Culture in the Progressive Era* (Notre Dame, Ind.: University of Notre Dame Press, 2006).

23. See Nancy G. Ford, *Americans All! Foreign-Born Soldiers in World War I* (College Station: Texas A & M University Press, 2001), 16–44.

24. On the connection between Protestant fundamentalism and anti-Catholicism in the southern United States, see Norman F. Furniss, *The Fundamentalist Controversy, 1918–1931* (New Haven, Conn.: Yale University Press, 1954).

Many of the anti-Catholic organizations and periodicals that enjoyed great success in the southern states during the first half of the 1920s had emerged on the eve of the Great War. In Missouri, the widely read anti-Catholic weekly *The Menace,* founded by Wilbur F. Phelps in 1911, was replaced by the more radical *Torch.* A new model of associationism, mostly secret but better structured compared with previous fundamentalist organizations such as the Guardians of Liberty, the Knights of Luther, and the Covenanters, began to take hold, and it showed from the very outset its capacity to influence not only public opinion, but also the decisions of the political establishment. There were frequent cases, at various levels, in which the discriminatory and anti-alienist policies of such organizations, mainly directed at Catholics, became the main points declared from electoral platforms and the policies of local administrations. In 1919, the prohibitionist governor of Alabama Thomas Kilby set up a commission of enquiry into activities in convents and, on the model of a similar law passed in Pennsylvania in 1913, passed a law requiring the compulsory reading of the Bible in public schools.[25] The following year, during the elections in Georgia, the Democratic candidate to the Senate Tom Watson made antipapism the focus of his campaign and went so far as to accuse President Wilson of not responding firmly enough to Benedict XV's attempts to manipulate American Catholics in a time of war. Again in 1920, the secret society of True Americans, which mainly devoted itself to the anti-Catholic cause, even checked out the government of the densely populated city of Birmingham, Alabama, causing the expulsion of all municipal employees who were Catholic.[26] Again, in Florida, the Democratic governor Sidney J. Catts used a series of meetings and public speeches to warn the population against an alleged plan of the pope's to invade the state and transfer the Apostolic See there.[27]

Outside the southern states, anti-Catholic nativism did not ex-

25. See Higham, *Strangers in the Land,* 180, 265, 292.
26. This episode was reconstructed by Charles P. Sweeney, "Bigotry in the South," *The Nation,* November 24, 1920, pp. 585–86.
27. See Higham, *Strangers in the Land,* 292.

ist with the same level of violence and intolerance. On a national scale, it was less evident but much more effective. The introduction of quotas to regulate migratory flows and, before that, the Eighteenth Constitutional Amendment, ensured notable exclusion of Catholics from the most important public offices, so confirming that they were considered not only to be drunkards, criminals, and foreign agents, but also second-class citizens: anti-American subjects to be fought using first the political and juridical means of Republican institutions, and then force. The Ku Klux Klan (KKK) itself, which reemerged in Georgia in 1915 and then spread along the Pacific coast, throughout the Midwest, and in the northern Atlantic states—burning crosses, plundering, mutilating and sometimes killing Catholics, Jews, and blacks—reached the height of its success when the brutal practices with which it began gave way to a more pragmatic strategy of applying pressure within the two main national political parties.

Given this political and cultural climate dominated by more-or-less aggressive forms of nationalism of which anti-Catholicism in general and antipapism in particular were the most shocking manifestations, it is natural to wonder what the attitude of America's elite was toward the large Catholic community. What were the repercussions of relations with the Holy See? And above all, what was the reaction of American Catholics? As we have seen, none of the Republican administrations of the 1920s did much to oppose the nativists who, whether or not members of the various secret societies, managed to take with them into Congress the increasingly anti-alienist hysteria of the time and obtain the approval of laws restricting immigration.

In this as in many other matters, Warren Harding maintained a noncommittal attitude in spite of his memberships in the KKK.[28] Unlike Wilson, however, he was certainly not an outright antipapist. His lack of interest in the possibility of a renewal of relations with the Vatican, occasionally raised during his brief presidency, seemed to be dictated more by political opportunism than by any real ideo-

---

28. See Wyn C. Wade, *The Fiery Cross: The Ku Klux Klan in America* (New York: Oxford University Press, 1987), 165.

logical leaning. In no way, should the normalcy promised to his electors have meant an improvement in relations with the pope, taken as a symbol of the "old" traitor and of warmonger Europe; in actual fact, his diplomatic cold-shouldering of the Holy See had been going on for more than seventy years and no president had questioned it. And yet it was during the three years or so of Harding's presidency that something began to change. Not because there had been some brief sign of rapprochement, but because—even while the winds of nativism were blowing strongly—the American Catholic Church gave its own response to the profound social, economic, and cultural changes of the time, so beginning a radical phase of change both in its own internal structure and in its way of operating. In this it was encouraged, and to a certain extent driven, by Rome, which was also involved in this important period of change.

## THE AMERICAN CATHOLIC CHURCH FROM BENEDICT XV TO PIUS XI

In May 1922, at the First Presbyterian Church in New York, Harry Emerson Fosdick delivered a provocative sermon entitled "Shall the Fundamentalists Win?" This prominent figure of liberal Protestantism in the early twentieth century accused the most extreme fringes of the American fundamentalist movement of allowing their message of hatred and intolerance to distance many "moderate" believers from Christianity.[29] A similar assessment of the consequences of fundamentalist radicalism is expressed by Eldon Ernst in his history of the Interchurch World Movement, where he notes that in the early postwar years "crusading Protestantism was losing its traditional hold on the American people as a whole and on the social and cultural tone of the nation."[30]

---

29. On this subject, see Robert M. Miller, *Harry Emerson Fosdick: Preacher, Pastor, Prophet* (New York: Oxford University Press, 1985), 112–49.

30. Eldon G. Ernst, *Moment of Truth for Protestant America: Interchurch Campaigns Following World War One* (Missoula, Mont.: American Academy of Religion, 1972), 170–71.

In effect, although postwar nativism had voiced exclusivist and xenophobic sentiments in the American WASP culture and, thanks to political support, had had notable success on the legislative level, this did not prevent forces defined as "alien" and "anti-American" from developing. On the contrary, it was the survival instinct that helped to bring together those groups for whom the label of "undesirables" was decidedly unsuited. With an often notable dynamism and desire for renewal, they began to reflect on their role within the troubled American society of the 1920s, claiming their right to give full expression to their respective cultures and religions. The Catholic component, being the nativists' favorite target for invective, was probably the most involved in this phenomenon of change.

At the time the country entered the First World War, the American Catholic Church had no organized structure at the national level. The last plenary council had been held at Baltimore in 1884 and since then, as a result of the promulgation of the apostolic letter condemning Americanism, *Testem Benevolentiae* (1899), its annual assemblies of bishops had been the only instrument of united action. But the issues relating to the war made necessary a reinforcement of connections between the ecclesiastical hierarchy and the various Catholic organizations in the country and at the front.

With the consensus of Cardinals Gibbons, O'Connell, and Farley, Father John J. Burke, editor of the Paulist periodical *Catholic World* and founder of the Chaplain's Aid Association, called a meeting in Washington of representatives from all the Catholic societies and churches and all the dioceses.[31] On August 11 and 12, 1917, four months after war had been declared on Germany, as many as 115 delegates from sixty-eight dioceses and twenty-seven organizations met at the Catholic University of America. At the end of the proceedings, Burke, flanked by an executive committee made up of exponents from each ecclesiastical province, from the Knights of Columbus, and the American Federation of Catholic Societies, announced the constitution of the National Catholic War Council. Its objective

---

31. See Hennesey, *American Catholics*, 226.

was "to study, coordinate, unify and put in operation all Catholic activities incidental to the war."[32]

Between November 1917 and January of the following year, the program drafted in Washington was definitively approved by the episcopate. In order to ensure the correctness of the War Council's actions, it was subjected to the supervision of an administrative council of bishops presided over by Peter J. Muldoon of Rockford, Illinois, assisted by Joseph Schrembs of Toledo, William Russell of Charleston, and Patrick J. Hayes, assistant to Cardinal Farley of New York and ecclesiastical supervisor of the military chaplains. John Burke immediately made contact with the Department of War and with the other Protestant and Jewish agencies, and was given the delicate task of managing the Committee on Special War Activities with its seven subcommittees.

During the war, the National Catholic War Council was extraordinarily successful. It made a substantial contribution to the most important collector of funds—the United War Work—of the period; financed the efforts of the Knights of Columbus, whose role had been decisive in the convocation of the August assembly and which, through its recreational activities, the diffusion of books, and psychological support afforded to soldiers, was the most significant Catholic presence in army camps throughout the country and in Europe; it was also patron to the institution of the Catholic School for Social Services in Washington, D.C., whose pupils, once the hostilities were over, were sent to Europe to assist in the reconstruction of the Old Continent.[33]

The Great War was therefore a kind of testing ground for American Catholicism: an occasion to find its potential and show that it was capable of making a contribution to the good of the country.[34]

---

32. Joseph McShane, *"Sufficiently Radical": Catholicism, Progressivism, and the Bishops' Program of 1919* (Washington, D.C.: The Catholic University of America Press, 1986), 72.

33. See Christopher Kauffman, *Faith and Fraternalism: The History of the Knights of Columbus, 1882–1982* (New York: Harper and Row, 1982), 190–227.

34. See Douglas J. Slawson, *The Foundation and First Decade of the National*

Or at least many promoters of the War Council were convinced that this was the legacy of the war; and in fact Burke and Muldoon, in the light of a more effective promotion of Catholic interests in times of peace, considered making the organization permanent, though it had been devised with the specific intention of ending its work as soon as the war ended.[35] However, this possibility met with great resistance and ended up by reviving the old disagreements within the ecclesiastical hierarchy that had emerged at Baltimore in 1884 and never been resolved.

Though aware of the fact that, by reinforcing its presence in the capital, the Church would have drawn considerable advantage from being able to exercise greater pressure on the decisions of the federal government, many bishops feared that the new structure of the organization led by Burke might in some way erode their local authority and even, in the long run, become an instrument in the hands of the Vatican to take more control of the episcopate, whose wish for autonomy had always preoccupied Rome.[36] These matters were bitterly disputed following the golden jubilee of James Gibbons, which took place at the Catholic University of America in Washington, D.C., on February 20, 1919.

The representative sent to the ceremony by Benedict XV was Archbishop Bonaventura Cerretti, secretary to the Congregation of Extraordinary Ecclesiastical Affairs. The undoubted importance of the event and the fact that Gibbons was the last living participant of the First Vatican Council were not Benedict's only reasons for such a prestigious choice. Being well versed in the dynamics of international affairs, the pope understood that only the United States possessed the resources necessary to help the peoples suffering from the effects of the war. Apart from its humanitarian aim, America's economic sup-

---

*Catholic Welfare Council* (Washington, D.C.: The Catholic University of America Press, 1992), 45–46.

35. The reasons for making the Catholic War Council permanent are analyzed by Elizabeth McKeown in "The National Bishops' Conference: An Analysis of Its Origins," *Catholic Historical Review* 66 (1980): 565–75.

36. See on this issue Camilla J. Kari, *Public Witness: The Pastoral Letters of the American Catholic Bishops* (Collegeville, Minn.: Liturgical Press, 2004), 35–36.

port would help to relax the great social tensions in European countries, thereby eliminating the risk of revolutionary ideas finding fertile ground in the wake of events in Russia.

Just before the surrender of the Central Powers, in fact, the Vatican secretary of state had asked the apostolic delegate Bonzano to "involve the American cardinals in the feeding of Germany" with the intention of "avoiding death by starvation and preventing to threaten the triumph of Bolshevism."[37] During the following weeks, there was a massive mobilization of the American Church and, in all probability, the pope himself put the matter to Wilson during their brief meeting in the Vatican in January 1919, immediately before the Conference of Versailles opened its doors without the participation of the Holy See.

In this way, Gibbons's golden jubilee became an occasion to discuss both the internal problems of the American Church and the role it should play in supporting the peace strategies of Vatican diplomacy. On both fronts, Cerretti's appeals for the unity of the ecclesiastical hierarchy were decisive in the attempt to make the plan to reconstruct the Catholic War Council a reality.[38]

Knowing that neither Bonzano nor even Gasparri was satisfied with the way he had handled relations with the Wilson administration, Gibbons did not hesitate to follow up the bishops' requests that the Holy See had sent to Washington. During the jubilee celebrations, in his role as senior member of the episcopate, he nominated a committee of three archbishops and four bishops—including Muldoon, Schrembs, and Russell—who the next day presented to the other bishops the first draft of a plan providing for the setting up of a permanent group to work side by side with the entire hierarchy.

On May 1, 1919, having received Benedict XV's approval of the plan, Gibbons sent the bishops a letter that reasserted the goal that the new organizational structure, "with adequate authority and the aid of sub-committees would accomplish more than any individu-

---

37. Pietro Gasparri to Giovanni Bonzano, Vatican, November 22, 1918, ASV, DASU, 5, pos. 63 b/2, f. 116.

38. See Fogarty, *The Vatican and the American Hierarchy*, 214–15.

al, however able or willing he might be"; the American Church, he added, "has been suffering from a lack of a unified force"[39] and this necessitated greater cohesion in approaching the centers of political power with the intention of preventing the approval of legislation that was hostile to the Catholic community.[40] On September 24, ninety-two of the one hundred and one American bishops took part in the meeting which was held once again at the Catholic University of America. It was here that they gave final approval to the plan set out in February by the War Council with the backing of Gibbons and the pope. The proposal presented by Muldoon provided for the setting up of an executive committee made up of seven prelates whose task it was to supervise five departments of a permanent character (instruction, social action, laity, press, internal and foreign affairs) which basically corresponded to the main Catholic interests. The bishop of Brooklyn, Charles McDonnell, raised particularly aggressive protests against the plan as a violation of the Code of Canon Law which has come into force only one year before; he went so far as to accuse its supporters of forging the pope's letter of approval. Those "in favor," however—Archbishops Edward J. Hanna of San Francisco, John Glennon of St. Louis, and some of the emerging figures of the hierarchy such as George Mundelein of Chicago and James Keane of Dubuque—managed to get the upper hand. Though they were unable to reach agreement on matters relating to financial management, the bishops' conference ratified the creation of the National Catholic Welfare Council (NCWC) in September 1919. John Burke was nominated general secretary while Edward Hanna was entrusted with the running of the executive committee.

A closer look suggests that what gave rise to the institution of the NCWC and which was to characterize its first few years was not simply the internal disagreement of the ecclesiastical hierarchy on two different ways of seeing the priorities of the American Church during the troubled postwar period. It was, in fact, the reflection at a lo-

39. James Gibbons to Bishops, Baltimore, May 1, 1919, ACUA, ANCWC, National Catholic War Council Files, box 12, fold. 39.

40. See McKeown, "The National Bishops' Conference," 575–76.

cal level of a worsening of the much deeper conflict within the Vatican between prominent cardinals such as Merry del Val, De Lai, Van Rossum, and Pompilj—all of whom had been Benedict XV's main detractors since the controversial conclave of 1914—and the secretary of state, Gasparri, the tireless "right arm" of the pope.

The death of James Gibbons on March 24, 1921, threatened the survival of the NCWC. As the last archbishop of Baltimore, the oldest of the American episcopal seats, to perform de facto the function of primate, he had been the Vatican's main interlocutor even before being made a cardinal (1886). During the Great War, in spite of his disputable line of conduct and his not always idyllic relationship with the apostolic delegate Bonzano, Benedict XV and Gasparri had laid their hopes in him to convince Wilson to reconsider the Roman question. Thanks to his usual management skills and persuasive powers, the reorganization initially warmly supported by Rome and a large part of the local clergy was soon accomplished. In brief, as the Jesuit historian Gerald Fogarty has said, for nearly half a century "the American Church had virtually meant Cardinal Gibbons."[41]

Two cardinals remained after Gibbons's death; it was William Henry O'Connell of Boston who seemed to be the one to become the new leader because, apart from his being the senior of the two, he was also the only one who intended to carry on in Gibbons's footsteps. The other cardinal, Dennis Dougherty of Philadelphia, suffered from being little known outside his own densely populated archdiocese. Of the archbishops, Patrick Hayes of the prestigious diocese of New York—aptly called the "cardinal of charity"—was exclusively involved in pastoral work.[42] O'Connell, who had been the voice of the strategy of the "romanization" of the episcopate as wished by Pius X and then gradually modified by Benedict XV, had never made a mystery of his preference for the conservative line of Pope Giuseppe Sarto with whom

41. Fogarty, *The Vatican and the American Hierarchy*, 220.
42. On Dennis Dougherty and Patrick Hayes, see James J. Walsh, *Our American Cardinals: Life Stories of the Seven American Cardinals McCloskey, Gibbons, Farley, O'Connell, Dougherty, Mundelein, Hayes* (New York: Books for Libraries Press, 1969), 223–48, 293–342.

he fully shared antimodernism and a strictly doctrinal approach.[43] Hence his strenuous opposition, during the special assembly of the episcopate in September 1919, to the setting up of the NCWC, which he considered to be a kind of congregationalist distraction and, after the death of Gibbons, the reason why the organization should be dismantled.

O'Connell was well aware that to achieve this objective the support of the Holy See was needed, but he had no illusions about being able to obtain it. In October 1921 he described the situation of the American Church to his old friend Merry del Val: "there is all around about an intangible something which would seem to emanate from too much politics, diplomacy and intrigue; too much mingling with affairs which don't concern us. How different in the days of Pius X when the chief concern was to God and when cheap politics and free-masons were kept in their place."[44]

Bitter words, these, evidently dictated by his having waited in vain for months for the rumor concerning the pope's possible change of mind about the agreement with the supporters of the NCWC to become a reality. And yet the chance to return to those yearned-for "splendors" of the time of Pius X came quite soon. On January 22, 1922, Benedict XV died.

### THE 1922 CONCLAVE AND ITS "AMERICAN" CONSEQUENCES

The College of Cardinals met on Thursday, February 2, 1922, to elect the new pope. It was a troubled and "poor" conclave,[45] the longest

43. On O'Connell, see James P. Gaffey, "The Changing of the Guard: The Rise of Cardinal O'Connell of Boston," *Catholic Historical Review* 59 (1973): 225–40; and Douglas J. Slawson, *Ambition and Arrogance: Cardinal William O'Connell of Boston and the American Catholic Church* (San Diego, Calif.: Cobalt Press, 2007), 16–52.

44. O'Connell's letter to Merry del Val, to be found in the Archives of the Archdioceses of Boston, M-850, is quoted by Fogarty, *The Vatican and the American Hierarchy*, 218–9. Fogarty dates it around October 24, 1921.

45. To solve the problem of lack of resources, Gasparri pointed out that "from

of the twentieth century. Four days and fourteen votes were needed before the "white smoke" was seen issuing from the roof of the Sistine Chapel.⁴⁶ The archbishop of Milan, Achille Ratti, received forty-two votes, six more than the necessary quorum. After the *accepto* ritual, he chose to be called Pius XI in memory of the fact that he had entered the seminary under Pius IX and that it was thanks to Pius X that he had been transferred to Rome to indulge in his great love of culture, first as vice-prefect and then as a prefect of the Vatican Library; but also because Pius was a name symbolizing peace, to the furtherance of which Ratti was dedicated, just like his predecessor.⁴⁷

With Ratti on the throne of St. Peter and Gasparri as secretary of state, the hopes of Merry del Val and the other "traditionalists" were dashed. In the view of William O'Connell of Boston, this added insult to injury. Just as had happened in 1914, in fact, accompanied by the other American cardinal Dennis Dougherty, O'Connell arrived late at the Vatican, about half an hour after the new pope had blessed the crowd from the balcony of the Basilica of St. Peter's. Since O'Connell was a close friend of Merry del Val, he and Dougherty would certainly have given their support to avoid Ratti's election. Their votes would almost certainly not have influenced the outcome of the election, but it was also true that for the second time running the heads

---

North America the balance of the last third of the previous year had not yet been received," and asked Giovanni Bonzano to arrange for the sum to be sent; see Pietro Gasparri to Giovanni Bonzano (cipher), Vatican, January 20, 1922, ASV, DASU, 1, pos. 118, f. 16. Bonzano replied immediately: "You will be telegraphed two hundred and ten thousand, four hundred dollars and nine cents. Please destroy the three cheques and advise me by telegraph"; see Giovanni Bonzano to Pietro Gasparri (cipher), Washington, D.C., January 21, 1922, ibid., f. 20.

46. This information on the conclave of 1922 is taken from Max Liebmann, "Les Conclaves de Benoit XV et de Pie XI," *La Nouvelle Revue* 38 (July–August 1963): 46–53.

47. See Carlo Confalonieri, *Pio XI da vicino* (Turin: Editrice SAIE, 1957), 26. On Ratti's papacy, see also Carlo Puricelli, *Un papa brianzolo: Le radici culturali di Achille Ratti, Pio XI* (Milan: Ned Editrice, 1991); Emma Fattorini, *Pio XI, Hitler e Mussolini: La solitudine di in papa* (Turin: Einaudi, 2007); and Jean Dominique Durand, "Lo stile di governo di Pio XI," in *La sollecitudine ecclesiale di Pio XI: Alla luce delle nuove fonti archivistiche*, ed. Cosimo Semeraro (Vatican City: Libreria Editrice Vaticana, 2010), 44–66.

of the American Church had not been able to take part in a conclave.

O'Connell called on Gasparri the same day as his arrival in Rome (February 6), and protested about not receiving either from the Apostolic Delegation, or directly, news of the decline in Benedict XV's health. He also complained about there having been no attempt to put off the beginning of the conclave for a few days.[48] These were harsh words to use with Gasparri, as if he were insinuating that there had been a plot to exclude the American cardinals; but this is proved untrue by the correspondence between the secretary of state and Bonzano,[49] and his words are incomprehensible given the articles on the illness of Benedict XV that appeared in American newspapers.[50]

A few days later, during the first audience conceded him by Pius XI, O'Connell repeated what he had said to Gasparri. Like most of the American hierarchy and the American public, O'Connell did not know Achille Ratti very well. He knew about contacts with Henry Hyvernat, the professor of biblical archeology and Oriental languages at the Catholic University of America; but he could not have imagined that the new pope knew so much about the situation in Boston, which had been at the center of the Holy See's interest for some time. So he was caught out by the questions Ratti asked about his nephew, James P. E. O'Connell, protagonist of the scandals that

48. See Dorothy G. Wayman, *Cardinal O'Connell of Boston: A Biography of William Henry O'Connell, 1859–1944* (New York: Farrar & Co., 1955), 178–81.

49. Pietro Gasparri to Giovanni Bonzano, Vatican, January 20 and 21, 1922, ASV, DASU, 1, pos. 118, ff. 7, 21, prot. n. 4530-f, 4538-f; Giovanni Bonzano to Dennis Dougherty, and Giovanni Bonzano to William H. O'Connell, Washington, D.C., January 20 and 21, 1922, ibid., ff. 8–9, 23–24.

50. See, for example, "Pope Benedict XV, Must Stay in Bed," *Washington Post*, January 19, 1922; "Pope Dying Receives Last Rites," *Washington Times*, January 20, 1922; "Crowds Kneel Outside Vatican Expecting Death News at Any Time," *Washington Herald*, January 21, 1922; "Pope Is Close to Death This Morning," *New York Times*, January 21, 1922. The reason for the two cardinals' late arrival was clarified by Dougherty himself in a letter sent to the Apostolic Delegation from the ocean-going liner *Lorraine* on which he was traveling with O'Connell: "Our small and narrow boat is in a storm. Ever since our departure from New York we have had winds and high waves. The outlook for an early arrival is bad. It is thought we may not arrive there before the 7. Our boat is slow"; see Dennis Dougherty to Giovanni Bonzano, February 2, 1922, ASV, DASU, 1, pos. 119, f. 4.

had involved the diocese of Boston, who had secretly married while holding the important post of chancellor. This was a matter that the American cardinal thought had been closed but which, because of the way it had been handled, had attracted the interest of the pope—not without a certain annoyance—since the thick "Boston dossier" had appeared on his desk the day after his election.[51]

Nevertheless, taking advantage of this moment of transition, O'Connell managed to obtain from his troubled stay in the Vatican an important decree signed by his friend, secretary of the Holy Consistorial Congregation Cardinal Gaetano De Lai, which provided for the immediate breakup of the NCWC. This had been a priority for O'Connell and those of the American ecclesiastical hierarchy who would have like to have seen a different outcome to the conclave. Dated February 25, 1922, the document was delivered to Dennis Dougherty who made an early return to the United States.[52]

At first, Pius XI did not oppose the step. In all probability, he had not yet had the time to look into the controversial question of the new American organization, neither had he expressed himself on the role of episcopal conferences and, more in general, interprovincial and national meetings of bishops.

The NCWC's reaction to the decree was vehement. On April 6, all members of the Administrative Committee except Edward Hanna met in Cleveland at the home of Bishop Schrembs. They unanimously decided to send a cablegram to the pope asking him to reconsider the decision of the Consistorial Congregation. The council's suppression, the bishops argued, would be counterproductive not only to the interests of the American Church, but also to those of the Holy See. The step taken would eventually jeopardize any development of the fragile relations set up by the bishop of Portland, Louis Walsh, and by other members of the committee with the fed-

---

51. See Gerald P. Fogarty, "Pius XI and the Episcopate in the United States," in *Achille Ratti, Pape Pie XI,* 549–50 (Rome: École Francaise de Rome, 1996); and Paula M. Kane, *Separatism and Subculture: Boston Catholicism, 1900–1920* (Chapel Hill: University of North Carolina Press, 1994), 13–21.

52. See Fogarty, *The Vatican and the American Hierarchy,* 220.

eral government and with Herbert Hoover's American Relief Administration in order to protect Catholic citizens bitterly opposed by the Russian Soviet regime.[53] President Harding also played a prominent part in this; Ellis notes that, under pressure from Father Burke,[54] he had spoken to the American ambassador to Italy, Richard Child, to send a delegation to Rome to reinforce his own action. It would be headed by Joseph Schrembs who was due to pay the customary *ad limina* visit to the Vatican. While he was on his way the night of April 25–26, the committee met again, this time in Washington, and decided to consult the Administrative Board of the Catholic University of America, asking them to draft a petition in defense of the council to be sent to the pontiff.[55] The text was submitted to Bonzano, and on his suggestion the members of the committee quickly circulated the petition among the other exponents of the hierarchy in order to collect more signatures. The next day (April 27) the document, translated into Italian by Filippo Bernardini (professor of canon law at the Catholic University of America, advisor to the Apostolic Delegation at Washington, and nephew of Cardinal Gasparri), was delivered to the archbishop of Cincinnati, Henry Moeller, who was about to visit Schrembs in Rome.[56] The petition, which Fogarty has described as being "a poignant expression of the pain felt at the dawn of a new pontificate,"[57] stated: "Upon the whole Hierarchy of our country, the decision taken by the Consistorial Congregation seems to put the stigma of a suspected loyalty and of incompetence; and it suppresses our most cherished organization upon which we had founded the greatest hopes for the defense and prosperity of religion in our country."[58] Its signatories (about 90 percent of the ecclesiastical

53. Administrative Committee, April 6, 1922, ACUA, ANCWC, OGS, box 60, fold. 28: 32–33.

54. See Ellis, *Documents*, 607–13.

55. Administrative Committee, April 26, 1922, ACUA, ANCWC, OGS, box 60, fold. 28: 34.

56. Administrative Committee, April 27, 1922, ibid., 35–36.

57. Fogarty, "Pius XI and the Episcopate in the United States," 552.

58. Administrative Committee, Petition to His Holiness, Pope Pius XI, April 25, 1922, ACUA, ANCWC, OGS, box 60, fold. 29. For a comment on the petition,

hierarchy) also complained that they had received neither warning nor explanation of why the decision had been taken so hurriedly, reached in fact only eleven days after the election of the pope.[59]

Once at the Vatican, Schrembs delivered the petition to Pius XI on May 30 during the first audience he was granted. Following this, he met first Vladimir Ledochowski, the Jesuit General, who warned him that many cardinals, above all Merry del Val, continued to suspect the promoters of the NCWC of modernism and even feared a schism,[60] and then Tommaso Pio Boggiani, a member of the Consistorial Congregation, who said he had known nothing of the decree before its publication. Basically, Schrembs was now sure that it had been the result of the concerted action of O'Connell, Merry del Val himself, and De Lai, who did nothing to hide from the bishop of Cleveland their fear that the new organization that had emerged in Washington in 1919 could make control of the American episcopate by the Holy See more difficult because of its considerable increase in members.[61]

All of Gasparri's diplomacy and persuasive powers were needed to get Pius XI to instruct the Consistorial Congregation of his intention to retract the order to suppress the NCWC. On June 22, the Consistorial Congregation had to annul the previous decree and authorize the American bishops to meet again in September. Furthermore, in the instructions that followed on July 4, the Vatican advised that the meetings of the episcopate should not be held annually and that attendance should be voluntary; that their decisions should immediately be made public; and above all, that the word "Council," which had a specific connotation in canon law, should be replaced by a more generic term in order to make unequivocal the nonple-

---

see Elizabeth McKeown, "Apologia for an American Catholicism: The Petition and Report of the National Catholic Welfare Council to Pius XI, April 25, 1922," *Church History* 43 (1974): 515.

59. Ibid., 516.

60. Ledochowski's warning is referred to by Hennesey, *American Catholics,* 230.

61. See John B. Sheerin, *Never Look Back: The Career and Concerns of John J. Burke* (New York: Paulist Press, 1975), 74–78.

nary, nonlegislative, but simply consultative character of the organization.[62]

At the preliminary meeting in Chicago (August 11–12), the executive committee proposed replacing "Council" with "Conference" because—as reported in the minutes—this was the word that the Consistorial Congregation had used in its July recommendations.[63] At the general meeting of the episcopate held at Washington on September 27 and 28, the motion was tenaciously supported by the bishop of Portland, Walsh, and in spite of O'Connell's and Dougherty's firm opposition, finally approved by the assembly.[64] The next year (October 1923) all seven members of the executive committee were reconfirmed.

Officially, the newly named National Catholic Welfare Conference (NCWC) retained a purely consultative function.[65] However, John Tracy Ellis notes that "through its Administrative Board of ten of the leading prelates of the country, it has become the highest authoritative body within the American Church."[66] Rather than a simple, though necessary, place for discussing matters regarding the territory, the NCWC therefore became an effective instrument of pressure on the federal government. In the 1920s and, above all, over the next decade, it was to play a crucial role of mediation between the Holy See and the American political establishment. Gerald Fogarty, in fact, points out that the success of the new organization, "horizontal" in structure, was a return to the traditional collegiality of the American Catholic Church; but above all it meant a definitive departure from the rigid pyramid model of the hierarchy that had affirmed itself in the wake of the anti-Americanist reaction of the late nineteenth and early twentieth century and which, as we have seen, had become totally ineffec-

62. Ibid., 78–82.
63. Administrative Committee, April 26, 1922, ACUA, ANCWC, OGS, box 64, fold. 3.
64. Bishops' General Meetings, Minutes, Washington, D.C., September 27–28, 1922, ibid., box 70, fold. 7.
65. On this point, see Gerald P. Fogarty, "Independence: The Anomaly of the American Church," *America*, June 1, 1974 pp. 430–32.
66. Ellis, *American Catholicism*, 141.

tive both in softening antipapist invective and in reactivating some form of dialogue with the White House.[67]

Apart from guaranteeing an objective, though slow and problematic, reinforcement of Catholicism in the troubled American scenario of the years following World War I, the question of the NCWC seems paradigmatic in the context of Ratti's attitude to the local episcopates which, as Giorgio Feliciani notes, "had caused considerable problems"[68] ever since his election as pope. The main reason for this is chronological. The consistorial decree of June 22, 1922, came four years before the first official pronouncement of the Holy See on the matter of general meetings of the bishops. One June 10, 1926, the mixed Plenary Assembly of Consistorial Congregations, Extraordinary Ecclesiastical Affairs and the NCWC came to the conclusion that the "General Conferences of the Episcopate should not be disciplined by a single regulation of a public character, but appropriate special instructions should correct abuses introduced in the various regions and recall such conferences to their original spirit and character."[69] That is, precisely as had happened in the United States.

It is important to note, too, that with regard to the function of the nuncios and the apostolic delegates—a question to which Ratti, having experienced difficulties in Poland, immediately dedicated a great deal of attention—the specific case of the United States anticipated a trend that was to characterize the twenty years between the wars. While requiring the ad hoc regulations of the various meetings of bishops to be laid down "in an acceptably wide sense, avoiding what might in any way offend the episcopates as being a kind of breach of trust,"[70]

---

67. See Fogarty, *The Vatican and the American Hierarchy*, 223.
68. Giorgio Feliciani, "Tra diplomazia e pastoralità: Nunzi pontifici ed episcopato locale negli anni di Pio XI," in Cosimo Semeraro, ed., *La sollecitudine ecclesiale*, 69.
69. The minutes of the Plenary Congregation are to be found in ASV, ACV, pos. 229/24, doc. 27, in particular f. 6. For an analysis of the juridical type, see Julio Manzanares, "Las conferencias episcopales en tiempos de Pio XI: Un Capitulo inedito y decisive de su historia," *Revista Espanola des derecho canonico* 36 (1980): 15–56.
70. Sacred Joint General Congregation, Vatican, June 18, 1925, ASV, ACV, pos. 229/24, doc. 16a, f. 5.

Pius XI imperatively required the nuncios and the delegates to take an active part in such general assemblies. This, as Eugenio Pacelli said, would have considerable advantages: the pontiff's representative, "on many serious issues about which the bishops do not have perfectly clear ideas, would be able to put the Holy See on the right lines,"[71] and so avoid "the risk of the President or a group of bishops getting the upper hand over others."[72]

This was an important step in the attempt to "officialize" the institution of episcopal conferences that would be completed only with Vatican Council II. The promotion of synergy between the apostolic delegation and the ecclesiastical hierarchy in the United States became a priority for the Holy See, which saw it as a way of opposing growing hostility to Catholicism and at the same time to encouraging better relations with the government in Washington. In actual fact, following the death of Gibbons and the advent of Pius XI, responsibility for overseeing the interests of American Catholic citizens and interfacing with the White House "shifted elsewhere," as James Hennessy says with insight, "to the pope's Apostolic Delegate, to the American cardinals, and in diffused fashion to the NCWC and its administrative board."[73]

71. Ibid., doc. 26, f. 40.
72. Ibid.
73. Hennesey, *American Catholics*, 240.

## 4

# THE INTERLOCUTORY STAGE

### FIRST SIGNS OF CONVERGENCE

Giovanni Bonzano proved to be a discreet but convincing supporter of the reorganization that culminated in the setting up of the NCWC.[1] During his years spent at the head of the Apostolic Delegation of Washington, and especially during the war, he had been immersed in the difficulties of reconciling the work of various Catholic associations in the country and that of the episcopate with directives from Rome; he had also had to give in when faced with the ostracism of Wilson and his administration at the time the Holy See had tried to win America's goodwill in resolving the Roman question at the Versailles negotiations. In particular, he believed that greater dynamism in the Church could, in the long run at least, improve the image of Catholicism in the eyes of a people greatly conditioned by the nativist stereotype. At the same time, he had no illusions about a possible "change of the guard" in the country's leadership bringing about a substantial and sudden improvement in relations with the federal establishment.

Although the Republican Party had the consent of most of the extremists of anti-Catholic nativism, its leaders appeared at once to wish to establish peaceful relations with the representatives of the Church of Rome. In form if not in substance, their attitude was a step

---

1. See Fogarty, *The Vatican and the American Hierarchy*, 220–28.

forward compared with that of the outgoing administration. This, as Bonzano said to Gasparri when reporting on the content of a meeting with the Republican J. Callan O'Loughlin, was confirmation of how "at the time of elections all politicians try to appear to be our friends," but at the same time put on an unexpected, though instrumental, show of helpfulness.[2]

As for the choice of a presidential candidate, the Apostolic Delegation did not fail to express its reservations to the Vatican secretary of state when commenting on the outcome of the summer 1920 conventions. Harding "is considered to be an able politician, but also weak, and his nomination would seem—putting aside the capitalist interests of the Party—to be due to there being serious accusations against the other most promising candidates."[3] Bonzano added: "he is of course Protestant, and it is rumored that he was initiated into the Masonry, but that he later left it. What politicians fear is that he does not have the strong character of a Roosevelt or a Wilson."[4] As for the Democrats, James Fox seemed to be a better choice of candidate. Bonzano said of him: "he is a good speaker, an able and energetic administrator, is good mannered and holds quite advanced views, and as the Bishop of Columbus [James J. Hartley] once assured me, he is well-disposed toward the Church";[5] "there is, however," the delegate bitterly remarked, "a negative point which unfortunately goes against him, and that is that he is divorced."[6] His eventual election would therefore not be "a very edifying spectacle,"[7] and it would be the first time it had happened in America.

2. Giovanni Bonzano to Pietro Gasparri, Washington, D.C., December 24, 1919, ASV, DASU, 2, pos. 206, f. 6.
3. Giovanni Bonzano to Pietro Gasparri, Washington, D.C., June 23, 1920, ibid., f. 20.
4. Ibid.
5. Giovanni Bonzano to Pietro Gasparri, Washington, D.C., July 10, 1920, ibid., f. 24.
6. Ibid.
7. Ibid. On the matter of Cox's divorce, the apostolic delegate also said that "this fact is certainly displeasing to Catholics and also to traditionally conservative Protestants, but it has little or no importance for most of the American people for whom divorce is legal and part of the country's customs." See Giovanni Bonzano to Pietro Gasparri, Washington, D.C., October 20, 1920, ibid., f. 39.

Even before Warren Harding entered the White House, the press has circulated the news of a possible renewal of relations between the United States and the Vatican. Given the climate of widespread anti-Catholic hysteria and the certainly nonreassuring diplomatic precedents, this was extraordinary. Bonzano himself—to whom the rumors seemed "totally unfounded"—thought it was the British Foreign Office that was dealing with this matter through the secretary of the British Embassy in Washington, Count de Salis, who had visited him in January 1921. According to de Salis, diplomatic relations with the Holy See would increase the "moral prestige both of the Church and of the United States"; moreover, "it was true that many honest, open-minded Protestants would not be against such relations." More than anything else, he feared the "strong" reaction of the more "diehard and fanatical" antipapists. He added that "such relations, if ever reestablished, would be similar to those between Brazil and the Holy See, unless the United States, in view of the interests of the almost exclusively Catholic peoples of Puerto Rico and the Philippines, preferred to conclude an accord in their favor." This was something which, apart from being difficult to bring about unless "the United States constitution were changed," did not seem to be so very urgent given the fact that "the Church cannot complain of its conditions in this country, and that its attitude to the Government—that of all Catholics—was one of loyalty and devotion."[8]

It is clear that Bonzano did not wish to compromise himself. He was aware of the leanings of public opinion with regard to relations with the Vatican and he did not intend to take any risks. A few days after his meeting with Count de Salis, he repeated to a British journalist (who had informed him that Harding, twice questioned on the matter, has expressed himself personally to be indifferent and that "it all depended on the Catholics")[9] that he had "never thought about the matter and had no reason to believe it."[10]

It was, however, impossible not to react to such news. "The involvement of the British Embassy," Bonzano said, "makes me think

8. Ibid., f. 41.
10. Ibid., f. 41.
9. Ibid., f. 42.

that there could be some truth in these rumors, and that the articles in American magazines could be a way of preparing public opinion." He added: "I think that Mr. Harding, who is not unaware of owing his landslide victory to the Catholic vote, is trying to secure it for the future by taking steps to attract our sympathy."[11] The Vatican secretary of state sent no special instructions, only a request to keep him informed "on such an important subject."[12] There was no alternative but to talk to Harding.

Bonzano and Harding met on April 29, 1921. The delegate went to the meeting with much clearer ideas than he had before. A few days earlier, he had had an opportunity to talk to the influential Republican senator Joseph McCormick about a possible renewal of diplomatic relations with the Holy See, and his "clear rebuttal" gave him to understand that "the rumors were without foundation."[13] This was confirmed by Harding himself during their private conversation at the White House. The president "began by saying that in a country so vast in size there is no lack of Protestants who make more noise than others and get alarmed by anything not in line with their views."[14] He said that he had replied to the many letters "asking whether there was any truth in the rumors," saying that so far nothing had been said on the matter, and anyway a ruling on it "depended on Congress, and as far as he knew, Congress had not dealt with, and had no intention of dealing with, such matters."[15] However, given the vehemence of the opponents, he had decided "to cut short these worries by contradicting the rumors"[16] publically. The president also pointed out that the United States had diplomatic relations "only with Powers with temporal supremacy, and not with spiritual heads of religions," so that "he saw no reason why, among so many religious denominations, the United States should have relations with only one of them in preference to others."[17]

11. Ibid., f. 42.
12. Pietro Gasparri to Giovanni Bonzano, Vatican, February 18, 1921, ibid., f. 49.
13. Giovanni Bonzano to Pietro Gasparri, Washington, D.C., May 3, 1921, ibid., f. 59.
14. Ibid.
15. Ibid., f. 61.
16. Ibid.
17. Ibid.

All these considerations were contained in the draft of an official statement prepared by Harding and his advisors. However, Bonzano was invited to "modify any part of it that Catholics might find offensive."[18] As a result, the reference to the purely spiritual sovereignty of the pope was removed from the final version. This, said Bonzano, was "really providential" since the wording of the draft, "if made public, would have seriously invalidated the Roman question."[19] The White House's official statement was issued on May 3.[20] The same day *L'Osservatore Romano* published an article entitled "Harding Does Not Believe It Necessary to Renew Diplomatic Relations with the Vatican." Among the many who were against this step was Maurice James Eagan, former minister of the United States at Copenhagen, "whom many thought would be the new Minister representing the American government."[21]

Although all the difficulties that militated against an improvement in relations between Washington and the supreme pontiff had emerged, Bonzano could be satisfied both with the way he had handled the delicate matter and, above all, with the attitude that Harding had adopted. Compared with the recent past, relations with the administration were decisively more cordial. "Now," pointed out the apostolic delegate after receiving his umpteenth invitation to the White House on the occasion of the ceremony in honor of South American diplomats in May 1921, "it is the President of the United States who—admittedly for his own ends—calls me."[22] This was an impor-

18. Ibid.  19. Ibid.
20. Dispatch from the White House, Attached to Bonzano's report to the Vatican secretary of state, May 3, 1921, ibid., f. 63. "Many inquiries have come to the president relative to a contemplated nomination of a diplomatic representative to the Vatican, and the president has thought it best to answer all of them by the public statement that no consideration has been given to such a step, and there will be no occasion to consider it unless Congress by the enactment of law provides for such representation. The president does not understand that any such proposal has been made to Congress."
21. *L'Osservatore Romano*, May 3, 1921, ibid., f. 58. According to Eagan, "neither the needs of the Church, nor the good of the American Nation, require such an important innovation."
22. Giovanni Bonzano to Pietro Gasparri, Washington, D.C., May 9, 1921, ibid., f. 65.

tant step forward for Bonzano: by assiduously frequenting the places of political power, he might have been able to carry out much more effectively the task of acting as a link between Washington and the Vatican; although formally speaking this was his position, it had been to a large extent ignored during Wilson's presidency.

### THE INTERNATIONAL PERSPECTIVE

In the intricate postwar scenario, scarred by the continuing divergences between European states, the Holy See did all it could to promote the Europe stabilization strategy supported—though not always coherently—by the American political and financial élites.[23]

On January 4, 1922, during the Washington Conference on the Reduction of Naval Weapons, Giovanni Bonzano paid the customary New Year's visit to Harding. The main discussion point during their half-hour talk was arms reduction. The president "expressed his gratitude for the message from the Holy Father"[24] received in May the previous year from which he learned of his decision to return to a discussion of the problem of naval disarmament.[25] He agreed with Bonzano's observation that the only way to deal with the German situation was to solve as soon as possible the question of reparations, and "he showed willing[ness] to cooperate, though apparently he did not yet have a plan ready, and saw France as being an insurmountable hurdle."[26]

Harding's words were an encouragement to the Holy See. They not only showed goodwill toward Catholics, "recently put into positions, especially in the post office, for which he himself chose the holders,"[27]

23. A more detailed study of this topic is to be found in D'Agostino, *Rome in America*, 158–66.
24. Giovanni Bonzano to Pietro Gasparri, Washington, D.C., January 12, 1922, ASV, DASU, 5, pos. 63 b/3, f. 245.
25. Pietro Gasparri to Giovanni Bonzano (cipher), Vatican, May 25, 1921, ibid., f. 238, prot. n. 3073-f. "All our hopes are in America especially after our acceptance to take part in the conference."
26. Giovanni Bonzano to Pietro Gasparri, January 12, 1922, ibid., f. 249.
27. Ibid., ff. 246–47.

and, not least, his solidarity for the relation set up by Bonzano. Above all, his words were proof of how the U.S. administration intended to deal with the European situation, and the extent to which it agreed with the position of the Vatican.

Occupied until the end of the war with the delicate work of mediation, above all to ensure that Italy and Germany were offered better conditions for repayment of their war debts,[28] pontifical diplomacy, through Bonzano, turned to Harding as "the father and the savior of Europe and the world,"[29] having been reassured that this was true immediately after his entering the White House.[30]

This "harmony at a distance" between Washington and the Holy See became evident on the occasion of the Genoa Conference in April 1922.[31] On March 8, 1922, the United States formally declined the invitation to the conference, contesting its main aims.[32] The Holy See was represented at the final stage by an external observer. This was Monsignor Giuseppe Pizzardo, deputy to the secretary of state, to whom Pius XI—elected pope only a few weeks before—sent via Gasparri a letter and a memorandum to deliver to the delegates from the various countries. The pope's message asked the assembly to request the Soviet authorities to return to the Church the properties confiscated during Lenin's violent anticlerical campaign[33] to elimi-

---

28. On which subject see, especially, Carlo Felice Casula, "Le segreterie di stato tra le due guerre," in *Il papato e l'Europa*, ed. Gabriele De Rosa and Giorgio Cracco (Soveria Mannelli: Rubbettino, 2001), 417–28.

29. Giovanni Bonzano to Pietro Gasparri, Washington, D.C., March 12, 1921, ASV, DASU, 2, pos. 206, f. 54.

30. Giovanni Bonzano to Pietro Gasparri, Washington, D.C., March 12, 1921, ibid., 5, pos. 63 b/3, f. 228, prot. n. 2576-f. "The new President of the United States has asked me to pay homage to and thank the Holy Father and to assure His Holiness that he is dealing with the situation in Europe in a way which will not compromise the position of the United States."

31. On the origins of the Genoa Conference see, in particular, Carole Fink, *The Genoa Conference: European Diplomacy, 1921–1922*, 2nd ed. (Syracuse, N.Y.: Syracuse University Press, 1993), 5–14.

32. Charles E. Hughes to Vittorio Rolandi Ricci, Washington, D.C., March 8, 1922, FRUS, 1922, vol.1: 393.

33. Pius XI to Pietro Gasparri, Vatican, April 29, 1922, ASV, SS, AES, America (fourth period), pos. 232, fasc. 56, ff. 19–21.

nate from Russia what the historian Richard Pipes has described as "the last relic of the old order."[34] The document was read at the margins of the conference on May 2, but according to the *New York Times* neither Lloyd George nor the representatives from France and Italy could agree on what the pope meant by asking for respect for freedom of worship on the part of the Bolshevik government.[35]

Having collaborated with Benedict XV in 1917 on the creation of an autonomous Congregation for the Oriental Churches, Pius XI did not hesitate to table discussions with Moscow once he had been elected pope. As early as December 1921, the "unofficial" Soviet representative to Italy, Vaclav Vorovsky, and Monsigor Pizzardo had begun to negotiate a possible modus vivendi. An agreement between Gasparri and Vorovsky was reached on March 12, 1922. Moscow did not obtain the formal recognition from the Holy See on which it counted to escape from diplomatic isolation, but conceded the entry into Russian territory of the Pontifical Relief Mission that was guaranteed immunity; in exchange, the Holy See assured the Soviet government that the mission would have exclusively humanitarian aims, and that its envoys would refrain from all political activity and religious teaching.[36] In this way, the Vatican could continue its work of protection of Russian Catholics and at the same time use its mission "as a means of showing the people of the Orthodox Church the real face of the Catholic Church, so favoring conversion."[37] However, only a few weeks after the agreement with Vorovskij had been reached, the Holy See came to know of the requisitioning of the Church's properties ordered by Lev Trockij and the consequent execution of many exponents of the Orthodox clergy. In protest, Piz-

---

34. Richard Pipes, *Russia under the Bolshevik Regime, 1919–1924* (New York: Alfred Knopf, 1993), 347.

35. "Russia's Answer Held for Changes Suggested by Italy," *New York Times*, May 11, 1922, p. 2.

36. On these points, see Giorgio Petracchi, "La missione pontificia di soccorso alla Russia (1921–1923)," in *Santa Sede e Russia da Leone XIII a Pio XI*, ed. Massimiliano Valente (Vatican City: Libreria Editrice Vaticana, 2002), 122–80.

37. Yves Chiron, *Pio XI. Il papa dei Patti Lateranensi e dell'opposizione ai totalitarismi* (Cinisello Balsamo: Edizioni San Paolo, 2006), 201.

zardo left the Genoa Conference, but did so to the total indifference of the delegations, and he limited himself to repeating to the journalists of the Associated Press the Holy See's request for the properties confiscated by the Russian authorities to be granted the same treatment as that promised to other states. In spite of the escalation of violence toward the Catholic clergy and the growing discontent of some cardinals of the Roman curia with the "soft" approach of the pope and the secretary of state, the Vatican decided not to interrupt its relief mission.

The Pontifical Mission made it possible for the Holy See to operate in the hostile Russian environment in close contact with the American Relief Administration (ARA) which, on the basis of the Riga Agreements between the American and Russian governments, had the function of coordinating all rescue activities in Russia. On the suggestion of the NCWC, Pius XI entrusted leadership of the mission to the Jesuit father Edmund Walsh, director of the School of Foreign Service at Georgetown University in Washington, D.C. During his year and a half spent in Russian territory, Walsh was able to win the esteem of the director of the ARA, Colonel William N. Haskell, who admired both his organizational skills and, above all, the determination with which he had carried out his delicate assignment.

In the United States, this collaboration with the Pontifical Relief Mission was not looked on favorably by the public. While condemning the Soviet leaders' indiscriminate use of violence, exponents of the various Protestant denominations, expressing themselves in widely read periodicals such as the *Nation* and the *New Republic*, even began to doubt the truthfulness of the number of arrests and executions of Russian Catholic citizens communicated by Father Walsh and made generally known during those months by the news service of the NCWC.[38] These conjectures, however, were soon proved incorrect by the facts. The Bolshevik government's further

38. On the relationship between the ARA and the Pontifical Relief Mission and on the reactions of the American public, see Patrick H. McNamara, *A Catholic Cold War: Edmund A. Walsh, S.J., and the Politics of American Anticommunism* (New York: Fordham University Press, 2005), 23–61.

acts of repression convinced both Washington and the Holy See that their dialogue with Moscow, though only for humanitarian ends, had to be interrupted. The ARA brought its Russian activities to a halt in August 1923 and three months later, in November, Pius XI decided to recall Walsh to Rome, while the last operational center of the Pontifical Relief Mission was closed down the following year.[39]

For different reasons and objectives, the United States and the Vatican had attempted to overcome ideological, rather than political, incompatibility with Moscow by pragmatically looking for some form of coexistence. Both, however, drew from the experience of those years the conclusion that the barriers could not easily be removed. Anticommunism, therefore, became a further factor of convergence between the Holy See and the North American republic, and they were already on the same wavelength on the issues of disarmament and reparations. Encouraged by Rome, the American Catholic Church had the merit of contributing to raising public awareness of a matter destined to become extremely important in the years preceding World War II, so giving the idea that the reorganization strategy that culminated in the founding of the NCWC was able, by its greater dynamism, to have the "voice" of Catholics taken into greater consideration.[40] These were certainly encouraging signs. And yet there was still a long way to go in removing the obstacles that had cluttered the history of relations between the United States and the Holy See.

Giovanni Bonzano, the key figure in the renewal of the American Church as well as Vatican diplomacy's effective interlocutor with

39. On this topic, see Evghenia S. Tokareva, "Le relazioni tra l'URSS e il Vaticano: Dalle trattative alla rottura (1922–1929)," in Massimiliano Valente, ed., *Santa Sede e Russia*, 199–261.

40. On September 25, 1924, at the same time as the final closure of the Pontifical Relief Mission in Russia, the NCWC approved the following resolution: "Speaking in the name of twenty millions of Catholics of this republic, we condemn the wholly unjust attitude of the present Russian government, opposed as it is to the fundamental principles of justice and repugnant to the best sentiments of all Christian people"; see ACUA, ANCWC, OGS, box 65, fold. 20, Annual Reports, 1924.

the Harding administration, was recalled to Rome by Pius XI to be made cardinal in the Consistory of December 11, 1922. His successor as head of the Apostolic Delegation in Washington was Pietro Fumasoni Biondi, titular archbishop of Dioclea, former nuncio to the East Indies (1916–19) and then to Japan (1919–21), as well as secretary of the Congregation for the Propagation of the Faith (1921–22). In spite of the timid signs of openness and greater willingness to engage in dialogue shown at that time by the government, the task set him immediately turned out to be a tough one.[41] His arrival in the United States coincided with what was probably the most "radical" phase of the anti-Catholic invective of various American nativist groups, and preceded by only a few months the sudden ascent to power of Calvin Coolidge, who turned out to be a fervid supporter of an outburst of nationalistic conservatism.

### FUMASONI BIONDI, THE "FENCE-SITTER"

In the summer of 1926, Fumasoni Biondi was charged by Cardinal Gasparri with the task of finding out "with the greatest prudence and discretion"[42] the real intentions of the United States government which, according to the Rome representative of the Knights of Columbus, Edward Haern, was thinking of sending "an American observer to the Holy See similar to the one at the League of Nations in Switzerland." Fumasoni Biondi cautiously replied that it would be "better to wait," adding that "if the government wanted anything, they would say so."[43] The Vatican secretary of state had been reassured of the fact that "there was no secret, and that it would be published." Given these conditions, the Holy See would certainly have welcomed an American representative, "but," he added, "there was

41. Pietro Fumasoni Biondi to Luigi Cossio, Vatican, January 13, 1923, ASV, DASU, 1, pos. 122, f. 29.
42. Pietro Gasparri to Pietro Fumasoni Biondi (personal), Vatican, May 31, 1926, ibid., 2, pos. 343, f. 2r.
43. Pietro Fumasoni Biondi to Pietro Gasparri, Washington, D.C., August 16, 1926, ibid., f. 3v.

one doubt, and that was that Mr. Hearn had reported well what the American government had in mind."[44] In fact, there was a need further to verify the intentions of Coolidge's administration.

To this end, the apostolic delegate spoke to the NCWC's secretary, John J. Burke, who said he had never heard the matter discussed and the fact that Hearn had not replied to his invitation convinced Fumasoni Biondi that "the idea of the Observer had been cooked up by the Knights of Columbus."[45] For this reason, he continued by maintaining that "the person who could say anything noteworthy" on the subject "was the Secretary of State Mr. Frank Kellogg, apart from the president," and if they wished to "suggest such an idea to the Vatican" they would only need to use "their good channels, persons the government trusted"[46] such as Father W. Lyons, rector of the University of Georgetown, and Father John Burke of the NCWC himself. Hence the suggestion that they should wait for the White House to act officially, and the decision to exploit the opportunity for a meeting with Gasparri to inform him that "the Episcopate in general was against the constitution of any form of American government agency in the Vatican."[47] Suspecting that the closer relationship between Washington and the Holy See would bring about a progressive erosion of its jealously guarded autonomy, many of the ecclesiastical hierarchy were of the opinion that "an agent, or Observer, in Rome would do nothing but favor this or that plan, this or that candidate, for merely political ends."[48]

Fumasoni Biondi had only few years' experience of the United States, but he seems to have fully understood the dangers inherent in the delicate question raised by the Knights of Columbus. Any further pressure from the ecclesiastical hierarchy in support of sending an American observer to the Vatican would not only stir up the aggressive reactions of antipapists, but—as Cardinal Patrick Hayes of New York said—would weaken the results obtained by the Church at the International Eucharistic Conference that had taken place in Chica-

44. Ibid., f. 2r.
46. Ibid., f. 3r.
48. Ibid.
45. Ibid.
47. Ibid.

go (June 18–25, 1926), the first ever to be held in the United States.⁴⁹

As well as symbolizing the remarkable growth of the Midwest dioceses, the Eucharistic Congress of 1926 represented the definitive consecration of Cardinal Archbishop of Chicago George Mundelein and, above all, an occasion for American Catholicism to show its muscles at the time of the great success, also at a political level, of antipapist nativism of which the KKK was the main expression.⁵⁰

From the KKK's point of view, Calvin Coolidge was certainly the best candidate for the 1924 presidential elections. Coolidge's rectitude and his support for traditional values were the best guarantee of preserving the old Puritan virtues being threatened by social upheavals and the cultural Babel of those years. All this was profoundly worrying to American Catholics. Much more than in the past, and thanks to the rise of Hiram Evans, the behavior of the KKK was markedly antipapist. On October 25, 1923, the *Washington Post* published excerpts from a speech given by Evans in Dallas the day before, a speech in which he explained why the KKK contested American Catholicism. "No nation can endure that permits a higher temporal allegiance than its own government"; but, declared the imperial wizard, "the hierarchies of Roman and Greek Catholicism violate that principle."⁵¹ Stating, too, how illiteracy and economic backwardness in Europe were for the most part limited to Catholic countries, he exhorted the government to speed up the process of blocking immigration and setting up special commissions of enquiry into the conduct of naturalized Catholics. His was an out-and-out condemnation of Catholicism in both its spiritual (allegiance to the pope) and its institutional dimensions (the role of the ecclesiastical hierarchy).

John J. Burke gave the only reply to Evans's provocations. Pat-

49. Ibid. "Cardinal Hayes," wrote Fumasoni Biondi, "points out to me that having an Observer would do damage at present because it would give a political significance to the Eucharistic Congress that had taken place and ruin its effect."

50. Of the main studies on this topic, see especially Rory McVeigh, *The Rise of the Ku Klux Klan: Right-Wing Movement and National Politics* (Minneapolis: University of Minnesota Press, 2009), 167–79.

51. *Washington Post*, October 25, 1923, ACUA, ANCWC, OGS, box 78, fold. 24, Organizations: Ku Klux Klan (1923–1939), press clippings.

rick H. Callahan, treasurer of the Knights of Columbus, reported his statements in a memorandum of October 29, 1923. This was not so much a counteroffensive as a defense of the Catholic contribution to the country's interests. In Burke's view, apart from being obviously "wicked," Evans's insinuations were not even worth considering because disavowed by the declarations of the episcopate in support of Wilson's decision to enter the war in 1917 and by the fact that thousands of Catholics had been killed at the front. It was therefore up to the American people, added Burke, to decide whether to take sides with their country, implicitly accused of weakness by Evans, or with the KKK.[52] Between the lines, the message seemed to be that the American Church would avoid responding to such provocations and simply express its loyalty to republican institutions and ensure that its followers did likewise.

Thanks to documents found in the archives of the NCWC, it is possible to establish that the line of "cautious neutrality" adopted by the ecclesiastical hierarchy with regard to Evans's attacks remained the same during the controversial campaign of 1924, when the most important episodes of political conflict revolved around the question of the KKK. Once again, it was Father Burke who confirmed this.

First in February and then in March, the general secretary of the NCWC felt he should clarify the position of the episcopate. It would have been a mistake, which Burke described as fatal, for the Church to expect the Republicans or the Democrats directly to condemn the KKK from their electoral platforms, or to publically take an initiative of some kind. This conclusion was reached for many reasons. The main one was the belief that they should steer clear of the perverse world of political competition, but also the idea for which the Church would gain much more in terms of credibility, leaving the citizens, in the exercise of their right to freedom of expression, to judge the KKK phenomenon.[53]

52. Statements by John J. Burke, quoted by Patrick H. Callahan, treasurer of the Knights of Columbus, Louisville, October 29, 1923, ACUA, ANCWC, OGS, box 78, fold. 24, Organizations.

53. Memorandum Burke, February 2, 1924, ACUA, ANCWC, OGS, box 78,

Whether Burke's words were simply a façade or a sincere statement, they did clearly express the position of the episcopate in the early postwar years and at the same time its limitations and contradictions.

The American Church had dedicated its efforts to the care of immigrants for decades, focusing on the consolidation of its own institutional structure just after World War I. From this point of view its success was considerable, especially in the field of education. In Philadelphia alone, during the decade 1921–31 the Church inaugurated ninety-one parishes and eighty-nine parish schools, as well as three diocesan high schools, fourteen academies, a women's college, and a seminary. The universities grew both quantitatively and qualitatively, thanks to the conspicuous donations of the faithful and the teaching of the Jesuits, they were able to extend their curricula and modernize their buildings.[54]

These developments, however, ended up by becoming inward-looking, with the hierarchy creating greater isolation rather than integration of Catholics into the rest of society. The ecclesiastical leaders directed their zeal at performing their pastoral tasks while remaining silent on the many economic and social problems that afflicted not only Catholics but all Americans.[55] Apart from the episcopate's sometimes passive and conservative attitude, another of their great limitations was the almost total lack of Catholic leaders at the national political level capable of collating the needs emerging from the "bottom" and of bringing them together to form a more general overview.[56]

---

fold. 24, Organizations, prot. n. 345-a; and John J. Burke to John A. Ryan, Hot Springs, June 3, 1924, ibid.

54. See McAvoy, *A History of the Catholic Church,* 395–96; J. William Sanders, *Education of the Urban Minority: Catholics in Chicago, 1833–1965* (New York: Oxford University Press, 1977).

55. See Francis L. Broderick, *Right Reverend New Dealer John A. Ryan: The Biography of a Priest Professor and Social Reformer Extraordinary* (New York: Macmillan, 1963), 93–139; and also Raymond L. Bruckberger, "The American Catholics as a Minority," in *Roman Catholicism and the American Way of Life,* ed. Thomas T. McAvoy (Notre Dame, Ind.: University of Notre Dame Press, 1960), 40–48.

56. The question of Catholic leadership in the United States is analyzed in Ellis, *American Catholicism,* 146–55; and Hennesey, *American Catholics,* 235–60. See

What was it that prevented the roughly twenty million Catholics from making themselves felt in American political life? Pietro Fumasoni Biondi's view on this was very clear: beside the ostracism experienced in large sectors of public life that he had come up against ever since his arrival in Washington, the Church itself was partly to blame. "First of all," he said to Gasparri in August 1923, "the episcopate has done nothing about it," and then he argued that "I believe that this deficiency is due to the failure of Catholic universities to train Catholic leaders."[57] Continuing incapability to educate a class of leaders able, even minimally, to overcome prejudice toward Catholicism was, in the apostolic delegate's view, not something they could afford at that point in history. They could not expect the same "goodwill" shown by Harding from Calvin Coolidge, "a man of few words and strong character" who belonged to the "Congregationalist sect which does not recognize the clergy as having any other authority than that which comes straight from the people, and reduces faith to a minimum."[58] Although it had been said that the new president respected the potential of Catholicism, Fumasoni Biondi thought it impossible that he should find room for Catholics in his administration. If a new generation of Catholics were to be introduced into the highest levels of national politics or were to take part in debates on the important social and economic topics, they would have a long time to wait, and at the very least the ecclesiastical hierarchy would have to try to put pressure on the White House, especially where the orientations of the government might coincide with those of the Holy See.

The Chicago Eucharistic Congress of June 1926 therefore became the occasion to ask Coolidge to put an end to religious persecution in Mexico.[59] On October 27, 1915, in spite of the confiscation of Ameri-

---

also Philip Gleason, "American Catholics and Liberalism, 1789–1960," in *Catholicism and Liberalism: Contributions to American Public Philosophy*, ed. Bruce Douglass and David Hollenbach (New York: Cambridge University Press, 1994), 60–63.

57. Pietro Fumasoni Biondi to Pietro Gasparri, Washington, D.C., August 7, 1923, ASV, AES, America, fourth period, pos. 176, fasc. 21, f. 16v.

58. Ibid., f. 16r.

59. See Elizabeth A. Rice, *The Diplomatic Relations between the United States*

can citizens' property following the 1911 revolution, Woodrow Wilson had recognized the legitimacy of the ruthless government presided over by Venustiano Carranza, whose anticlericalism found full expression soon after in the text of the Constitution of Queretaro, promulgated on February 5, 1917. In those years, the archbishop of San Francisco, Edward Hanna, had used the local press to denounce the violence of the Mexican government, harshly criticizing the American administration's attitude to Carranza, but he was not listened to.[60] After a period of relative calm, at the time of the presidencies of Adolfo de la Huerta and Alvaro Obregon, the situation precipitated again with the election of Plutarco Elias Calles in 1924. Calles demanded the immediate application of Article 27 of the Constitution of Queretaro, which provided for the nationalization of the land, including that owned by the Church. From then on far more bishops and priests were arrested; in February 1925 the apostolic delegate Ernesto Filippi was deported; and a year later, his deputy, the archbishop of Maltese origin George Carnana suffered the same fate.[61]

Having no direct channel of communication with Washington, the Holy See relied on the mediation of the American Church in solving the thorny issue of Mexico. In May 1921, Giovanni Bonzano had informed the Vatican secretary of state of the Harding administration's intention to recognize the government of Obregon, but pointed out that this was subject to the Mexican leaders respecting certain conditions, "the most important of which was respect for the lives and property of American citizens and above all the protection of their petroleum investments."[62] He intended to approach the U.S. authorities "to get them to insist on the Mexican government's guar-

---

*and Mexico, as Affected by the Struggle for Religious Liberty in Mexico, 1925–1929* (Washington, D.C.: The Catholic University of America Press, 1959), 93.

60. See Richard Gribble, "Roman Catholicism and U.S. Foreign Policy, 1919–1935: A Clash of Policies," *Journal of Church and State* 50, no. 1 (2008): 82–83.

61. See Robert E. Quirk, *The Mexican Revolution and the Catholic Church, 1910–1929* (Bloomington: Indiana University Press, 1973), 21.

62. Giovanni Bonzano to Pietro Gasparri, Washington, D.C., May 25, 1921, ASV, DASU, 5, pos. 65, f. 30.

antee of religious liberty."⁶³ To this end, he spoke first to a person who was close to the secretary of the interior, Albert Fall, who agreed on the fact that "apart from the revolutionary forces, the Mexican people are largely Catholic, and that without religious liberty there could never be peace in Mexico."⁶⁴ On May 23 he was received by the secretary of state, Charles Hughes, who, having listened attentively, assured him that "it was also the desire of the United States government to work for true appeasement, including religious liberty."⁶⁵

Bonzano's successor, Fumasoni Biondi, played a similar role. On instructions from the Holy See, the new delegate mobilized some of the most influential members of the episcopate and, above all, kept his superiors in the Vatican updated on the efforts made by the NCWC, whose pressure was insistent from 1926 onward.⁶⁶ Having dismissed the possibility of the Mexican people's support in the form of armed resistance, the Administrative Committee of the NCWC took note of the report from Archbishop Hanna, which confirmed the Mexican hierarchy's decision to use passive resistance to the persecutions of Calles's government,⁶⁷ and in April 1926 presented a four-point action plan: to send a letter of protest to President Coolidge; to publish a report explaining in detail to American Catholics the situation of the Church in Mexico; to set up a national committee to keep the public informed of developments; and to involve the National Council of Catholic Men and Women in the organization of a discussion forum at the local level.⁶⁸ In spite of Archbishop Hanna's attempts to convince the new secretary of state, Frank Kellogg, to intervene in the Mexican situation and the fuss caused by

63. Ibid.    64. Ibid., f. 31.
65. Ibid.
66. Pietro Fumasoni Biondi to Dennis Dougherty, Washington, D.C., March 14, 1923, ibid., f. 34; Pietro Fumasoni Biondi to George Mundelein, Washington, D.C., March 19, 1923, ibid., f. 37.
67. ACUA, ANCWC, OGS, Administrative Committee, Annual Reports, box 65, fold. 21, September 25, 1925.
68. The statement of the NCWC of April 15, 1926, is quoted in Raphael M. Huber, ed., *Our Bishops Speak: National Pastorals and Annual Statements of the Hierarchy of the United States, 1919–1951* (Milwaukee, Wis.: Bruce Publications, 1952), 269–70.

the American hierarchy's pastoral letter of December 1926, Washington had not seemed to have any intention of revisiting the decision taken in 1924 to recognize the government of Obregon.[69]

Meanwhile, the Holy See's expression of appreciation for the work of the NCWC continued to arrive,[70] and Father Burke decided to intervene directly to escape from the impasse. His work on this, from the end of 1927 to the following year, was decisive. Having met Coolidge and the undersecretary of state, Robert Olds, with the help of Fumasoni Biondi, in January 1928 he joined the new ambassador to Mexico Dwight Morrow in order to take part in negotiations with Calles. Talks with the Mexican government, which promised to end well both in the interests of American petroleum investments and in terms of a revision of anticlerical laws, underwent a sudden interruption in July following the assassination of Obregon (just elected as Calles's successor) by a Catholic fanatic. In spite of this unfortunate incident, Burke, Morrow, and the two Mexican archbishops, Pascual Diaz and Leopold Ruiz, continued their diplomatic work. Thanks to the approachability of the provisional government headed by Porters Gil, in Mexico City on June 21, 1929, the Catholic Church and the Mexican State signed an agreement that promised respect for Catholic freedom of worship and permitted the return to the country of the apostolic delegate, a position for which Ruiz was chosen.[71]

This solution to the Mexican problem seemed momentarily to set aside the difficulties that continued to assail American Catholicism and relations between Washington and the Vatican. As with the case of Soviet Russia, the issue of freedom of worship in Mexico had brought about a convergence of the positions of the United States

69. John Burke to Joseph Schrembs, Washington, D.C., December 12, 1926, ACUA, ANCWC, OGS, International Affairs, Mexico, box 44, fold. 5.

70. Donato Sbarretti to Edward Hanna, Vatican, February 7, 1927, ACUA, ANCWC, OGS, box 64, fold. 4, Bishops' General Meetings, Minutes (1925–1927); Pius XI to William O'Connell, Vatican, August 10, 1927, ibid., International Affairs, Mexico, box 44, fold. 5.

71. See Douglas J. Slawson, "The National Catholic Welfare Conference and the Church-State Conflict in Mexico, 1925–1929," *Americas* 47 (July 1990): 55–93.

and the Catholic Church. At least on issues that related strictly to internal affairs, the NCWC gave every sign of being able to handle mediation with the government, for which the Vatican had had great expectations since that institution had been set up; furthermore, the negotiation skills of Father Burke and the regularity with which he had kept the Holy See informed at such a delicate time confirmed that fact that Pietro Fumasoni Biondi could be considered a valid successor to Bonzano. But it was a momentary success. The 1920s—as Francis Broderick says—remained "an age of retreat when holding actions, limited counteroffensives, and prayer were the only recourse."[72]

Fumasoni Biondi's wait-and-see policy made him aware of the inherent weaknesses of American Catholicism, the need to get to know the reasons for the widespread antipapism of the times, and to prepare for better times, hopefully with an administration more open to dialogue in which there might even be room for Catholics who could therefore become "first class citizens." After all, as Cardinal Gasparri said in the above-mentioned exchange of letters with the apostolic delegate on the eve of the Eucharistic Congress in Chicago, it "would not be a bad thing" to postpone the arrival of an American observer in the Vatican. In 1926, in fact, Vatican diplomacy was concentrating all its energies on Ratti's "concordatarian" strategy and such an expert in law as Gasparri well knew that an agreement with the United States was out of the question because the U.S. Constitution did not permit favoring a religious confession to the disadvantage of others.

## THE PRESIDENTIAL ELECTIONS OF 1928

On August 2, 1927, Calvin Coolidge announced that he would not stand as a candidate in the following year's presidential elections. In July the Italian ambassador to Washington, Giacomo De Martino, had sent to the Italian Ministry of Foreign Affairs a long report on

---

72. Broderick, *Right Reverend*, 126.

the candidature of Alfred Smith, who had been nominated by the Democrats in Houston. "The Convention," De Martino stated, "is of great interest because it shows that—contrary to the expectations of many—in recent years there had been a profound change in attitudes to religious questions in this country."[73] At Houston, continued the Italian diplomat, "the anti-Catholic position has been defended only by Senator James T. Heflin, the Alabama representative, a loony fanatic of the Ku Klux Klan; it is known that he receives funding and he is discredited all over the country for his grotesque attacks on Catholicism and for the campaign he conducts against the presumed interference of the Roman Pontiff in American politics."[74]

In many ways, the picture that De Martino painted of American politics of the time was correct. First and foremost, Smith had few opponents inside his party; and then he was the symbol of the America that was alienated, marginalized, relegated to the outskirts of the Northeast industrial cities where people were forced to do the most humiliating jobs. A Catholic of Irish origin, he had made his way up in the Lower East Side of New York, winning the affection of millions of immigrants and the respect of the Tammany Hall at Albany. During his four terms as governor of New York he had not left behind him his past as "a boy of the sidewalk," and he had fought to improve the standard of living of the less well-off. By becoming the Democratic candidate, he no longer represented the party of the South—he became the symbol of the ethnic, linguistic, and religious growing pluralism, whose voice had not been heard for a very long time.

But the Italian ambassador's statement on the religious issue was absurdly wrong. Much more than the errors in terms of electoral strategy and noncommitment to main socioeconomic matters, Smith had to pay in the end for being a Catholic like the vice-president he chose: John J. Raskob.[75]

---

73. Giacomo De Martino to MAE, Washington, D.C., July 3, 1928, ASMAE, AP1, SU, b. 1605, Rapporti Politici, First Semester.

74. Ibid.

75. See Allan J. Lichtman, *Prejudice and the Old Politics: The Presidential Elections of 1928* (Chapel Hill: University of North Carolina Press, 1979), 40–76.

Pietro Fumasoni Biondi, who knew all too well how deeply anti-Catholic prejudice was rooted in America, foresaw this when he said that the 1928 elections would undoubtedly be "an occasion for the enemies of the Church to take up the old arms of intolerance and bigotry."[76] The editors of the main American dailies were of the same opinion: while appreciating the official disclaimer of the apostolic delegate concerning the presumed involvement of the Holy See in Smith's nomination, they pointed out that those who were prejudiced against the Catholic Church would continue to nurse suspicions of Vatican interference.[77] There had already been a clear demonstration of this attitude in a letter by the New York attorney Charles G. Marshall to Smith, published in the *Atlantic Monthly* on April 18, 1927.[78] Fumasoni Biondi translated this into Italian and sent it to the Vatican secretary of state. In Marshall's view, there was "a note of doubt, a malicious tone of enquiry," not in the rectitude and moral intentions of Smith, but "in certain ideas" that many Americans attributed to his position "as a loyal and faithful Roman Catholic" and that in their minds were "irreconcilable with the Constitution's defense of civil and religious freedom on which the institutions were based."[79] Smith replied by asserting that he believed "in the absolute separation of Church from State, and in the basic value of the constitutional provision that Congress should not pass any law that supported any one religion or that prohibited its freedom of worship."[80]

The press reacted favorably to Smith's assertions. The *Herald Tribune* thought the ex-governor of New York had "ably handled religious issues"; the *New York Times* considered his reply "vigorous, clear, and forceful"; and even the *Star* of Indianapolis, a bastion of

76. Pietro Fumasoni Biondi to Pietro Gasparri, Washington, D.C., May 16, 1927, ASV, SS, AES, America, pos. 214, fasc. 45, f. 42, rep. n. 5776-g.

77. *Washington Post*, May 11, 1927; and *New York Times*, May 12, 1927, ibid., ff. 43–44.

78. C. George Marshall, "An Open Letter to the Honorable Alfred E. Smith," *Atlantic Monthly* 139, (1927): 540–49.

79. Pietro Fumasoni Biondi to Pietro Gasparri, April 18, 1927, ASV, SS, AES, America, pos. 214, fasc. 44, ff. 40–65.

80. Alfred E. Smith, "Catholic and Patriot. Governor Smith Replies," *Atlantic Monthly* 139 (1927): 721–28.

Puritanism, said that Smith's Catholicism was not a "handicap."[81] The ecclesiastical hierarchy also made its voice heard. The episcopate's concern, said Fumasoni Biondi in August 1927, was simply to dispel once and for all "the prejudice of Protestants, and at the same time to protest against the slanderous insinuations against the sanctity of Our Religion imposed by the laws of our own country, without intruding in the politics of other nations."[82]

Al Smith was soundly beaten by Hoover on November 6, 1928. Ambassador De Martino quickly had to change his mind, therefore, about the forecast he had made: "the importance of the religious issue, which seemed to have been set aside in the American political battle, has raised its head again."[83] In effect, the outcome of the elections left millions of American Catholics deeply embittered; as Fumasoni Biondi pointed out, "they felt despised, offended and trodden on without their having shown the least provocation."[84] Even Texas, Florida, and Virginia, three states that were Democratic by tradition, had preferred to give their vote to Hoover rather than elect a Catholic president.

The White House was to remain a dream for Smith, but the 1928 elections were not a completely negative experience either for the Democratic Party or for Catholics. Forty of the forty-eight states went to the Republicans, as did some bastions like Oklahoma City, Atlanta, Dallas, and Houston which, having a large Lutheran majority, voted for Hoover. Smith, however, did win both in the twelve largest cities of America (which in 1920 and 1924 had guaranteed the Republican candidates an advantage of over one million votes) and in the 122 northern counties with a large immigrant Catholic population. The fact that immigrants, especially Italian-Americans,

---

81. *Herald Tribune,* April 19, 1927; *New York Times,* April 18, 1927; *Star,* April 18, 1927, ASV, SS, AES, America, pos. 214, fasc. 45, press clippings, ff. 24, 13, 14.

82. Fumasoni Biondi to Gasparri, Washington, August 6, 1927, ASV, SS, AES, America, pos. 214, fasc. 45, f. 48v, rep. n. 6306-g.

83. Giacomo De Martino to MAE, Washington, D.C., November 14, 1928, AS-MAE, AP1, SU, Rapporti Politici, First Semester.

84. Pietro Fumasoni Biondi to Pietro Gasparri, Washington, D.C., November 26, 1928, ASV, SS, AES, America, pos. 214, fasc. 45, f. 59v, rep. n. 1702-h.

went over to the Democrats was to turn out to be of extraordinary importance to the party during and after the disastrous economic crisis that was soon to overwhelm the country. The year 1928 saw the last great cultural, as well as political, battle between religious, ethnic, and geographical opposites: the Catholicism of immigrants against native Protestantism; cities against rural areas; prohibitionism against antiprohibitionism. Now that the decade was over, together with the economic prosperity vaunted by the Republicans, it was by basing themselves on the consensus won by Smith that the Democrats were able to begin the most extraordinary socioeconomic redevelopment plan in U.S. history.

In the opinion of the apostolic delegate in Washington, the outcome of the elections confirmed the fact that the rural areas were "still immersed in the gloom of Protestantism, feeling the deepest hatred for the Pope and for Rome."[85] He also accused the Republican Party of giving support to "corruption and calumny" against the Church by financing the publication of "brochures and newspapers intent on slandering Catholics and especially the Holy Father, attributing to him malicious intentions which were offensive to American freedom."[86] As for Hoover, the apostolic delegate accused him of limiting himself to hinting at religious intolerance without "ever denouncing, as he should have, the campaign against the Catholic Church," in order not to "miss out on the votes of a very large number of Protestant bigots."[87] Hence Fumasoni Biondi's suggestion to "put off sending congratulations"[88] for the electoral victory until the inauguration of the new administration.

It was clear, therefore, that from then on the hierarchy would look elsewhere both to find ways of restoring its image in the country and of encouraging Washington to come closer to the Holy See. In the meanwhile, the news was about to arrive from the Vatican that the Roman question had at last been resolved by the stipulation of the Lateran Treaty. This was a new era for Vatican diplomacy, as it was for relations with the United States.

85. Ibid., f. 60.
87. Ibid., f. 60.
86. Ibid., ff. 59rv.
88. Ibid., f. 60v.

## AMERICAN REACTIONS TO THE LATERAN TREATY

In the United States, where the government had gradually moved to positions of wary "benevolence" toward fascism,[89] the Catholic press followed the orientations of the Holy See. Until 1923, in fact, there appeared in the Jesuit magazine *America* and in that of the Paulist fathers, *Catholic World,* article after article against Benito Mussolini; while the magazine of the archdiocese of Chicago, the *New World,* went as far as to compare Fascist violence in the campaigns of northern Italy with that of the KKK in the American Bible belt.[90]

Following the breakup between the Vatican and Don Luigi Sturzo's People's Party, these publications began a formidable American campaign for the new "marriage" between the Church of Rome and the Fascist regime. Editorials exalting the March on Rome appeared in almost all the main American Catholic newspapers.[91] The same support was given on the occasion of the crisis caused by the assassination of the Socialist Party leader Giacomo Matteotti. This time, *Commonweal,* the main publication of American lay Catholics, even assumed an apologetic tone to the Duce and freed him of all direct responsibility for the killing, accusing the uncontrolled extreme fringes of the Fascist National Party. *America* and *Catholic World* took the same line, pointing out that Mussolini had blocked the expansion of communism in Italy.[92]

From that moment on, the American ecclesiastical hierarchy intensified its efforts to legitimize the Fascist regime. A synergy was

---

89. See John P. Diggins, *Mussolini and Fascism: The View from America* (Princeton, N.J.: Princeton University Press, 1972), 3–262; and David F. Schmitz, *The United States and Fascist Italy, 1922–1940* (Chapel Hill: University of North Carolina Press, 1988), 36–110.

90. "The Naples Conference," *America,* May 15, 1920, p. 76; "The Rise of the People's Party in Italy," *Catholic World,* May 1921, pp. 35–41; *New World,* August 4, 1922, p. 11.

91. See "With Fascists in Italy," *Catholic World,* March 1923, "Mussolini and the Vatican," *America,* December 2, 1922, p. 147; and *New World,* February 1, 1924, p. 4.

92. See "Mussolini and the Law," *Commonweal,* November 26, 1924, pp. 42–43; "Premier Mussolini," *America,* October 25, 1924, p. 28; "The High-Handed Mussolini," *Catholic World,* June 1925, p. 408.

created between the episcopate and the Italian diplomats which, as the historian Peter D'Agostino has pointed out, found in the rituals of public demonstrations a means of closely relating the "Italian spirit" with the "Catholic spirit."[93]

Such posturing, however, eventually dampened the enthusiasm of the rest of the American people, above all that of the Protestants. In October 1927, a United States citizen who wished to go by the name of "sincere observer" wrote to Mussolini asking him provocatively whether he intended to use his extraordinary power for the good of Italy which, thanks to its Risorgimento heroes, had managed to unify the country, or whether he wished to act in the interests of the Church, which had used its despotic, obscurantist regime to keep large areas of the peninsula in a state of total backwardness.[94] This was only the beginning. As soon as the rumors about the secret negotiations between the Fascist government and the Holy See to solve the Roman question began to spread, the American people's attitude to the Duce became increasingly hostile.

Mussolini was informed of the American public's attitude toward the possibility of a reconciliation with the Church. On February 28, 1928, Giacomo De Martino wrote to him: "every time the news highlights an improved relationship between the Italian government and the Holy See, there is a favorable reaction in Catholic circles and an unfavorable one in Protestant circles, who repeat their conviction that Fascism strengthens Catholicism and that Fascism in the United States, therefore, could be a threat to the Protestant Church. News of the disagreement between the government and the Vatican produces the opposite effect."[95] The ambassador attached to his letter an article from the weekly *Independent* entitled "Il Duce Visions a Pope King." He had been told by the consul of Boston, Agostino Ferrante, that, especially in New England, where there were still strong "Anglican and Puritan traditions, the war against the Fascist government

---

93. See D'Agostino, *Rome in America*, 174–83.
94. Sincere Observer to Benito Mussolini, October 25, 1927, ASMAE, API, SU, b. 1604.
95. Giacomo De Martino to Benito Mussolini, Washington, D.C., February 28, ibid., b. 1607.

is fuelled by the traditional hatred of the Anglican Church for Rome, the papacy and the Catholic Church."[96]

Once American Catholics knew of the signing of the Lateran Treaty, through which the Holy See and Fascist Italy resolved the Roman question and formally recognized one another, their joy was unbounded. The front pages of Catholic newspapers and magazines were filled with enthusiastic comments. *Sign*, the monthly of the Passionists fathers, called the event the most important of the century, and did not miss the opportunity to "take revenge" on all those who had offended the pope during the 1928 presidential elections.[97] Unanimous support for the Lateran Treaty also came from Catholic intellectuals. Carlton J. H. Hayes, professor of history at Columbia University, called the accord the best possible application of Church-State separatism; Father Ryan of the Catholic University of America thought the treaty made it possible for Italy to approach the United States on the subject of religious liberty; the editor of *America*, the Jesuit Wilfred Parsons, spoke of a "return to normality."[98]

Protestants, Jews, and the liberal world in general were of an opinion diametrically opposed to that of Catholics. The view of the weekly *Christian Advocate* was that the Lateran Treaty paved the way to the illegitimate ambition of the pope to become part of the League of Nations. The *Baptist*, the media voice of the Northern U.S. Baptist Conference, and the *Christian Observer* expressed fears that the return of a pontifical state might induce the U.S. government to renew diplomatic relations with the pope. But more than anything else, most Americans accused the Fascist government of not providing, at least initially, for any form of safeguard for religious minorities.[99] The White House was more worried than anything else about the effect of the financial agreement stipulated between Rome and the Holy See, on the fragile Italian economy, to which American investors

96. Agostino Ferrante to Giacomo De Martino, Boston, February 24, 1928, ibid.
97. "The Independence of the Holy See," *Sign* 7 (March 1929): 451–53.
98. See D'Agostino, *Rome in America*, 214–19.
99. See "Mussolini Bargains with the Vatican," *Christian Advocate*, February 14, 1929, p. 196; "The More Prince the Less Priest," *Baptist*, March 16, 1929, p. 343; "Pope to Be Temporal Ruler," *Christian Observer*, February 20, 1929, p. 2.

had exposed themselves in the last few years. In this regard, the U.S. government had been much reassured also by Ambassador Henry P. Fletcher in May 1929.[100]

It would therefore seem that the question of reconciliation between the Kingdom of Italy and the Holy See resulted only in restoking anti-Catholicism in the United States. This may have been the immediate effect, but many events of the 1930s demonstrated the contrary. As we shall see, the Lateran Treaty marked an important transition in the pontificate of Pius XI, not only because the treaty brought the Roman question to an end, but also because it was followed by a profound renewal of the curia corresponding to an equally evident change in the Holy See's approach to international affairs. From this point of view, Gasparri's resignation from the position of secretary of state in September 1929 took on a fundamental role. Pope Ratti looked for someone to replace him who would be capable of "putting the emphasis once and for all on the 'pastoral' aims of the Holy See's diplomacy, which should not seem to be subordinate to the interests of any state."[101]

Gasparri's successor, certainly not chosen at random, was Eugenio Pacelli. Mindful of his long years of experience in Germany during and after the Great War, when he had got to know the enormous influence exercised by the United States over European affairs, he would eventually reinforce the link between the Vatican and Washington, first through the work of the American hierarchy, and then, when Europe was on the point of plunging into another war, by direct contact with President Franklin Delano Roosevelt. His tireless "right hand man" was to be Monsignor Francis Spellman to whom, before returning to his native Boston as auxiliary bishop, Pacelli gave the delicate task of taking to Paris—in avoidance of Fascist censorship—the text of the encyclical *Non Abbiamo Bisogno* and to translate it for the benefit of Anglo-Americans.[102]

---

100. Henry Fletcher to the secretary of state, Rome, May 21, 1929, NARA, DS, RG 59, 765.66/49. The ambassador stated: "It is an exaggeration, however, to see in these polemics the reopening of a breach between the Church and the State."
101. Coco, *Eugenio Pacelli*, 87.
102. The archbishop's reference to the task assigned to Spellman is John W. Garrett to the secretary of state, Rome, July 10, 1931, NARA, DS, RG 59, 765.66A/28.

# 5

# TOWARD RAPPROCHEMENT

The 1930s

---

### FRANKLIN DELANO ROOSEVELT, THE "APOSTLE OF REDEMPTION"

On the afternoon of July 2, 1932, the fifty-year-old governor of New York, Franklin Delano Roosevelt, landed at Chicago Midway Airport. The previous evening, the Democratic Party's national convention had elected him as candidate to the presidency and, breaking with all tradition, he wished to receive the investiture in person. In constrast to Hoover, whom the Republican Party had renominated its candidate in spite of his incompetent management of the economic crisis, Roosevelt had dispelled the skepticism within his party and won the confidence of the public who saw in his indomitable enthusiasm a hope of escaping from the poverty they had suffered for a number of years.[1] He was certainly no great thinker, just as he was no ideologist, but he did know how to warm the hearts of "forgotten Americans" who received the message of relief he conveyed during his many journeys before the elections to areas that had most felt the deep economic recession.[2]

1. See William E. Leuchtenburg, *Franklin D. Roosevelt and the New Deal, 1932–1940* (New York: Harper, 2009), 1–17.
2. On the New Deal coalition, essential reading is David Plotke, *Building a*

A mutually beneficial alliance established itself between Roosevelt and the Catholic world. Even at critical moments, this meant the creation of a convergence of the ideas behind the New Deal, its concrete realization, the social doctrine of the Church of Rome as revised and in large part put into practice by the encyclicals of Pius XI, and the needs of millions of American Catholics, who were among those who had suffered most in the Great Depression.[3]

In the early 1960s, Francis J. Lally's book *The Catholic Church in a Changing America* pointed out that during the period of the New Deal American Catholics reached "a new level of association indicating a change in the 'official' American attitude to the Church, and equally important, in the Church's disposition toward the government." He added that it was only from that moment in time that it became possible to speak "in realistic terms of a widespread Catholic social consciousness and with it a willingness not simply to adapt to community life but also to work to transform it."[4] A few years later, in 1968, the historian George Q. Flynn described Franklin Delano Roosevelt's ascent to power as, for Catholics, the beginning of a "new era in their Church's place in American society."[5]

Roosevelt became aware of the strength of the Catholic component in the Democratic Party from the very beginnings of his political career. He was born into the upper-class families of the New York hinterland, and in Manhattan had to measure up to a radically different social environment. The early twentieth-century Tammany Hall was to a large extent controlled by Catholics, most of them Irish, and Roosevelt had known the breed until then only as rough and semiliterate house servants. His impact with New York could only be

---

*Democratic Political Order: Reshaping American Liberalism in the 1930s and 1940s* (New York: Cambridge University Press, 1990), 77–91.

3. See Luca Castagna, "I cattolici statunitensi e il riformismo rooseveltiano: Il New Deal come occasione di riscatto," in *Studi di storia in onore di Gabriele De Rosa*, ed. Luigi Rossi (Salerno: Plectica, 2012), 589–604.

4. Francis J. Lally, *The Catholic Church in a Changing America* (Boston: Little, Brown and Co., 1962), 48.

5. George Q. Flynn, *American Catholics and the Roosevelt Presidency, 1932–1936* (Lexington: University of Kentucky Press, 1968), ix.

disastrous. Like his cousin Theodore, the young Franklin fought to eradicate so-called bosses from the Democratic Party, and therefore came up against the corrupted leaders, many of whom were, in fact, Catholic. In the presidential elections of 1904, for example, instead of voting for the Democratic candidate, Alton Parker, who had been nominated thanks to the support of one of the most powerful bosses of the party, the Irish Catholic Charles F. Murphy, he voted for the Republican Teddy Roosevelt.[6]

However, Roosevelt became one of Alfred Smith's main supporters during the troubled political events of the 1920s. They already agreed on their objectives in the State of New York, and their alliance was sealed on the occasion of the 1924 National Democratic Convention at Madison Square Garden, where it was Roosevelt who made the concluding speech in favor of Smith's nomination, a speech in which he described him as a "happy warrior." It was only four years later, however, that Roosevelt fully experienced the issue of anti-Catholicism in American public life. Before the presidential electoral campaign of 1928, he did not think that Al Smith's being a Catholic could be a problem. But as soon as he realized that the "religious question" had come to the fore in the systematic violent attacks on the Democratic candidate, he reacted with great zeal both privately and in public.[7] At an electoral rally at Buffalo on October 20, 1928, when referring to his experience in Europe during the war, he urged the public not to forget that there had been many Catholics among those who fell in the name of freedom.[8]

Roosevelt continued to receive solid support from Catholics from 1928 to 1932. For example, the Catholic press warmly welcomed his decision to sign the Love-Hayes Bill in March 1932. This was a

6. See Charles LaCerra, *Franklin Delano Roosevelt and Tammany Hall of New York* (Lanham, Md.: University Press of America, 1997), 43–54.

7. See on this point Robert A. Slayton, "Al and Frank. The Great Smith-Roosevelt Feud," in *FDR, the Vatican and the Roman Catholic Church in America, 1933–1945*, ed. David B. Woolner and Richard G. Kurial (New York: Macmillan, 2003), 55–66.

8. See Samuel Rosenman, ed., *The Public Papers and Addresses of Franklin D. Roosevelt* (New York: Random House, 1938), 1.36–38.

measure that made it illegal to ask those applying for teaching posts in public schools what religion they belonged to.[9] Three years earlier, in June 1929, Roosevelt had received an honorary degree from Fordham University, and on that occasion he spoke in appreciation of the men and women who had chosen to serve God and performed charitable works.[10]

Although the initial choice of Al Smith to run in the 1932 elections resulted in much of the Catholic public's dampening of enthusiasm for Roosevelt,[11] he managed in the end to win over the Catholic electorate thanks to the support of a number of influential Catholic politicians including James "Jim" Farley, Edward J. Flynn, the senator of Montana Thomas J. Walsh, James M. Curley of Boston, and the businessman of Kentucky, Colonel Patrick H. Callahan.[12] Of great importance, especially or its symbolic significance, was the fact that Roosevelt, at the Detroit meeting of October 2, 1932, quoted the encyclical of Pius XI, *Quadragesimo Anno,* calling it "one of the greatest documents of modern times ... just as radical as I am."[13] Until then, he had never shown any great interest in the social doctrine of the Catholic Church, nor in Pope Pius XI's position in this regard. His private correspondence, however, reveals that during the summer of 1932 he was advised to read the pope's social encyclical more carefully as it suggested useful points for his anticrisis measures; it is also worth noting that Roosevelt had oriented his collaborators in this

9. *Brooklyn Tablet,* March 26, 1932, p. 1.
10. This episode is reported in Frank B. Freidel, *Franklin D. Rosevelt: The Triumph* (Boston: Little, Brown & Co., 1952), 3.72.
11. See Charles W. Thompson, "Today and Next November," *Commonweal,* June 1, 1932, p. 119; and *Extension,* June 1932, pp. 24–25.
12. On these aspects, see especially Daniel Scroop, *Mr. Democrat: Jim Farley, the New Deal, and the Making of Modern American Politics* (Ann Arbor: University of Michigan Press, 2006).
13. Quoted in Rosenman, ed., *The Public Papers,* 1.778. Roosevelt added: "The accumulation of power, the characteristic note of the modern economic order, is a natural result of limitless free competition, which permits the survival of those only who are the strongest, which often means those who fight, more relentlessly, who pay least heed to the dictates of conscience." Examples of enthusiastic reactions to Roosevelt's words in the Catholic Press are the *Catholic Herald,* December 5, 1932, p. 4, and *America,* October 15, 1932, p. 31.

direction,[14] and asked the director of the NCWC's Department for Social Action, Father Ryan, to recommend the best way of making reference to the encyclical during the electoral campaign.[15] On the other hand, he certainly did not fail to make reference to *Quadragesimo Anno* in the months following the elections. In August 1933, for example, Michael O'Shaughnessy, founder of the Catholic League for Social Justice, received a letter—later published by the NCWC News Service from Secretary of Agriculture Henry Wallace, who said that he had discussed the encyclical with the other members of the administration.[16] Wallace again expressed himself publically at least twice on the subject of the analogies between New Deal legislation and the pope's ideas: first in New York in April 1934 during the assembly of the World Alliance for International Friendship, and then a few months later, in October, before the National Conference of Catholic Charities at their meeting in Cincinnati.[17] There were, however, as George Flynn had pointed out, many other reasons that prompted Catholics to side with Franklin Delano Roosevelt. First, there was the economic crisis and consequently the hope that the New Deal would get them through it. Second, there was an inevitable tendency to realize that Hoover had exploited the anti-Catholic campaign during the 1928 elections. And third, there was Roosevelt's decision to give two Catholics, Flynn and Farley, key roles in the organization of his political "machine." These explain the overwhelming electoral victory of Roosevelt in 1932, and especially his remarkable success in areas with dense Catholic populations, areas where, in many cases, he even bettered Smith's 1928 results.[18]

14. Richard Skinner to Franklin D. Roosevelt, New York, August 3, 1932, and Franklin D. Roosevelt to Richard Skinner, December 27, 1932, FDRPL, PPF, Roosevelt Papers, box 229.

15. Franklin D. Roosevelt to John A. Ryan, New York, September 1, 1932, ACUA, ANCWC, RP, Series 1, Correspondence, box 31, fold. 27.

16. NCWC News Service, August 14, 1933, ibid., OGS, Information Media: Press, box 31, fold. 26.

17. National Conference of Catholic Charities, Cincinnati, October 7–10, 1934, ibid., Organizations: Lay, box 123, fold. 21.

18. See Flynn, *American Catholics*, 17. See also Samuel Lubell, *The Future of American Politics*, 3rd ed. (New York: Harper & Row, 1965), 43–44.

## THE NEW DEAL AND AMERICAN CATHOLICS

Catholics mainly belonged to the lower-middle class of American society and were among those who were worst hit by the Great Depression that began in the late 1920s; above all, they seemed not to possess the means necessary to deal with it. The few political leaders they could rely on at the local level appeared to be incapable of planning reforms that might in some way protect them, just as the ecclesiastical hierarchy, caught up in the inward-looking exaltation of its own institutions, had until then shown itself to be unwilling to encourage its flock to become more politically and socially active. And yet American Catholicism reacted with unprecedented energy to the economic disaster, even before the *Quadragesimo Anno* encyclical excited the interest of the American public.[19]

On November 12, 1931, the ecclesiastical hierarchy issued a Joint Statement under the auspices of the NCWC. Apart from appealing for the study and wider application of the precept contained in *Quadragesimo Anno*, the episcopate called for a minimum subsistence wage for workers and a more equitable distribution of profits, and proposed talks between trade union, industrial, and federal government representatives to discuss measures to adopt against the growing crisis.[20] Between the spring and summer of 1932, two of the most influential American Catholic figures, Reverends Francis J. Haas, director of the National Catholic Conference of Social Work, and Edmund A. Walsh, vice-president of Georgetown University, made their voices heard in protest against the anticrisis policies of the Hoover administration. At a conference held in Philadelphia on July 1, Haas called for the adoption of a massive federal spending program and the application of a surcharge on the highest incomes and revenues; while Walsh, speaking at the Independence Day celebrations organized by the American Legion in Washington, D.C., maintained that the best

---

19. See Paul L. Blakely, "The Schools and Rerum Novarum," *America,* May 9, 1931, pp. 111–12; and J. Thomas McNicholas, "Justice and Present Crisis," *Catholic Mind,* October 22, 1931, pp. 473–81.

20. This document is quoted in full in Huber, *Our Bishops Speak,* 194–96.

way of preventing the spread of Marxist ideology among American workers was to raise the minimum wage and introduce a system of unemployment benefits.[21] At the annual convention of the National Conference of Catholic Charities held at Omaha, Nebraska, Reverend Aloisius J. Muench, rector of the Seminary of St. Francis (Wisconsin), stressed the need for prompt redistribution of resources in favor of the less well-off and touched on the subject of talks between workers and management. Two lay Catholics who were present at this event, the director of the New York Power Commission, Frank P. Walsh, and James Fitzgerald, a member of the St. Vincent de Paul Society of Detroit, bitterly criticized the way the government was dealing with the recession.[22]

Other interpretations of the Great Depression, however, were much more radical and the identification of the means necessary to combat it more explicitly linked to the need for a widespread knowledge of the encyclicals of Leo XIII and Pius XI.

In August 1932, the 77th General Convention of the Catholic Central Verein of America held in St. Louis approved a resolution proposing that government reconstruction programs should be based on the contents of *Quadragesimo Anno*.[23] At New York on November 20 of the same year, similar proposals were made by the assembly of the National Catholic Alumni Federation that was engaged during those months on the promotion of meetings to discuss topics relating to social justice. The leading speakers at this New York meeting were the editors of *Catholic World* and *America*, James M. Gillis and Wilfred Parsons, respectively, together with Father John A. Ryan, all three of whom agreed that the best antidote to the Great Depression was the text of the social encyclical of Pope Ratti, described as the most radical of public figures of the time.[24] Of the same opin-

21. *Brooklyn Tablet*, July 9, 1932, p. 1, and July 16, 1932, p. 2.
22. National Conference of Catholic Charities, Omaha, September 25–28, 1932, ACUA, ANCWC, OGS, Organizations: Lay, box 123, fold. 21.
23. See Flynn, *American Catholics*, 31–32.
24. For a detailed account of the meeting, see *New York Times*, November 21, 1932, p. 19. On the "radicalism" of Pius XI, see Wilfred Parsons, "The Pope and the Depression," *Catholic Mind*, June 22, 1952, p. 244.

ion was another leading figure, the mayor of Detroit Frank Murphy, who maintained that the encyclical was directly "applicable" to the United States' deeply serious economic situation.[25]

The early 1930s, therefore, saw a general proliferation of forums in which the various segments of American Catholicism expressed the bitterness they felt at the failure of the capitalist system and the obstinate nonintervention policy of the Hoover administration. Consequently, the presidential elections of 1932 were held at a crucial moment in U.S. history. As David O'Brien notes, there were "a clear confrontation between those who saw the Depression as the result of economic laws beyond human control and those who felt it resulted from greed and stupidity."[26] Hence Catholic hopes that Roosevelt's charisma and the New Deal that he had promised during the electoral campaign would realistically enable the country to leave the crisis behind them. This expectation, following Roosevelt's overwhelming victory, became an explicit invitation to quickly make real the electoral promises and between 1933 and 1936 turned into more or less unconditional support for the administration's reforms.

One of the most interesting aspects of this encouraging Catholic support for the president was the wide spectrum of public opinion that it represented until the spring of 1933. William C. Murphy wrote in the *Commonweal* that the New Deal was proof that democracy provided the means necessary to combat any type of emergency. One year after Roosevelt's taking up office, the president of the Extension Society of Chicago, Reverend William D. O'Brien, even called him the "apostle" of America's new way.[27]

Overall, and especially in 1933, the Catholic press presented the New Deal reforms as the American version of the pope's social encyclicals. This was how *Catholic World* and the *Catholic Register* of

25. *Brooklyn Tablet*, November 26, 1932, p. 1.
26. David J. O'Brien, *American Catholics and Social Reform: The New Deal Years* (New York: Oxford University Press, 1968), 51.
27. See William C. Murphy, "The New Deal in Action," *Commonweal*, May 5, 1933, pp. 11–13; William D. O'Brien, "The New Deal in Religion," *Extension*, May 1934, p. 34.

Denver interpreted Roosevelt's inaugural speech;[28] while the London *Catholic Times*, which was widely read in the United States, invited a direct comparison between the words of the newly elected Roosevelt and Pope Ratti's *Quadragesimo Anno*, pointing to the precise convergence of the two positions, especially where the causes of the crisis were concerned.[29]

This initial enthusiasm for the New Deal was also felt by a large number of Catholic organizations. Both the International Catholic Truth Society, headed by Edward L. Curran, and the National Catholic Alumni Federation praised Roosevelt's efforts. Similar expressions of esteem came from the leader of the Catholic Daughters of America's Mary C. Duffy, who informed the president of the general consent for his program expressed by the majority of the assembly of the organization's meeting in Colorado Springs on July 7, 1933; the *Social Justice Bulletin* of the Catholic League for Social Justice stated that the influence of Pius XI's encyclical on the New Deal program was evident; and equally emphatic, the Knights of Columbus said they were impressed by the resolute manner in which the new administration was dealing with the problem of economic reconstruction.[30]

It became apparent, too, that Roosevelt was extremely good at encouraging such enthusiastic support. Inverting a trend that deprived Catholics of any chance of holding institutional or political posts at the national level, many of them were admitted to the new administration, sometimes at the highest level. James Farley and Thomas Walsh, for example, were respectively made general director of Postal Services and attorney general. These nominations, which William Shannon has described as an opportunity to prove the groundlessness of the Catholic stereotype of a rough local party leader, made Catholics feel proud, and the news filled the front pages of Catholic newspapers all over the country.[31] Catholics were also let

28. *Catholic World*, April 1933, p. 107, and *Catholic Register*, March 2, 1933, p. 1.
29. The London *Catholic Times* article is quoted in Flynn, *American Catholics*, 44.
30. See ibid., 45–46.
31. See, for example, *Tablet*, March 4, 1933, p. 1, and *Pilot*, March 11, 1933, p. 1.

into the front doors of the diplomatic corps: the mayor of Detroit, Frank Murphy, was made governor general of the Philippines, and Robert Hayes Gove governor general of Puerto Rico. A few years later, in 1937, Joseph Kennedy was given the prestigious post of ambassador to Great Britain.

Apart from lay members of the Catholic Church, Roosevelt appointed numerous members of the Catholic clergy to important positions in the New Deal reform programs. John A. Ryan and Francis J. Haas were undoubtedly the most notable. Having been engaged in the study of issues connected with social justice and in the promotion of Catholic social action, Ryan was invited by the White House in 1933 to discuss with presidential staff issues relating to the industrial sector.[32] In July, the Public Relations Office of the National Recovery Administration (NRA) asked him to draft for the president a request for support addressed to the members of the episcopate.[33] Over the months that followed, his relations with the administration were gradually strengthened. He accepted participation in the consultative body of the U.S. Employment Service (August 1933) and became director in 1934.[34] In September 1933, Secretary of the Interior Harold Ickes nominated him as a member of the National Advisory Council of the Subsistence Homesteads Division.[35] At the suggestion of Father Maurice Sheehy, moreover, President Roosevelt appointed Ryan a member of the NRA Industrial Appeals Board and consultant for the drafting of the Social Security Act, which saw the light in August 1935.[36]

Similarly involved with issues relating to employment, Father Francis Haas became a member of the National Labor Board in Oc-

32. Francis Perkins to John A. Ryan, Washington, D.C., March 29, 1933, ACUA, ANCWC, RP, box 29, fold. 14.

33. John A. Ryan to William Sweet, Washington, D.C., July 18, 1933, ibid., box 35, fold. 16.

34. Frances Perkins to John A. Ryan, Washington, D.C., August 5, 1933, ibid., box 29, fold. 14.

35. Harold Ickes to John A. Ryan, Washington, D.C., September 22, 1933, ibid., box 17, fold. 45.

36. Maurice Sheehy to John A. Ryan, June 28, 1934, and John A. Ryan to Maurice Sheehy, Washington, D.C., July 3, 1934, ibid., box 34, fold. 8.

tober 1933,[37] and from December 1935 was one of the three members of the Labor Policies Board of the Work Progress Administration (WPA). All this was a true "revolution," and Father Ryan himself stated at the end of September 1934: "there are more Catholics in public positions, high and low, in the Federal Government today than ever before in the history of the country."[38]

The ecclesiastical hierarchy, too, established a relationship of close collaboration with the president and his entourage, and shared from the very beginning both the style of government and the program of reforms. In a speech made in April 1933, Cardinal William O'Connell of Boston publically expressed his appreciation of Roosevelt and called him a man sent by Providence for the good of the nation. At a dinner at Jim Farley's house before the newly elected president took up office, Cardinal York Patrick Hayes of New York reassured the new administration that the Catholic community would give it all possible support; and the following year, at a Manhattan College ceremony, he said he was sure that the New Deal would produce remarkable results for the country. No less explicit were the expressions of approval of various members of the episcopate for the government's action during the months following the launch of the first anticrisis measures.[39]

Frank Delano Roosevelt's main supporter in the hierarchy during his first years as president was Cardinal George Mundelein of Chicago. Although the closure of the archives of the archdiocese of Chicago prevents our knowing more, the relationship between Mundelein and Roosevelt is one of the most significant examples of the new relaxed climate between the U.S. government and the Catholic Church from the 1930s onward.[40]

37. Franklin D. Roosevelt to Francis Haas (telegram), Washington, D.C., October 6, 1933, ibid., box 27, fold. 31.
38. John A. Ryan to James Moran, Washington, D.C., September 28, 1934, ibid., box 23, fold. 21.
39. On these aspects, see Flynn, *American Catholics*, 37–40.
40. The best reconstruction of the figure of George Mundelein is by Edward R. Kantowicz, *Corporation Sole: Cardinal Mundelein and Chicago Catholicism* (Notre Dame, Ind.: University of Notre Dame Press, 1983).

The relationship with Roosevelt began informally for reasons quite unconnected with politics. The Massachusetts senator David J. Walsh told a White House secretary, Marvin McIntyre, that the cardinal was an enthusiastic collector of presidential autographs, and that it would please him greatly if Roosevelt were to send him his. On the eve of St. George's Day (April 22, 1933), Mundelein's name day, the president responded to his request. Struck by the fact that the busiest man in the country should have found the time to send him his wishes and such a welcome gift, the cardinal proposed they should meet in person in Washington, where he would have the pleasure of staying on the occasion of a visit to his old parish in the State of New York. Roosevelt and Mundelein met at the White House on May 17, 1933.[41] This was the first of a long series of conversations and exchanges of ideas which continued until the cardinal's death in 1939; Mundelein wisely cultivated it both in private and on the numerous occasions that he sided with presidential policies in public.[42]

Roosevelt greatly needed Mundelein's support, as also that of Catholics in general, when from 1934 American Catholicism began to feel a certain disappointment with the results of the New Deal. Initial enthusiasm for Roosevelt's program of reforms was sealed by his being presented with an honorary degree of doctor of law from the Catholic University of America on June 14, 1933, and by the speech delivered on that occasion by the cardinal of New York Patrick Hayes,[43] but began to fade over the months that followed. Most of the isolated dissenting voices were those of Catholic magazine and newspaper editorials such as *Catholic World*, the *Tablet*, and the *Monitor* of San Francisco.[44] At times, however, criticism was more in-

41. David I. Walsh to Marvin McIntyre, Washington, D.C., April 18, 1933, FDRPL, PPF 321; Franklin D. Roosevelt to George Mundelein, Washington, D.C., April 22, 1933; and George Mundelein to Franklin D. Roosevelt, Chicago, April 26, 1933, ibid.

42. Cf. Harold Ickes, *The Secret Diary of Harold L. Ickes* (New York: Simon & Schuster, 1954), 3.53.

43. The complete program of the ceremony and Cardinal Hayes's speech are to be found in ASV, DASU, 5, pos. 153, ff. 24–26, June 14, 1933.

44. *Monitor*, August 16, 1933, p. 1; "Our Unconventional President," *Catholic*

cisive and induced some of the strongest early supporters, such as the Jesuits who published *America*, and even some of the ecclesiastical hierarchy, to stigmatize the excessive expansion of federal power to the detriment of the states.[45]

All in all, however, many segments of American Catholicism poured praise on the "apostle of redemption," especially in the most critical phases when the very mainstay of the New Deal were caught in the crossfire of the Supreme Court and conservative propaganda. There was the work of proselytism of John Ryan and Raymond McGowan, the support of the Knights of Columbus, and the main Catholic organizations such as the Catholic Conference on Industrial Problems, all backed by politicians close to the president, men like Jim Farley, Joseph Kennedy, and Frank Walsh; and above all for their great symbolical significance, the words of Ryan who, on the eve of the 1936 presidential elections, stated that if Roosevelt did not have a second term of office the country would fall into the hands of the "Bourbons."[46] In these elections, the percentage of Catholics who voted for Roosevelt was around 70–80 percent, and as Colonel Patrick H. Callahan of Kentucky pointed out after the consultations, reached an even higher percentage in the twelve main urban districts of the country.[47]

In the second half of the 1930s Roosevelt's attention moved gradually from the internal problems of the United States to international issues, and especially those relating to Europe, which was slipping inexorably into a new war. The American Catholic world's attitude to the foreign policy of the Democratic administration during Roosevelt's first four years was generally favorable and, though it did not have the substantial unanimous consent to the New Deal reforms,

---

*World*, February 1936, pp. 513–23; "The Nestors in Washington," *Tablet*, January 10, 1936.

45. Paul Blakely, "Hold to the Constitution," *America*, July 13, 1935, p. 314.

46. John A. Ryan, "An Open Letter to the Editor," *Catholic World*, April 1936, 22–26.

47. Patrick H. Callahan to Joseph Polin, 1936, ACUA, ANCWC, RP, box 7, fold. 3. For a thorough analysis of the elections and the Catholic vote in urban areas, see Lubell, *The Future*, 62–64, 78–79.

contributed to further reinforcing links with the president; but that attitude became decisively more critical when he began to think about a greater involvement of the United States in European affairs.

Collaboration with Roosevelt to put a stop to the escalation of Nazi-Fascism became one of the objectives of the Holy See, which during the final phase of Achille Ratti's pontificate, demonstrated "a noticeable and growing rejection of totalitarianism movements."[48] So Vatican diplomacy, seeing the war as imminent, decided to strengthen its relations with Washington.

It was without any doubt Eugenio Pacelli who conducted the overall strategy. He was for a long time, and to some extent still is, considered to be responsible for the Church's silence on the subject of Nazi-Fascist abominations, or at least that he had a role to play in the blunting of the perception that the Vatican had of the dangers of Hitler's insane plan to eliminate all Jews. As Pius XI's secretary of state, Pacelli worked with the circumspection and pragmatism he was known for to ensure that the greatest democracy in the world should give its full contribution to combating the German Reich and Fascist Italy. On the eve of the war, when he had been made pope, he was able to reap the harvest of his efforts, and at the same time Roosevelt decided to resume relations with the Holy See, recognizing as he did that the Vatican played a strategic role that had for too long been sacrificed to antipapist prejudice.

### HEALTHY PRAGMATISM

Like millions of their fellow citizens, American Catholics largely shared Roosevelt's initial approach to foreign policy.[49] In some cases, as with the diplomatic recognition of the Soviet Union and Washington's attitude to the recrudescence of Mexican anticlericalism, this support was in no sense immediate, but ended up by determining

---

48. Fattorini, *Pio XI, Hitler e Mussolini*, ix.

49. On reasons for the isolationism of American Catholics in the 1930s, see George Q. Flynn, *Roosevelt and Romanism: Catholics and American Diplomacy, 1937–1945* (Westport, Conn.: Greenwood Press, 1976), 3–28.

an important convergence of opinion between the administration, the American Catholic Church, and the Holy See on the subject of religious liberty and the approach to Latin American issues.

The question of the possible penetration of communism into the United States had been one of the main preoccupations of the Catholic Church since the Bolshevik Revolution of October 1917, and it became particularly worrying after the war, during the so-called Red Scare of 1919–20. It returned menacingly during the Great Depression[50] and became one of the main topics of discussion between the Roman curia and the Apostolic Delegation in Washington.

In a letter of April 14, 1932, to the apostolic delegate Pietro Fumasoni Biondi, the Vatican secretary of state Eugenio Pacelli wrote that "Communist propaganda at present is one of the greatest dangers to social order in general, and to the Catholic Religion in particular"; therefore, "it is natural that the Holy Father should concern himself with this threat and make it the business of his universal pastoral care to look for the means to stem it." He added that, to this end, it would be "useful for the Holy See to be precisely informed of all manifestations, propaganda and signs of development of Communism." The delegate's task would therefore be to "communicate detailed and precise information with the caution" he was noted for, making use whenever he felt it opportune "of the collaboration of the Bishops and others of the clergy or lay Catholics whose confidence he had, especially those in contact with the Government."[51] In his reply, Fumasoni Biondi admitted to having had "many occasions to deal with this matter" in his years spent in Washington, especially when he had come into contact "with the arduous problems relating to the nationality and race of various groups of immigrants from European countries and Mexico, above all Blacks, who are impregnat-

---

50. The American ambassador in Riga, Frederick Coleman, for example, reported information about a supposed plan organized in Moscow with the help of French communists to speed up the infiltration of communism into U.S. trade unions; see Frederick Coleman to Department of State, Riga, January 9, 1930, NARA, DS, RG 59, 711.61/184.

51. Eugenio Pacelli to Pietro Fumasoni Biondi, rep. n. 967/32, Vatican City, April 14, 1932, ASV, DASU, 2, pos. 412, f. 4.

ed with Communist propaganda."[52] Thanks to the collaboration of Reverend Raymond McGowan, a "specialist on the subject," he was able to give Pacelli a detailed overview of the American communist phenomena, calling his attention above all to "youth organizations and their Press," and noting that in spite of "a great awakening to social studies and employment problems following the *Quadragesimo Anno* encyclical," it was still "a difficult task to which few people dedicate themselves to making known and making triumph Catholic principles on economic and social matters in America."[53]

These exchanges continued incessantly over the following months, even after Fumasoni Biondi was called to Rome and made a cardinal by Pope Ratti in the Consistory of March 13, 1933. On April 4 of that year, alarmed by a report from the Pontifical Commission for Russia, who had come to the conclusion that "the Communist danger that threatens the whole world is extremely serious, given the powerful and totally up-to-date means that the enemy forces have at their disposal to poison and pervert public opinion,"[54] Secretary of the Congregation for Extraordinary Ecclesiastical Affairs Giuseppe Pizzardo communicated to Paolo Marella, the chargé d'affaires of the delegation in Washington, that the situation in the United States was "particularly serious especially because of the repercussions to be had by the hotbed of subversive ideas created and encouraged in that country."[55] These observations were confirmed by the new apostolic delegate Amleto Giovanni Cicognani, and to which Pizzardo returned soon after when he maintained it was necessary "to organize and develop Catholic Action and spread knowledge of the Church's social doctrine, the only effective way of protecting the people from Communism."[56]

52. Pietro Fumasoni Biondi to Eugenio Pacelli, rep. n. 3459-i, Washington, D.C., December 3, 1932, ibid., f. 97, with the attached Memorandum by McGowan, "Communism in the United States," ibid., ff. 9–95.

53. Ibid., ff. 98–99.

54. Giuseppe Pizzardo to Paolo Marella, rep. n. 927/33, Vatican City, April 4, 1933, ibid., f. 102.

55. Ibid.

56. Amleto Cicognani to Giuseppe Pizzardo, rep. n. 4506-i, Washington, D.C.,

Given this premise, the Vatican's reaction to the news that the newly elected president Roosevelt intended to propose negotiations with Moscow is not surprising: Pacelli immediately stamped on the idea in January 1933 as being gravely damaging to the "cause of civilization because it encouraged recognition of Bolshevism."[57] In effect, apart from the basic ideological incompatibility between American liberal-democratic principles and Marxist doctrine, concern about the spread of communist subversive ideas had always been an obstacle to the effective process of relaxation of tension with the Soviet government.[58] As on many other foreign affairs matters, Roosevelt had been vague about the "Russian question" during the 1932 electoral campaign, so attracting the immediate attention of Catholics who were absolutely against rapprochement between Moscow and Washington. In October of that year, in fact, the vice-president of Georgetown University and former director of the Pontifical Commission for Russia, Edmund A. Walsh, said that he expected the president to take up an unambiguous position on the matter as soon as possible.[59]

Instead of disclaimers, however, rumors of a possible exchange of ambassadors with the Soviet Union were often heard after the 1932 presidential elections. The American Catholic press published a whole series of articles expressing more or less vehement opposition to the diplomatic recognition of the Union of Soviet Socialist Republics (USSR). From the *Tablet* of Brooklyn to the *Catholic Messenger* of Davenport (Iowa), all the leading newspapers distanced themselves from the administration's strategy.[60] Criticisms that were just as

---

April 25, 1933, ibid., ff. 109–17; Giuseppe Pizzardo to Paolo Marella, rep. n. 1418/33, Vatican City, May 20, 1933, ibid., f. 124.

57. Eugenio Pacelli to Pietro Fumasoni Biondi (copy), rep. n. 3741/32, Vatican City, January 9, 1933, ibid., V, pos. 157, f. 2v.

58. See Robert Browder, *The Origins of Soviet-American Diplomacy* (Princeton, N.J.: Princeton University Press, 1953), 18–22; and Katherine A. Siegel, *Loans and Legitimacy: The Evolution of Soviet-American Relations, 1919–1933* (Lexington: University of Kentucky Press, 1996), 89–109.

59. Cf. *New York Times*, October 15, 1932, p. 9.

60. See *Tablet*, December 10, 1932, p. 10; *Catholic Messenger*, March 4, 1933, p. 1; *America*, November 4, 1933, p. 97.

harsh came from Catholic organizations, above all from the National Council of Catholic Men and the Knights of Columbus.[61]

In the meantime, the Holy See had already started to move. At the end of January 1933, the Vatican secretary of state had arranged for the Apostolic Delegation to sound out the views of the American episcopate on the Soviet question.[62] On April 20, just two months later, Marella was at last in a position to send a detailed report. Although some of the letters sent by the bishops contained "useful and quite explicit statements," he maintained that the replies received could not "be considered to express the opinion of the hierarchy in general." It was therefore decided to consult other bishops who were "more able to give a solid considered opinion on the subject."[63] The outcome of the survey was in some respects surprising. Many of the bishops, in fact, replied to the questions asked by the Apostolic Delegation pragmatically, with absolute realism. Many held that "the dangers and the harm they already faced" concerning the spread of communist ideology "would not be increased by diplomatic recognition." But many argued quite the reverse, in fact: such threats "would be diminished because diplomatic relations with Russia would make it easier for the United States to have control of and therefore repress subversive propaganda."[64] Along these lines, the bishops pointed out that any official taking up of a different position by the ecclesiastical hierarchy would undoubtedly provoke "great ill feeling, not only on the part of those in favor of the recognition of Russia, but those who, though against it, were in principle against the Church's interference in political matters."[65] Consequently, they maintained that even a pastoral letter on communism from the episcopate "would have no

---

61. See *Tablet*, April 1, 1933, p. 1.

62. Eugenio Pacelli to Pietro Fumasoni Biondi (cipher n. 289), Vatican City, January 27, 1933, ASV, DASU, 5, pos. 157, f. 4.

63. Paolo Marella to Eugenio Pacelli, rep. n. 4498-i, Washington, D.C., April 20, 1933, ibid., f. 116. The letter was sent to the cardinals of Boston, Chicago, New York, and Philadelphia; to the archbishops of Baltimore, Cincinnati, Milwaukee, St. Louis, St. Paul, and San Francisco; and to the bishops of Cleveland, Fall River, Fort Wayne, Kansas City, Omaha, and Toledo.

64. Ibid., f. 119.

65. Ibid., f. 120.

other effect than to inflate the importance of Communism, so giving Soviet propaganda new life blood."⁶⁶ Anyway, as Marella wrote, Patrick Hayes, the cardinal of New York, was sure that Roosevelt would soon deal with the matter. The president's view was that "it was not possible to take any positive step toward peace and the economic recovery of countries involved if one country which accounted for such a conspicuous part of the Earth's population was left out of international negotiations promoted by the United States."⁶⁷

Roosevelt wanted Catholics and the Holy See itself to be in some way involved in the plan to give diplomatic recognition to the Soviet Union, and hoped that they should at least be reassured on the fact that the question of freedom of worship would not be sidestepped. On this subject, Cicognani sent Pacelli a translation in Italian of Roosevelt's speech delivered at the end of the Catholic Charities Congress in New York on October 4, 1933. On that occasion the president implicitly stigmatized communist atheism, stressing the importance of religion.⁶⁸

On October 10, the same day that it was made public that a request had been made to Mikhail Kalinin, the president of the Central Executive Committee of the USSR, to send a representative to begin negotiations,⁶⁹ Roosevelt invited to the White House Edmund Walsh, who until then had been one of the most bitter opponents of the diplomatic recognition idea. In a further meeting on October 20, the president stressed "his wish to insist on Russia's agreement to religious liberty and freedom of worship,"⁷⁰ and urged Walsh to let him view a memorandum summarizing the Holy See's position on the matter.

Pacelli responded almost immediately. Through the Apostolic

66. Ibid., f. 123.
67. Paolo Marella to Eugenio Pacelli, rep. n. 4716-i, Washington, D.C., May 24, 1933, ibid., SS, AES, Russia, pos. 656, fasc. 37, ff. 24–26.
68. Amleto Cicognani to Eugenio Pacelli, rep. n. 6104-i, Washington, D.C., October 17, 1933, ibid., DASU, 5, pos. 157, f. 250.
69. Franklin D, Roosevelt to Mikhail Kalinin, Washington, D.C., October 10, 1933, NARA, DS, RG 59, 711.61/287A.
70. Amleto Cicognani to Eugenio Pacelli (cipher n. 228), Washington, D.C., October 21, 1933, ASV, DASU, 5, pos. 157, f. 285.

Delegation, he asked Walsh to insist on two points raised eleven years previously by Pius XI at the Conference of Genoa: freedom of conscience for all Russian citizens and nonresidents in the Soviet Union, and freedom of public and private practice of religious belief. The Vatican secretary of state added that "as a first and urgent condition," it was necessary to obtain from the Russians "a written commitment ensuring the end of persecution, of propaganda against God in and outside Russia, and the release of those who had been imprisoned for religious reasons, especially priests."[71] Having read the report "Religion in Soviet Russia" put together by Father Walsh,[72] which Cardinal Hayes had had delivered to the White House by his assistant Robert Keegan, Roosevelt said "that he would adhere to" the document, which he considered official, and that he would do his best "to improve conditions in Russia as to religious liberty."[73]

The agreement signed by Roosevelt and Litvinov on November 16, 1933, though covering the two salient points of religious liberty and freedom of worship, was limited to respect by the Soviet authorities only for American citizens resident in the USSR.[74] The American Catholic press maintained its hostile attitude toward the Russians, but declared itself satisfied with the outcome of the talks.[75] Monsignor Keegan congratulated the president and Father Walsh.[76]

There was, however, a net divergence of opinion between the Holy See and the Apostolic Delegation in Washington. On November 19, Amleto Cicognani described the accord between the United States and the USSR as "a good precedent for other states to imitate

---

71. Eugenio Pacelli to Amleto Cicognani (cipher n. 380), Vatican City, October 23, 1933, ibid., f. 286.

72. Edmund Walsh to Franklin D. Roosevelt, Washington, D.C., November 4, 1933, FDRPL, OF 220-A, Russia, box 4.

73. Amleto Cicognani to Eugenio Pacelli, rep. n. 6289-i, Washington, D.C., November 1, 1933, ASV, DASU, 5, pos. 157, ff. 312–14.

74. See "Text of the Communications Accompanying Our Recognition of Russia," *New York Times*, November 18, 1933, p. 3.

75. See *Commonweal*, December 1, 1933, p. 117; *America*, December 2, 1933, p. 193.

76. Robert Keegan to Franklin D. Roosevelt, November 18, 1933, FDRPL, PPF 628.

in their dealings with Soviet Russia."[77] Pacelli's comment, however, was harsh. "America's recognition of the Soviet Union," he wrote to Cicognani, "unfortunately involves a notable increase in the prestige of the Soviet Union and an enhancement of its activity, which includes propaganda for atheism in the world."[78]

His reaction was "off the cuff," almost instinctive, dictated more than anything else by his disappointment that the assurances obtained by Roosevelt with respect to religious liberty were limited to American citizens. As the days went by, the Vatican came to accept the idea that the result obtained by Roosevelt was the only one realistically achievable and that, after all, no other U.S. president had given so much attention to the opinion of the Holy See in matters of foreign affairs. Consequently, on January 4, 1934, *L'Osservatore Romano* published an article that underlined the fact that "on more than one occasion president Roosevelt had stressed the importance of religion and religious principles for the wellbeing of a nation."[79] The intention, between the lines but unmistakable, was that there should be no interruption of the dialogue carried out at a distance with the White House.

To this end, the Roosevelt administration's Latin American policy undoubtedly contributed. The so-called good neighbor[80] was the subject of two confidential memoranda drawn up by Father John Burke at the beginning of 1936 and sent to the Apostolic Delegation in Washington, intended for Cardinal Eugenio Pacelli in Rome. Burke went into the details of possible advantages to the Catholic Church of the administration's planned meeting with South American states at Buenos Aires at the end of the year. "The United States," he wrote,

77. Amleto Cicognani to Eugenio Pacelli (cipher n. 234), Washington, D.C., November 19, 1933, ASV, DAU, titolo 5, pos. 157, f. 415.

78. Eugenio Pacelli to Amleto Cicognani, rep. n. 3321/33, Vatican City, December 16, 1933, ibid., SS, AES, America, pos. 232, fasc. 57, f. 11.

79. "I valori religiosi del Cristianesimo esaltati dal presidente Roosevelt," *L'Osservatore Romano*, January 4, 1934, in ibid., DASU, 5, pos. 153, f. 76.

80. On this topic, see in particular Lester D. Langley, *America and the Americas: The United States in the Western Hemisphere*, 2nd ed. (Athens: University of Georgia Press, 2010), 141–55.

"could secure liberty of religious worship and right of religious ministration for its own citizens in other countries, and it could possibly work thereby for the common recognition of religious liberty of worship by all nations for the citizens of all."[81]

Burke had been one of Roosevelt's main supporters when, in 1934–35, his decision not to intervene directly to placate the fresh outbreak of anticlericalism in Mexico during Lazaro Cardenas's government had triggered a wave of violent protests among Catholics, involving the press, many lay organizations, and even many members of the ecclesiastical hierarchy. At this juncture, it was first and foremost the Knights of Columbus who fanned the flames. The supreme committee of that organization had drawn up a petition that urged the Roosevelt administration to suspend diplomatic relations with the Mexican government. According to the treasurer of the Knights, some Catholic senators including McCarran, Walsh, O'Mahoney, Murphy, and Murray, had expressed themselves in favor of the proposal put forward by the isolationist William Borah of Idaho to charge the Senate Commission on Foreign Affairs with the setting up of a special committee to investigate the atrocities perpetuated by the Cardenas government.[82] Roosevelt submitted the question to the attention of the Department of State. In a memorandum of May 11, 1935, Robert W. Moore repeated what Cordell Hull had already said at the Conference of Montevideo in December 1933: though deploring the Mexican government's conduct, Washington would not interfere in any way with the internal affairs of that country.[83] However, the memorandum did nothing to placate Carmody. In fact, the secretary of state decided on June 26 to agree with the Knights of Columbus to a private audience at the White House.[84] At

81. Memorandum by Burke given to the apostolic delegate (confidential), March 26, 1936, ACUA, ANCWC, OGS, box 152, fold. 7.

82. Report by Father Burke, "The Knights of Columbus and Mexico," January 22, 1935, ASV, DASU, 2, pos. 455, ff. 8–9.

83. Memorandum by the Assistant Secretary of State, Washington, D.C., May 11, 1935, FDRPL, OF 146, Mexico 1933–1940, box 1.

84. Memorandum by the Secretary of State, Washington, D.C., June 26, 1935, ibid.

the meeting on July 8, Roosevelt listened carefully to the grievances of the organization's delegates, and a few days later, on July 17, he spoke to Congress in the hope of putting an end to the controversy. In response to another petition from some Catholic congressmen, among whom were Clare Fenerty of Pennsylvania and Hamilton Fish of New York, he stated that it was not the duty of the U.S. government to interfere in the affairs of another state, but he wished to stress that the White House believed in the principle of religious liberty both at home and abroad.[85]

Despite the attacks of Congress and the Knights of Columbus, Roosevelt and his staff were able to count on the direct support of a number of individuals belonging to national Catholic circles, and indirectly on the Holy See. Father Burke was one of the most important. Knowing that Burke acted as intermediary with the Vatican,[86] the president was in the habit of consulting him whenever a bishop pronounced himself on the Mexican issue. Another of Roosevelt's great supporters on the matter was George Mundelein, the cardinal of Chicago. Through the *New World,* Mundelein contested the legitimacy of the request for the dismissal of the ambassador to Mexico, Josephus Daniels, advanced at the end of 1934 by many sectors of the Catholic public, after the diplomat had applauded reforms introduced by President Calles.[87] Above all, it was Mundelein who presided over the ceremony at which the University of Notre Dame conferred on Roosevelt an honorary degree. On that occasion, to the cardinal's words of appreciation for his perseverance and courage, the president replied by stressing the absolute inviolability of the right to religious liberty.[88]

85. Roosevelt's speech of July 18, 1935, is quoted in Rosenman, ed., *The Public Papers,* 4.305.

86. Marvin McIntyre to Franklin D. Roosevelt (confidential memorandum), Washington, D.C., May 27, 1935, FDRPL, OF 146, box 1.

87. See *New World,* October 12, 1934, p. 4.

88. Walter Trohan, "President Gets Honor Degree at Notre Dame," *Chicago Daily Tribune,* December 10, 1935, p. 9. A draft of Roosevelt's speech written by Father Burke is in ACUA, ANCWC, OGS, box 153, fold. 1, Washington, D.C., December 9, 1935.

The repeated attacks on Roosevelt induced the Holy See to mobilize the Apostolic Delegation in Washington, so Cicognani began to gather information on the Knights of Columbus. On February 23, 1935, he asked the auxiliary bishop of Boston, Francis Spellman, how in his opinion they could exercise some form of control over the organization which, at that time especially, seemed to be completely out of tune with episcopal authority.[89] The Apostolic Delegation's choice of Spellman was by no means casual. Having been relegated by Cardinal O'Connell to minor positions on the editorial staff of the newspaper of the Boston archdiocese, he had become friends with Francesco Borgongini-Duca, prefect of the Congregation for Extraordinary Ecclesiastical Affairs, having translated into English some of his writings in the early 1920s. In November 1925, Borgongini-Duca had called him to Rome, where he remained until 1932 in charge of the oratory of the local section of the Knights of Columbus. This organization was subject to the authority of the congregation, so Spellman became a member of the staff of the Vatican secretary of state. It was in the Vatican that he became personally acquainted with Cardinal Gasparri, and at the same time he became an assiduous frequenter of the "Casa del Sole," the Roman residence of the Bradys, a husband and wife who were generous American Catholic benefactors. Some of the most influential individuals of the Holy See used to meet there, among them the nuncio in Germany, Eugenio Pacelli. The relationship between Spellman and Pacelli became closer during the controversy between the Vatican and the Fascist regime over the Catholic Action issue. In this rather tricky situation, Spellman worked mostly as a translator, which earned him the respect of Pius XI as well as that of Pacelli, who entrusted him with the delicate task of taking to Paris the encyclical *Non abbiamo bisogno* in July 1931. Returning to Boston in September the next year, less than two months before the presidential elections, as auxiliary bishop, in spite of the resistance of Cardinal O'Connell, he quickly made his way up in the American hierarchy.[90] Spellman had

89. Amleto Cicognani to Francis Spellman, rep. n. 234/35 (confidential), Washington, D.C., February 23, 1935, ASV, DASU, 2, pos. 455, f. 17.
90. See Robert I. Gannon, *The Cardinal Spellman Story* (Garden City, N.Y.:

clearly understood the need to support the good neighbor policy, and replied to Cicognani by pointing out the mistakenness of the Knights of Columbus and of the cardinals themselves, O'Connell among them, of opposing the administration's line on the Mexican issue.[91] Apart from anything else, his opinion precisely reflected that of the Holy See. This can be deduced from the long note sent on April 8, 1935, by the auditor of the Apostolic Delegation, Egidio Vagnozzi, to Cicognani: "the Vatican is not in favor of political agitation in solving the Mexican problem and the alleged approval that the Knights of Columbus are requesting is only a figment of their imagination."[92]

Cardinal Pacelli was aware of the influence the United States could exercise on European affairs because of his experience in Germany during and after the First World War, and he gave great importance to improving relations with them. As the skies of Europe darkened with the threat of nazism-fascism, he realized that it was necessary to step up the dialogue with Washington, and with this in mind, as well as activating the channels that the Vatican could use in the United States, he became personally involved, finding in Roosevelt an interlocutor willing to put aside differences that were more or less "outdated" in the name of the mutual desire to avert a new war.

### THE "SPIRIT" OF HYDE PARK

"Transatlantic" and "Pan-American" were the adjectives used by Pope Pius XI in the dedication of a portrait of himself that he gave to Cardinal Eugenio Pacelli on November 14, 1936.[93] The words were

---

Doubleday, 1962), 31–89; and John Cooney, *The American Pope: The Life and Times of Francis Cardinal Spellman* (New York: Times Books, 1984), 18–79.

91. Francis Spellman to Amleto Cicognani, Boston, March 2, 1935, ASV, DASU, 2, pos. 455, ff. 46–56; Francis Spellman to Amleto Cicognani, Boston, March 15, 1935, ibid., ff. 203–4.

92. Egidio Vagnozzi to Amleto Cicognani, Vatican City, April 8, 1935, ibid., ff. 282–83.

93. This dedication is quoted in "Come il giovane popolo d'America è apparso al Card. Pacelli," *L'Osservatore Romano,* November 22, 1936, ASV, DASU, Press Clippings, f. 267, pos. 194.

in no way casual. In fact, the Vatican secretary of state received the pope's gift on his return from the United States of America, which in appearance was simply another of his numerous journeys, but which was in reality a historical occasion destined to bring about profound change not only in relations between the Holy See and the North American republic, but also in the diplomatic strategy of the Vatican at the most crucial time after the end of World War I.

Tempered by the vicissitudes of diplomatic life, as soon as he became secretary of state, Pacelli presented himself "as the heir of the *venerated masters* Rampolla and Merry del Val," and therefore as a "synthesis of these diverse approaches to the actions taken by the Church of Rome which had for so long divided the Curia, a dualism expressed as Pius X/Merry del Val and Benedict XV/Gasparri, and which was thought by many to be irreconcilable."[94]

This was the reason for Pius XI's choice; in the former nuncio in Berlin he recognized a new equilibrium, a mirror almost of his own policies, both pastoral and diplomatic. So it was that between the strong-willed and emotional pope Pius XI and the dignified and cautious Cardinal Pacelli there was born a relationship that Emma Fattorini defines as "special" because of that sort of complementarity that allows for "the intemperance of one to be dampened and resolved more diplomatically, and the indecisiveness of the other to be made more resolute."[95]

Increasingly disillusioned by the ineffectiveness of the concordat regulating relations between the Church and the German Reich, and concerned about Fascist politics and the inevitable approach between Mussolini and Hitler, toward the end of his papacy the sick and aging Pius XI clearly showed a rejection of nazism-fascism. Pacelli feared the pope's intransigence and often his spontaneous and imprudent character; he did, however, appreciate the reasons

94. Giovanni Coco, "Eugenio Pacelli: Cardinale Segretario di Stato, 1929–1930," in *I "fogli di udienza" del Cardinale Eugenio Pacelli Segretario di Stato*, ed. Sergio Pagano and Michael Chappin (Vatican City: Archivio Segreto Vaticano Ed., 2010), 93.

95. Fattorini, *Pio XI, Hitler e Mussolini*, xii.

and the necessity for such an attitude. This resulted in a tireless process of mediation, an attempt to tone down and soften the pope's position, and at the same time to use the tools of diplomacy that suited him and which he felt to be more effective because they were more indirect. It was his pragmatism, and his perception of the incapacity of European governments to restrain the mad aspirations of Hitler, that induced him to be increasingly obstinate in his wish to establish direct contact with the United States of America. Such a path had been paved more than once since the beginnings of Franklin D. Roosevelt's presidency, but it began to show promise—and certainly not by mere chance—following Eugenio Pacelli's visit to the United States in the fall of 1936.

With Roosevelt's victory in the presidential elections of 1932, the White House became much more accessible than in the past to Catholics, both laymen and clergy. This inversion of U.S. policy was mutually beneficial: for the administration it guaranteed a widening basis of its consensus, and for the various exponents of Catholicism it ensured greater participation in the national political life. There are various indications, including the report on the visit of Father Burke to the executive office of the White House,[96] that would seem to suggest that the president's intention to relax relations with Catholics were directed only internally, related exclusively to social reforms and therefore to the legitimization of New Deal legislation. However, Roosevelt went far beyond this when, a few months after taking office, he expressed the wish to revive diplomatic relations with the Holy See. This, at least, seemed to be the sense of what he said on June 12, 1933, on the occasion of his meeting with the apostolic delegate Amleto Giovanni Cicognani.

"Before my arrival in the United States, several people had spoken to Mr. Roosevelt about the new Delegate," wrote Cicognani to

96. Burke memorandum: "An Interesting Morning, or, Meeting Another President," Washington, D.C., April 13, 1933, ACUA, ANCWC, OGS, box 122, fold. 32. Roosevelt limited himself to thanking Burke for the support received during the elections and to underlining the importance of the Church at such a delicate time in the country's history.

Pacelli in a report of June 15, 1933, "and among these, according to what I have been told, was Cardinal Mundelein and Father Burke himself, and the President had given to understand that he would receive me with great pleasure."[97] Although it was "the custom to pay a courtesy visit and congratulations on every new President," he thought it necessary to report in detail "both on the formal occasion and on what was said."[98] In fact, much was new about this visit: "up to now Delegates had been received by the President in the Executive Office, which is annexed to the White House, and it was there that he took me, but he told me at once to go to the White House itself." Moreover, "both on arrival and departure there were none of the usual reporters and photographers, and it was clear that they had been given orders to this effect."[99] After a reference by Cicognani to the interest shown by the American Catholic press in the efforts made by the administration toward furthering the economic and social readjustment of the country, the president spoke with enthusiasm of the Holy Father, "praising his width of vision, his perfect understanding of the needs of peoples and the timeliness and beauty of his encyclicals, which, if more widely known, would greatly influence the social and economic thought of the United States."[100] Then the conversation moved on to questions of international politics, with regard to which Roosevelt expressed his "hopes in the Conference of London, saying that the United States would do their utmost to prevent a European war." He did not conceal the fact that he had welcomed "the signing of the Treaty of Four," and praised "both Mussolini (for his mediation work) and the representatives of foreign governments who had recently visited the United States."[101]

97. Amleto Cicognani to Eugenio Pacelli, rep. n. 4932-i, Washington, D.C., June 15, 1933, ASV, SS, AES, America, pos. 230, file 53, f. 83r. A first reconstruction of this episode based on Vatican documents is to be found in Luca Castagna, "La Delegazione Apostolica a Washington da Fumasoni Biondi a Cicognani, 1926–38," in *Ph.D. Rendiconti del Dottorato di Ricerca in Teoria e Storia delle Istituzioni*, ed. Gianfranco Macri and Antonio Scocozza (Naples: La Città del Sole, 2010), 166–69.
98. Amleto Cicognani to Eugenio Pacelli, June 15, 1933, ibid., f. 83v.
99. Ibid.
100. Ibid., f. 84r.
101. Ibid., f. 84v.

The very fact of having discussed, even in general terms, delicate themes of international politics with a Vatican representative was in itself something that had never happened before; what is even more surprising, however, is the way in which the president received Cicognani. "I wish to receive you," he said, "as an Ambassador; I hope that the time will soon come when I can greet you as an Ambassador."[102] Two days later, on June 14, in his speech at the Catholic University of America on receiving an honorary degree of doctor of law, Roosevelt spoke again of the delegate as a "new friend" whom he hoped "to see often during the next four years."[103] According to the report, Cicognani remained totally cautious, and thought of the possible start of diplomatic relations with the United States simply as "a demonstration of goodwill towards and liking for the Holy See," adding that "there would be serious arguments for and against."[104]

Cicognani's caution, however, was insufficient to avoid the interest of the press which, especially between the end of 1933 and the early months of the following year, began to speculate about the possible outcome. As usual, the staff of the Apostolic Delegation kept a careful eye on the situation and collected articles to keep the Vatican secretary of state informed.

It was a historian, Leo Francis Stock of the Catholic University of America, who first roused public opinion. In August 1933 he published a book that reconstructed the history of relations between the United States and the Papal States from the outbreak of the risings of 1848 to the end of the American mission to Rome in 1867. According to the News Service of the NCWC, this made it possible at last to discuss a matter that had been ignored for too long.[105] In the wake of Stock's work, on January 10, 1934, Giuseppe Della Torre, editor in chief of *L'Osservatore Romano*, readdressed the subject in a more con-

102. Ibid., f. 84r.  103. Ibid., f. 85v.
104. Ibid.
105. "U.S.-Vatican Relation Told," *NCWC News Service,* August 12, 1933, ASV, DASU, Press Clippings, pos. 178, f. 4. The work in question is Francis L. Sock, *United States Ministers to the Papal States: Instructions and Dispatches* (Washington, D.C.: The Catholic University of America Press, 1933).

cise form, but laid the emphasis on the fact that the solution to the Roman question had removed the legal obstacles to the revival of diplomatic relations.[106] The American press reacted immediately. According to *Il Progresso Italo-Americano* of New York, the Vatican's "desire to re-establish the official relations of the past" was evident; and this was a possibility, in the view of the Rome correspondent of the Denver newspaper the *Catholic Register*, which was "clearly implied" in the words of Della Torre. In the opinion of *Il Crociato*, a Brooklyn Catholic weekly, this would allow "the spiritual power of the Holy See and the political and economic power of the United States to exercise a decisive influence in international forums in favor of world peace." On February 4, 1934, Edward Folliard, one of the best known columnists in the United States, stated in the *Washington Herald* that, according to certain rumors in the capital's diplomatic circles, "a resumption of diplomatic relations between the United States and the Vatican is a distinct probability."[107] At the beginning of March, the *Catholic Register* and the *Chicago Daily News* even hazarded a guess as to the name of Roosevelt's possible choice of representative: Alexander Kirk, an advisor at the U.S. embassy in Rome. According to these two papers, in fact, a provisional agreement had already been reached by the administration and Eugenio Pacelli during Jim Farley's visit to the Vatican in December 1933.[108]

Since the government did not take up any official stand, the interest of the media in the question of the resumption of harmonious relations with the Vatican gradually faded. In spite of Roosevelt's expressed wish to deal directly with Cicognani when it was neces-

106. *L'Osservatore Romano*, January 10, 1934, in ibid., f. 2.
107. "I rapporti tra Santa Sede e Stati Uniti," *Il Progresso Italo-Americano*, January 11, 1934; "Open Hint Given by Osservatore about U.S. Envoy to Vatican City," *Catholic Register*, January 21, 1934; "La potenza spirituale di Roma e la potenza economica di Washington al servizio della pace," *Il Crociato*, January 27, 1934; Edward T. Folliard, "U.S. Accord with Vatican Believed Near," *Washington Herald*, February 4, 1934, ibid., ff. 4, 7, 12.
108. "Vatican Seeks U.S. Nod. Public Approval Needed," *Chicago Daily Tribune*, March 8, 1934; "U.S. Vatican Envoy May Be Chicagoan," *Catholic Register*, March 18, 1934, ibid, ff. 9, 13.

sary to communicate with the Holy See, Cicognani himself made no further reference to the subject. He therefore returned to occupying himself with the internal matters of the ecclesiastical hierarchy.

The question of dialogue between Washington and the Holy See came up again during the delicate time of international politics at the end of 1935, with the Italian-Ethiopian war. It is well known that Roosevelt became aware of the state of war between Italy and Ethiopia on October 5, 1935. Conditioned by pressure from the more hard-line isolationists in Congress, he went no further than to "morally" condemn the infamous Fascist atrocities in East Africa.[109]

The Holy See did everything possible to "take a line quite independent from that of Mussolini's government,"[110] and the idea of Roosevelt's mediation by exploiting Washington's influence on Great Britain was put forward by Bernardino Nogara, delegate to the Special Administration of the Property of the Holy See.[111] On October 12, the Jesuit general Wladimir Ledochowski, through Father Tacchi Venturi, made it known to the secretary of state that the American ambassador to Rome, the pro-Fascist Breckinridge Long, had confirmed Roosevelt's wish "to get into direct contact with the Holy Father to work for peace-keeping."[112] Pacelli charged the Apostolic Delegation in Washington with the task of finding out if there was any truth in the diplomat's statement and Cicognani approached Father Burke, whose meeting with Roosevelt turned out to be extremely disappointing. While the president appreciated the pope's attempts to keep the peace, he bitterly criticized the Fascist military attack on Ethiopia, describing it as a "national and international crime," but he gave no appearance of willingness to collaborate with the Holy

109. See David F. Schmitz, "Speaking the Same Language: The U.S. Response to the Italo-Ethiopian War and the Origins of American Appeasement," in *Appeasement in Europe: A Reassessment of U.S. Policies,* ed. David F. Schmitz and Richard D. Challener (Westport, Conn.: Greenwood Press, 1990), 75–102.

110. Lucia Ceci, *Il papa non deve parlare: Chiesa, fascismo e guerra d'Etiopia* (Rome: Laterza, 2010), 144.

111. See ibid., 152.

112. Wladimir Ledochowski to Pietro Tacchi Venturi, Vatican City, October 12, 1935, ASV, SS, AES, Italy, CI-E, pos. 967, vol. 2.

See.[113] In spite of this, Nogara did not give up. In a note of December 3 addressed to Pius XI, he repeated his conviction that Vatican diplomacy should convince Roosevelt to "take on the task of mediator in the dispute," and that the pope could achieve a great deal "with his moral authority." Just as optimistic at that time was Joseph Hurley, an American bishop employed in the secretary of state's office who was close to both Pacelli and Ambassador Long. Hurley wrote in a note of December 3 that he believed the involvement of the United States would favor a "conciliatory transaction."[114] The other side of the coin was the skepticism of the undersecretary of extraordinary ecclesiastical affairs Domenico Tardini, whose view was that, although Roosevelt's intervention would "without doubt be very useful" in terms of putting pressure on London, it had to be borne in mind that, "since the upper spheres of the United States were not usually very well-disposed to the Holy See," he would not easily accept to "side with a peacemaking action" promoted by the pope. In his view, therefore, the best course of action would be to insist on the fact that American mediation could be "decisive" and that the Holy See was "ready to use all its influence to facilitate the happy achievement of the initiative."[115] On December 7 the secretary of state drafted the negotiation to submit to Roosevelt. Pizzardo delivered this to Monsigor Giuseppe Fietta, then apostolic nuncio in the Dominican Republic, who was to visit Washington on December 21, and he asked him to tell the president that the pope would be ready "to do still more in favor of peace."[116]

No concrete action followed the indignation of Roosevelt and Pius XI against the Fascist war in Ethiopia; on the contrary, the pope's silence and America's supplying petroleum had the fatal result of assisting Benito Mussolini's imperialist plan. And yet Italy's aggression in Ethiopia marked the first and decisive breakup of rela-

113. Amleto Cicognani to Eugenio Pacelli, Washington, D.C., October 27, 1935, ibid.
114. Notes by Joseph Hurley, December 5, 1935, ibid., f. 214.
115. Notes by Domenico Tardini, Vatican City, December 6, 1935, ibid., ff. 215rv.
116. Notes and Observations by Domenico Tardini, Vatican City, December 7, 1935, ibid., ff. 217–29.

tions between Rome and Washington in the period between the two world wars. In the same way, Pius XI and his curia began to rethink the underlying strategy to adopt in dealing with the nazi-fascist regimes, partly in response to the German occupation of the left bank of the Rhine and the outbreak of the Spanish Civil War.

It was in this context that Eugenio Pacelli, who had underestimated the tragic consequences of Italian atrocities in Africa, made up his mind to pay a personal visit to the United States, where he probably hoped to make a breach in the wall of isolationism and inveterate antipapist prejudice in order to find some form of alliance with the most economically and diplomatically developed country in the world.

Francis Spellman was the great organizer of Pacelli's visit to the United States, an event which, as confirmed by Vatican archival sources, he planned in minute detail in collaboration with the architect Enrico Galeazzi—representative of the Knights of Columbus in Rome—and with Miss Brady, the papal duchess who owned the Manhasset residence where the Vatican secretary of state was to stay. Amleto Cicognani, in whom Spellman did not have much confidence, was kept in the dark as to the program until September 30, 1936,[117] when Domenico Tardini officially informed him of the visit.[118]

On October 8, 1936, the transatlantic liner *Conte di Savoia* with Cardinal Eugenio Pacelli and the new Italian ambassador in Washington on board docked at the Quarantine Port, New York, escorted by three steamboats crowded with personalities. Pacelli immediately made it clear that this was a private visit, saying that he simply wished "to see with my own eyes the Country and to feel the pulsations of its life and of its labor." He therefore chose to conclude his speech without even hinting at a position on the internal and international issues of those troubled times: "outside and above all conflict of parties whose interests are purely earthly," he said, "the

---

117. The hypothesis that the visit had been organized long before Cicognani was informed is confirmed by the fact that a bank transfer dated September 21 for $5,408.06 was made by the Vatican Secretary of State to Miss Brady's National City Bank account; see ASV, SS, AES, SE, pos. 430, fasc. 339, f. 33.

118. Domenico Tardini to Amleto Cicognani (cipher n. 36), Vatican City, September 30, 1936, ASV, DASU, 5, pos. 104, f. 2.

voice of the Father of Christendom is raised, amid the struggles of the present hour to warn humanity that it is following and that it will follow the wrong road if it refuse to recognize and to observe the noble and pure doctrine of the Gospel."[119]

"Although the Cardinal's lips remained buttoned up," wrote Italo Falbo in *L'Osservatore Romano*, the visit was "a dexterous diplomatic move."[120] The American press made a great deal of the event and began to speculate on Pacelli's real intentions. The idea put forward by some dailies, among them the *Evening Star*, the *Washington Post*, and *La Voce del Popolo* of Detroit, that the cardinal intended to resolve the "Coughlin case," was quickly set aside.[121] The *New York Times* correspondent Arnaldo Cortesi wrote that Pacelli "will almost certainly visit President Roosevelt with whom he may discuss the reported administration plan to call a world conference of the Heads of State immediately after the November elections."[122] Although the Vatican press office stressed that "a hasty move in that direction" could "upset the position that the Catholic Church has created for itself in the United States," the *Evening Star* had no hesitation in describing the visit as "preparatory to the recognition of the papal state by the United States government and establishment of a diplomatic mission."[123] The adviser to the Italian embassy in Washington, Alberto Rossi Longhi, was of the opinion that the real reason for the visit was to "look into the possibility of a renewal of diplomatic relations between the United States and the Holy See."[124]

119. Statement by Eugenio Cardinal Pacelli, New York, October 8, 1936, ibid., ff. 19–20.

120. *L'Osservatore Romano*, October 8, 1936, in ibid., Press Clippings, f. 81.

121. "Vatican Secretary Off to US Today," *Washington Post*, October 3, 1936; Charles Brown, "U.S. Recognition of Vatican Hinted," *Evening Star*, October 2, 1936; "Una petizione al Card. Pacelli," *La Voce del popolo*, October 6, 1936, ibid., Press Clippings, ff. 3, 8, 11.

122. Arnaldo Cortesi, "Papal Secretary of State Coming Here. Rome Speculates on Subject of Mission," *New York Times*, October 1, 1936, in ibid., Press Clippings, f. 3.

123. "Una smentita vaticana circa gli Stati Uniti," *La Corrispondenza*, October 20, 1936, in ibid., pos. 178, f. 39.

124. Alberto Rossi Longhi to MAE, Washington, D.C., October 3, 1936, AS-MAE, Affari politici 1931–1945, AP2, SU, b. 28, fasc. 37.

On his arrival in New York, Pacelli's habitual caution did not suffice to placate the comments of the press, and the newspapers even began to speculate about the supposed intention of the cardinal to persuade Roosevelt to agree to a "formal participation of this country in the catholic church's anti-commy campaign."[125] Amleto Cicognani tried to put the secretary of state on his guard: "at a time of deep political feelings," he wrote on October 9, "it is in the utmost interest of religion, as many bishops are stressing, not only to keep the Catholic Church out of the matter of the elections, but also to make it clear that, in fact as well as appearance, the Church is over and above political parties." It was absolutely necessary to be clear about this because some newspapers, and in particular *Our Sunday Visitor* of Baltimore, had spread the news that Pacelli was to call on President Roosevelt on October 10, and it was easy to foresee that this would inevitably provoke "strong reactions."[126] What also happened was that the headquarters of the Apostolic Delegation was flooded with hundreds of letters of protest from private citizens, almost all Catholics, who expressed various opinions on the conduct of Roosevelt's administration, but agreed on the need "to keep the Catholic Church out of the political campaign." Consequently, since Roosevelt was "in the midst of an electoral fight," a meeting with Pacelli, according to Cicognani, would be "very inexpedient and inopportune, and would be considered discriminatory."[127]

Anyway, the idea of a visit to the White House before the outcome of the elections was shelved. From October 9 to 21, Pacelli visited New York, Philadelphia, Baltimore, and Boston, Spellman's "stronghold," where he was greeted by a mass of people in the Church of the Sacred Heart in Newton Center. His arrival in Washington, planned for October 22, was preceded by another communication from Cicognani who—in spite of having received certain threats[128]—informed Pacelli

125. "Pacelli May Confer on Church's War to Halt Reds," *New York Evening Journal*, October 8, 1936, ASV, DASU, 5, pos. 194, Press Clippings, f. 66.
126. Amleto Cicignano to Eugenio Pacelli (personal), Washington, D.C., October 9, 1936, ASV, DASU, 5, pos. 194, ff. 70–71.
127. Ibid.
128. Anonymous Letter to Amleto Cicognani, October 20, 1936, ibid., ff. 216–

that the National Press Club had invited him to hold a press conference.[129] After receiving the honorary title of Juris Utriusque Doctor at Georgetown University and visiting the Congressional Library and the tomb of George Washington at Mount Vernon, Pacelli took part in the meeting with the press. Those who believed they might hear some clarification as to the reasons for the visit were profoundly disappointed. Pacelli did no more than briefly praise the professionalism of the American press, urging them to use their enormous influence over public opinion to act in the service of peace.[130]

The Vatican secretary of state left Washington and returned to New York. He took off on the morning of October 25 after presiding over the ceremony of Gotham400, a Catholic association directed by Miss Brady, to begin the second phase of his visit, which would take him to Chicago, South Bend (Indiana)—where he received an honorary degree of doctor of letters from the University of Notre Dame—St. Paul, San Francisco, Los Angeles, St. Louis, and lastly Cincinnati. Pacelli was warmly welcomed by the faithful as well as the local ecclesiastical authorities, and especially the archbishop of San Francisco John Mitty, who had taken the trouble on October 5 to invite him via the Apostolic Delegation since he was sure that his arrival in the city would be good for the image of the Church throughout the West Coast.[131]

Roosevelt's electoral victory on November 3 paved the way for what many believed was the main reason for Pacelli's visit: a meeting

---

17: "This is a solemn warning to you to get this Pacelli out of this country and get him out QUICK or there will be another Spain right here in America. The Ope of Rome and his horde of Spys headed by this Pacelli are getting dangerously bold of late here and must and will be stopped. As Spain so America is the slogan!"

129. Amleto Cicognani to Eugenio Pacelli (personal), Washington, D.C., October 16, 1936, ibid., ff. 129–30. Father Burke advised him to accept the press's invitation on October 15, and also drafted a speech for Pacelli to deliver (Memorandum by Father Burke, Washington, D.C., October 15, 1936, ACUA, ANCWC, OGS, box 152, fold. 5).

130. Transcript of Remarks by Eugenio Card. Pacelli, Washington, D.C., October 22, 1936, ibid., f. 193.

131. John Mitty to Amleto Cicognani, San Francisco, October 5, 1936, ibid., f. 18.

with the president. Contrary to the expectations of Cicognani, who with the help of Father Burke had done everything possible to organize the ceremony in Washington, the meeting (which the White House had scheduled for October 20)[132] was held at Roosevelt's private residence on November 5. Pacelli arrived at Poughkeepsie Station in the morning, accompanied by Joseph Kennedy, Bishop of New York Stephen Donahue, the ex-director of the National Emergency Council Frank Walker, and Francis Spellman. Before the delegation moved into the close-by Hyde Park with Roosevelt's secretary Marvin McIntyre, Spellman prevented the journalists who had gathered from asking questions, and when he communicated the outcome of the meeting to Pizzardo, he limited himself to underlining the climate of cordiality during the two-hour conversation.[133]

"With the total lack of official or unofficial information," the press attempted to "construct various descriptions of the event."[134] The *New York Times*, for example, described it simply as a kind of state visit probably to discuss subjects of various kinds.[135] According to the Italian ambassador to the Holy See Bonifacio Pignatti, however, there was no doubt: "the issue of diplomatic relations must have been discussed by President Roosevelt and Cardinal Pacelli." Both sides, but especially in America, "were looking into the question of how they could give credence to a North American representative at the Vatican for dealing with questions of a special nature."[136] Basically, the foundations had been laid for an opening of relations. What remained to be done was to carry out the negotiations, and quickly too. In Europe another war was looming.

132. Memorandum by Mcintyre, Washington, D.C., October 20, 1936, FDRPL, PPF 4129.
133. Francis Spellman to Giuseppe Pizzardo, New York, November 6, 1936, ASV, SS, SE, pos. 430, fasc. 339, ff. 59–61.
134. "Viaggio del Cardinal Pacelli negli Stati Uniti," *Annuario di politica Inernazionale*, 1936, p. 258.
135. "Pacelli Lunches with Roosevelt," *New York Times*, November 6, 1936, ASV, DASU, 5, pos. 194, Press Clippings, f. 242.
136. Bonifacio Pignatti to MAE, Vatican City, November 23, 1936, ASMAE, AP2, SU, b. 28, fasc. 37.

# 6

# A SHARED MISSION

## INTERLUDE, 1937–38

Neither the Neutrality Act of 1935 nor that of 1936 was applicable to civil wars. Nevertheless, fearing protests on the isolationist front on the eve of the presidential elections, Roosevelt applied an arms embargo on both sides after the *Alzamiento Nacional* of July 1936 and kept to it right up to the end of the Spanish Civil War. Like many members of his administration, who clearly disliked the Spanish radicals, the president initially saw Franco's attack as being essentially antisubversive. However, his perception of the Spanish situation and the repercussions it could have at international level quickly changed. He began to worry about the fact that Franco's victory in Spain would further reinforce the Nazi-Fascist link and that this would constitute a threat not only to the shaky European equilibrium but also to the national security of the United States if Nazi-Fascism should catch on in the American continent—that is, in Latin America, which was of vital interest to Washington in that it had always in the past given way to "flattering" authoritarianism. It was for this reason that he chose to exploit the Buenos Aires Inter-American Conference (December 1936) for maintaining the peace in order to solder the good neighbor policy with Latin American states, and, at the same time, put the whole international community on guard against the dangers of Nazi-Fascist escalation in Europe.[1]

---

1. See on this point, Richard P. Traina, *American Diplomacy and the Spanish Civil War* (Bloomington: Indiana University Press, 1968), 108; and Max P. Fried-

## A SHARED MISSION

At Chicago in October 1937, Roosevelt delivered a speech that drew on a vast series of age-old internationalist metaphors to denounce the world epidemic of illegality, and called for greater international collaboration to put aggressors in "quarantine." His words were vague, but they marked a renewed attention to the dynamics of international affairs and, with the caution typical of someone who is perfectly aware of the moods and attitudes of public opinion in his country, prepared the ground for what was to become the slow but inexorable process of the United States' entry into the war.

In this context of gradual antitotalitarian action, the dialogue between the White House and the Vatican began to play a part, and during the years 1937–39 they worked together to promote the relationship.

From the second half of the 1930s, the Holy See showed clearer signs of impatience with German National Socialism. In March 1936, irritated by the continual violations of the concordat between the Catholic Church and the Reich, Eugenio Pacelli bitterly commented on Hitler's decision to occupy the Rhine Basin: "There is no point in deluding ourselves," he said in conversation with the Italian ambassador, Bonifacio Pignatti, "for the Nazis treaties are not worth the paper they are written on."[2] The Spanish situation had also become a reason for concern for the Holy See,[3] from both the religious and the diplomatic points of view. What eventually happened in Spain was exactly what Pius XI and Pacelli so much desired, "to prevent harm being done to the Church and to find a formula that would in some way satisfy the government and at the same time protect the rights and liberty of the Holy See."[4] The question of the relationship between Franco and nazism, however, was by no means underestimat-

---

man, *Nazis and Good Neighbors: The United States Campaign against the Germans of Latin America in World War II* (New York: Cambridge University Press, 2003), 9.

2. Bonificio Pignatti to Benito Mussolini, Vatican City, March 13, 1936, AS-MAE, AP2, Holy See, b. 30.

3. See Giorgio Campanini, ed., *I cattolici italiani e la guerra di Spagna* (Brescia: Morcelliana, 1987), 41–59.

4. Notes by Eugenio Card. Pacelli, ASV, SS, AES, Sessioni, 1938, vol. 94, Spain, December 22, 1938.

ed. "And what about Nazi Germany? Are they not persecuting the Church?" wondered a worried Eugenio Pacelli in June 1937. "Even though it is not in the intentions of the Holy See, it would seem that, by supporting Franco, it is in agreement with a group which wishes to destroy religion and which worships Hitler."[5]

A few weeks before Pacelli pronounced these words, Pius XI, by then permanently bedridden, had condemned nazism in his encyclical *Mit brennender Sorge* (March 14, 1937). Contrary to the belief of various historians who have criticized Eugenio Pacelli's attitude to Hitler's regime,[6] he did in fact play a fundamental role in the writing of the encyclical, which he revised continually so that it was in the end much harsher than was liked by the cardinal of Munich, Michael von Faulhaber, who in the initial stage had been given the task of writing a draft. It was Pacelli, too, who conveyed the vehement protests of the Germans and suggested to the apostolic nuncio in Berlin, Cesare Orsenigo, to refrain from sending birthday wishes to Hitler in April 1937.[7]

*Mit brennender Sorge* echoed all around the world, resulting in a campaign of awareness raising and international solidarity. Like the American ambassador in Rome, William Phillips, his counterpart in Berlin, William Dodd, though appreciating the pope's boldness, expressed reserve to the Department of State when the Nazi authorities used their fury against German Catholics.[8]

One month later, on May 8, Cardinal George Mundelein of Chicago delivered a very provocative speech at the Quigley Preparatory Seminar of his archdiocese to over five hundred prelates in which he wondered how the German people could possibly have reduced

5. Views of Eugenio Card. Pacelli, ibid., (1937, Second Session), vol. 93, June 14, 1937.

6. This is the view of (among others) John Cornwell, *Hitler's Pope: The Secret History of Pius XII,* 2nd ed. (New York: Penguin Books, 2008), 130–78.

7. Eugenio Pacelli to Cesare Orsenigo, Vatican City, April 8, 1937, ASV, SS, AES, Germany, pos. 604, fasc. 114, f. 71.

8. William Phillips to Cordell Hull, Rome, March 23, 1937, NARA, DS, RG 59, 765.66A/199; William Dodd to Cordell Hull, Berlin, April 2, 1937, ibid., 862.404/203.

themselves to submission to Hitler, "an Austrian paperhanger and a poor one," and "two associates," Goebbels and Goring.[9] All the most important newspapers covered the story, pointing out that the words of a cardinal of German origin would meet the favor both of the episcopate and of Protestants and Jews.[10] On May 21 Pacelli asked Cicognani to send him the complete text of the "brave speech" that, according to the press, "the German Embassy had protested against." On the same day, the delegate corroborated the "vast favorable publicity" that the cardinal's assertion had received and made it known that the Reich's diplomatic representation in Washington had presented the case to the Department of State, "but without making any formal protest," and for this reason the American authorities had "thought it better not to reply."[11]

While the American press continued to stress the fact that the Vatican had not reprimanded Mundelein for his attack on Hitler,[12] on May 24, 1937, the German ambassador at the Holy See, Diego Von Bergen, was recalled to Berlin. The Nazi government's decision to take this action was discussed at length by the Congregation for Extraordinary Ecclesiastical Affairs on the following June 20. The minutes make it clear that the cardinals and the pope himself agreed on the fact that "in spite of the threats and despite the unforeseeable consequences, the Holy See must not give way to, not be alarmed by, and must not fall at the feet of the German government."[13] Pacelli, whose open talks with France during his visit to Paris and Lisieux

9. "Mundelein Rips into Hitler to Church's Attack," *Chicago Daily Tribune*, May 19, 1937, p. 7.

10. See, as examples, "Nazis Bid Vatican Rebuke Mundelein for His Criticism," *New York Times*, May 20, 1937, p. 1; "Catholic Bishops Challenge Nazis on Youth Groups," *New York Times*, May 24, 1937, p. 1; "Nazis Order 200 Catholic Papers to Cease Issue," *Chicago Daily Tribune*, May 28, 1937, p. 11.

11. Eugenio Pacelli to Amleto Cicognani (cipher n. 79), Vatican City, May 21, 1937, and with the same date, Amleto Cicognani to Eugenio Pacelli (cipher n. 154), Washington, D.C., ASV, DASU, 5, pos. 166b, f. 13.

12. Amleto Cicognani to Eugenio Pacelli, rep. n. 268/27, Washington, D.C., June 11, 1937, ibid., ff. 39–40.

13. View of Federico Card, Tedeschini, ibid., SS, AES, 1937, Second Session, Germany, June 20, 1937.

at the beginning of June were harshly criticized by the Nazi press,[14] showed clearly that he was in agreement with Mundelein, who had "illuminated the priests about the Germans' unilateral and deceitful propaganda."[15]

There followed a period of intense discussion on the need to strengthen ties between the Holy See and the United States. The meeting between Pacelli and Roosevelt at Hyde Park in November 1936 gave rise to rumors in some American newspapers of a possible exchange of ambassadors, in spite of disclaimers from both sides.[16] On February 16, 1937, Bishop Francis Spellman, who in November 1935 had told Pacelli that Joseph Kennedy had informed him of the president's intention to take steps in this direction, was invited to the White House. According to his personal diary, he was not able to raise the question on that particular occasion. Later, between August and September, he touched on the subject, but without any appreciable result, first with Thomas Corcoran, a White House assistant, and then with James Roosevelt, the president's son. At that time, however, the president seemed to prefer dealing with his great friend and supporter Cardinal Mundelein.[17]

On the same day as Roosevelt's "quarantine speech" (October 5, 1937), the president and Mundelein lunched together at the cardinal's home in Chicago; according to the press, they discussed the possibility of the Vatican's playing a part in an international movement for peace in Europe.[18] After the meeting, Mundelein immediately informed Amleto Cicognani that it was Roosevelt's intention to nominate a spe-

14. "Niemoeller Aide Held for Petition," *New York Times*, July 6, 1937, p. 11.
15. Eugenio Pacelli to Fritz Menshausen, rep. n. 2368/37, Vatican City, June 24, 1937, ASV, DASU, 5, pos. 166b, ff. 53–55.
16. "La Santa Sede avrà un Nunzio Apostolico a Washington," *Il Progresso Italo-Americano*, January 29, 1937; "Vatican Has New Rumors of Nuncio in Washington," *New York Times*, January 29, 1937, in ibid., pos. 178, Press Clippings, ff. 129–30.
17. See Gannon, *The Cardinal Spellman*, 154–55, and Fogarty, *The Vatican and the American Hierarchy*, 248–49.
18. Percy Wood, "Dedication Day Is a Busy One for President," *Chicago Daily Tribune*, October 6, 1937; Robert P. Post, "President Hits Out," *New York Times*, October 6, 1937, p. 1.

cial envoy to the Holy See: "not an ordinary priest or layman, but a man of ambassadorial rank."[19]

In spite of Roosevelt's intentions, however, the debate on how to begin formal relations was particularly heated and, initially at least, marked by a mutual unwillingness to compromise. Spellman and Pacelli's correspondence from the end of 1937 to early 1938, which can be reconstructed in its entirety thanks to the documents in the Vatican Secretary of State Archives, shows exactly this.

When on September 21 Spellman reported to Pacelli the content of the telephone conversation he had had with James Roosevelt, he said he had done his best to "explain everything from a juridical and historical point of view," and had pointed out "all the advantages" that it would "bring to the United States, the Holy See, and to the world in general." However, he had the impression that it would be "difficult to arrange for an eventual Nuncio to be recognized as the senior member of the diplomatic corps." The Vatican's consent to recognize the American ambassador to Italy also as the ambassador to the Holy See, continued Spellman, would facilitate an agreement and would avoid the opposition "of those in the Senate who were against a special fund to cover the cost of a new Embassy."[20] In his reply of November 26, Pacelli stressed that the position of the eventual apostolic nuncio to Washington as senior member of the Vatican's diplomatic corps could not be negotiated, and that he would prefer to keep the corps of Italy and that of the Vatican "separate," "in order to avoid confusion."[21] Following further discussions on the same subject, Spellman wrote on January 8, 1938: "Not wishing to seem too optimistic, I feel that in spite of all the serious difficulties, we should not exclude the possibility of a positive outcome." A few days later, on January 26, he stated that Roosevelt "was happy" with the arguments put forward in support of a revival of relations and

19. George Mundelein to Amleto Cicognani (confidential), Chicago, October 6, 1937, FDRPL, PPF 321.
20. Francis Spellman to Eugenio Pacelli, Newton Center, September 21, 1937, ASV, SS, AES, America, pos. 237, fasc. 65, ff. 33–34.
21. Eugenio Pacelli to Francis Spellman, rep. n. 4774/37, Vatican City, November 26, 1937, ibid., ff. 36–37.

now seemed persuaded of that fact that it would be difficult to find "a better occasion to take this step." As for the status of the U.S. representative, the president had asked "if the Holy See would prefer the nomination of a minister rather than an ambassador."[22] On February 26 Pacelli replied that, though it would be "more dignified for the United States to have a full ambassador," the Holy See would not "object if they preferred their representative to hold only the position of minister."[23]

This missive gave the impression that Pacelli wished to tone down his initial reluctance. While before it had not been negotiable, the request to institute an apostolic nunciature in Washington gradually gave way to a wish, decidedly more pragmatic, to exploit the signs of the White House having become more approachable on the matter; certainly Roosevelt opened to the possibility of abandoning the idea of making the ambassador to Rome, William Phillips, a representative to the Holy See and setting up a "special" representative in order to bypass the difficulties that Congress were sure to create. The rapprochement question was not followed by any concrete agreement, but came to the fore weeks later at the time of the events that led, on March 12, 1938, to Germany's annexation of Austria.

After the plebiscite of April 10, 1938, that ratified the *Anschluss*, Pacelli clarified the Holy See's position to the American ambassador to London, Joseph Kennedy. In a long memorandum translated into English by Enrico Galeazzi and sent on April 19 by the advisor to the embassy in London, Herschel V. Johnson, to the U.S. Department of State, the cardinal stressed that the Austrian episcopate's statements were a great surprise and had received no official or unofficial approval from the Holy See. Hence, at the end of the report, an appeal that the embassy should inform the White House of the Vatican's wish to follow up with a certain urgency the plan to renew diplomatic relations with the United States. "I think it will be very fine,"

22. Francis Spellman to Eugenio Pacelli, Newton Center, January 8 and 26, 1938, ibid., ff. 76–77, 83–84.
23. Eugenio Pacelli to Francis Spellman, Vatican City, February 26, 1938, ibid., f. 85.

Pacelli wrote to Kennedy, "if you will convey to your Friend at home [Roosevelt] these personal private views of mine," since there could not have been a better time "for trying to carry on the plan we had thought of while in America and that I know is amongst your aims." The accomplishment of the "plan" discussed at Hyde Park in November 1936 would, according to the Vatican secretary of state, have induced the rest of the international community to reflect "over the ever increasing necessity in the present troubles of keeping in touch with the Supreme Moral Powers of the world," intent on their efforts "against all political excesses from the Bolsheviks and the new pagans arising amongst the young 'Arian' generations"; and would also increase "the prestige of the American government which would appear solely directed to use all means for insuring the peace of all peoples."[24]

Pacelli received no official response from the United States, whose press had followed the polemic between Pius XI and the Austrian bishops.[25] Early in June, Amleto Cicognani drew up some notes that, on the basis of a comparison with the agreements that the Holy See had stipulated with other countries, dealt with the problem of compatibility between American constitutional principles and an eventual recognition of the Vatican. One could not, argued the delegate, speak of a concordat or a pact to regulate mutual relations because the First Amendment of the Constitution wisely stated that "Congress shall make no law respecting an establishment of religion, or prohibiting the free exercise thereof." Without violating this principle, therefore, the "renewal of diplomatic relations would have to be based simply on the fact that the Holy See, by virtue of the Lateran Treaty, occupies a position of sovereignty in the international context," and is "the perfect society that can contribute most effectively to the cause of peace between peoples and nations," and for this reason no state could ignore its "great and real importance."[26]

24. Memorandum from Cardinal Pacelli, NARA, DS, RG 59, 863.00/1744.
25. See Arnaldo Cortesi, "Vatican Rebukes Bishops of Austria for Nazi Plea," *New York Times*, April 2, 1938, p. 1.
26. Notes on Diplomatic Relations, Attached to the Report from Amleto

At this intriguing stage, Roosevelt, who had been impressed by the cold welcome given by Pius XI to Hitler on his visit to Rome in early May 1938,[27] began to give serious thought to taking a step toward the Holy See. According to what was reported at the end of April by the archbishop of Cincinnati, Thomas McNicholas, the president, convinced that the Vatican was the best place "to work out a Peace Program for the world," was ready to deal personally with the matter in the weeks that followed.[28] To do so, he decided once again to call on the collaboration of George Mundelein.

While certain American newspapers began to spread rumors about the imminent renewal of diplomatic relations,[29] Mundelein took the opportunity to speak to Francis Spellman about Roosevelt's intention to send a representative to the Holy See both on the occasion of the funeral of Cardinal Patrick Hayes of New York (September 9) and to attend the Eucharistic Congress of New Orleans (October 19), at which he participated in the role of pontifical legate.[30] Before Mundelein's departure for Rome on October 29, Roosevelt met him at the White House and instructed Ambassador Phillips to welcome him on his arrival at the port of Naples.[31]

In spite of official disclaimers, the most important American newspapers, and even the Nazi paper *Der Angriff,* reported the imminent announcement of diplomatic rapprochement with the Vatican.[32] Furthermore, in a report dated November 10, William Phillips

---

Cicognani to Eugenio Pacelli, n. 303/38, Washington, D.C., June 8, 1938, ASV, DASU, 5, pos. 178, ff. 78–92.

27. William Phillips to Franklin D. Roosevelt, Rome, May 5 and 13, 1938, FDRPL, PSF, 42.

28. Thomas J. McNicholas to Amleto Cicognani (personal), Norwood, August 30, 1938, ASV, DASU, 5, pos. 178, ff. 140–43.

29. "Si parla di una ripresa dei rapporti tra la Santa Sede e gli Stati Uniti d'America," *Il Corriere della Domenica,* Newark, September 4, 1938, ibid., Press Clippings, f. 145.

30. See Fogarty, *The Vatican and the American Hierarchy,* 253.

31. Franklin D. Roosevelt to William Phillips, Washington, D.C., October 1, 1938, FDRPL, PPF, 321; Memorandum from Franklin D. Roosevelt to Marvin McIntyre, Washington, D.C., October 11, 1938, ibid.

32. See: "Papal Nuncio to Washington Is Discussed," *Washington Post,* No-

assured the Department of State that the cardinal's mediation during the talks he had had in Rome had had positive results.³³

### ALEA IACTA EST

Pius XI died on February 10, 1939. In spite of his illness, which kept him bedridden for a long time, the final months of his life were very busy. On September 29, 1938, while the heads of state were in their second session at the Conference of Munich, the Vatican radio broadcast his emotional call for peace in response to the many appeals he had received over the previous months, appeals that he had repeatedly disregarded because he thought it would be useless and inopportune: a "heated-up soup," as he confided to Domenico Tardini.³⁴ The outcome of the conclave that followed his death was no surprise. Many European chancelleries, especially the English and the French, had never concealed their liking for Eugenio Pacelli, convinced as they were that he would provide continuity to the Vatican's antitotalitarian attitude of recent years.³⁵

Pacelli's natural inclination to compromise and, in general, his use of diplomatic means, together with his constant concern about the repercussions of a clash with the totalitarian regimes, induced him to get rid of all the signs of rigidity and impetuosity of his predecessor. Hence the decision, decidedly more in harmony with Benedict XV's approach at the outbreak of the First World War, not to take advantage of the opportunity, at that moment in time at least, to break with Nazi-Fascism, and to prefer an attempt to patch things up with both Mussolini and the German authorities. Pius XII's soft approach, with its underlying principle of caution, is the object of

---

vember 4, 1938, p. 15; "Vatican, Italy, U.S. Pat Honor to Mundelein," *Chicago Daily Tribune*, November 4, 1938, p. 10; "Have No Mission for Roosevelt, Mundelein Says," *Chicago Daily Tribune*, November 10, 1938, p. 15.

33. William Phillips to Franklin D. Roosevelt, Rome, November 10, 1938, FDRPL, PSF 42.

34. Quoted in Fattorini, *Pio XI, Hitler e Mussolini*, 198.

35. On which topic, see Owen Chadwick, *Britain and the Vatican during the Second World War* (New York: Cambridge University Press, 1986), 35–40.

many diverse interpretations which are not always objective, especially because of the continuing incompleteness of documentary sources relative to his papacy, but which, in the recent words of Philippe Chenaux, "was anything but passive resignation to the dramatic chain of events."[36]

Franklin Delano Roosevelt greeted the news of Pacelli's election with enthusiasm. From the cruiser U.S.S. *Houston* he sent a warm message of congratulations to the "transatlantic" and "pan-American" cardinal, whom he habitually called his good old friend.[37] "It is with true happiness," ran the message, "that I learned of your election as Supreme Pontiff. Recalling with pleasure our meeting on the occasion of your recent visit to the United States, I wish to take this occasion to send you a personal message of felicitation and good wishes."[38]

When Roosevelt was informed by William Phillips at the end of February that each of the thirty-eight countries represented at the Holy See would be sending a delegation to the coronation ceremony of the newly elected pope (March 12, 1939) and that Cardinal Mundelein had suggested there should be an American presence, he decided to nominate, for the first time in history, a special representative, the ambassador to London, Joseph Kennedy.[39]

Only three days after the coronation, on March 15, 1939, German troops invaded Czechoslovakia, so violating the accords signed in Munich the previous autumn. On March 18, the apostolic nuncio in Warsaw, Filippo Cortesi, announced that Hitler was preparing to invade Poland.[40] While Great Britain and France seemed determined to be

36. Philippe Chenaux, *Pio XII: Diplomatico e pastore*, 218. But see also Giovanni Miccoli, *I dilemmi e i silenzi di Pio XII* (Milan: Rizzoli, 2000); Michael Hesemann, *Pio XII: Il papa che si oppose a Hitler* (Cinisello Balsamo: Edizioni San Paolo, 2009); and Joseph Bottum and David G. Dalin, eds., *The Pius War: Responses to the Critics of Pius XII* (Lanham, Md.: Rowman and Littlefield, 2004).
37. See Harold H. Tittmann Jr., *Inside the Vatican of Pius XII: The Memoir of an American Diplomat during World War II* (New York: Doubleday, 2004), 4.
38. *New York Times*, March 3, 1939, quoted in Gannon, *The Cardinal Spellman*, 158.
39. U.S. Department of State to Franklin D. Roosevelt (confidential), cable n. 1609, February 24, 1939, FDRPL, PPF 4129.
40. Filippo Cortesi to Luigi Maglione, Warsaw, March 18, 1939, ADSS, vol. 1, 101–2.

firm and guarantee the safety of the Polish frontiers, the Holy See busied itself with calling for a diplomatic solution to the crisis. On May 3 the Vatican secretary of state ordered the nuncios to Paris, Warsaw, and Berlin, as well as the apostolic delegate in London, to sound out the governments in whose countries they were representatives on the possibility of calling an international meeting of five countries—Great Britain, France, Germany, Italy, and Poland—in an attempt to settle the situation peacefully.[41]

Ignored by all European powers with the exception of Great Britain,[42] Pius XII's plan included the involvement of the United States of America. The Department of State, in fact, informed the White House that the pope would like to consult with Roosevelt in the case of a conference, the idea of which had for the moment been set aside, being taken into consideration again.[43] The "signals" sent by Pacelli returned to the attention of the American establishment the question of reinforcing the channels of communication with the Vatican. Hull and Welles discussed rapprochement with the Vatican in the second half of July.

That the political climate had become decidedly more favorable to a step in this direction is demonstrated by a long letter sent to the Department of State by the Jewish New York congressman Emanuel Celler on July 24. The congressman's letter harshly criticized Congress's decision taken as long ago as 1867 to abruptly cut off relations with the pope's court and, noting Pius XII's efforts to force the peace, hoped for the beginning of a new phase of relaxation of tension, calling it "a clarion call to the civilized peoples of the world that religious and personal liberties are inherent in our Democracy."[44] Following up on Celler's letter, Sumner Welles acted without delay. On August 2 he wrote to Roosevelt: "I think it is unquestionable that the

41. Telegram from Secretary of State, Vatican City, May 3, 1939, ibid., 120.
42. Francis Osborne to Luigi Maglione, Vatican City, May 13 and August 17, 1939, ibid., 142, 218.
43. Sumner Welles to Franklin D. Roosevelt, Washington, D.C., May 16, 1939, FDRPL, PSF 51.
44. Emanuel Celler to Cordell Hull, Washington, D.C., July 24, 1939, ibid., PSF 51.

Vatican has many sources of information, particularly with regard to what is actually going on in Germany, Italy, and Spain, which we do not possess, and it seems that the question of whether it would be desirable for our Government to obtain access to this information was of considerable importance."[45]

Just as pragmatically, Cordell Hull pointed out to the president the advantages of an eventual diplomatic presence at the Holy See, and advised him to opt to send a personal representative whose nomination, unlike that of an ambassador, would not need the Senate's authorization.[46]

Roosevelt moved cautiously in an attempt to bring about diplomatic rapprochement that would not, dangerously on the eve of an election, reawaken the now dormant anti-Catholic and antipapist prejudice. He was successful in quickly dissipating these fears with the courage and propensity for risk taking that had always characterized him as much as his negotiation and political calculation skills. He decided to link the sending of his personal representative to the Holy See to the problem of war refugees; because of its "humanitarian" nature, such a mission would legitimize the predisposition of a direct means of communication with the Vatican.[47]

Between October and December 1939 Roosevelt's plan began to take shape. The president explained it in some detail to Francis Spellman who, a few months before, on April 24, Pius had nominated as archbishop of New York. In his account of his visit to the White House on October 24, Spellman got Cicognani to inform the secretary of state Luigi Maglione that Roosevelt had decided to set up a "special" mission and that in order to avoid the interference of Congress he would wait for the Christmas period when there would be no sessions. He warmly welcomed the president's proposal, which would mean the association of two "moral forces" for the good of

---

45. Sumner Welles to Franklin D. Roosevelt, Washington, D.C., August 2, 1939, ibid.

46. Cf. Tittmann, *Inside the Vatican*, 6.

47. Franklin D. Roosevelt to Cordell Hull, Washington, D.C., October 2, 1939, NARA, DS, RG 59, 121.866A/1b.

mankind.⁴⁸ As is seen from a letter from Spellman to Roosevelt sent the day after another meeting in Washington on December 7, the decision to make the arrangement official at Christmas time was certainly a good one.⁴⁹ Apart from the timing and the aims, there remained one more decision to take: who to entrust with the mission to the Vatican.

Roosevelt had in mind various people for the job: the ex-ambassador to Rome, Breckinridge Long, the secretary of war, Harry H. Woodring, and Myron Charles Taylor. In the end he chose Taylor. An Episcopalian belonging to an influential New York family, he had worked in the American industrial and financial sectors for the First National Bank, and then in the U.S. Steel Corporation, of which he was president from 1932 to 1938. His candidature seemed particularly appropriate for circumstances in which Roosevelt wished to emphasize the "humanitarian" nature of the diplomatic contact to be set up with the Holy See. Having thought of him as a possible successor to Joseph Kennedy at the London embassy, the president had charged him with the task of leading the American delegation at the conference called in July 1938 at Evian, in France, to discuss the problem of the massive migratory influx caused by disruptive European events, with special reference to the emigration of the Jews.⁵⁰

On December 23, 1939, in his Christmas message to Pius XII, Roosevelt officially announced his decision to send Taylor to the Vatican to "encourage a closer relationship between those in all parts of the world, in the religious field as well as that of government, who have a common objective," and so that "our common efforts for peace and the alleviation of suffering might be duly rewarded."⁵¹

As Roosevelt made clear to Taylor, this mission was not of a per-

48. Francis Spellman to Luigi Maglione, New York, October 25, 1939, ADSS, vol.1, 302–5.
49. Francis Spellman to Franklin D. Roosevelt, New York, December 8, 1939, FDRPL, PPF 4404.
50. See Di Nolfo, *Vaticano e Stati Uniti*, 14, 15–18.
51. Franklin D. Roosevelt to Pius XII, Washington, D.C., December 23, 1939, ADSS, vol. 1, 324.

manent nature.³² For the apostolic delegate Cicognani, however, who immediately informed the Vatican secretary of state, the die was cast ("*Alea iacta est*").⁵³

The enthusiasm of William Phillips and Francis Spellman, who were sure that the president's decision would bring benefits,⁵⁴ was accompanied for the first few months of 1940 by a series of demonstrations by Protestant bodies against the institution of the representation in the Vatican.⁵⁵

In this mixed climate of euphoria and opposition, Myron Taylor postponed his departure for a few weeks for health reasons, and arrived in Italy half-way through February 1940. He had impeccable style and was certainly astute, but the rank of ambassador was not made explicit in the first letter of his nomination that Roosevelt sent to him on January 30. In early February, however, Taylor applied pressure, and the head of White House protocol Stanley Woodward was authorized to modify the text as requested.⁵⁶ Apart from this, the solemn formality with which he was received by Pius XII on February 27, when he presented his credentials, and the fact that his name appears in the *Annuario Pontificio* as a member of the diplomatic corps, show that the Vatican considered Taylor to be much more than just a temporary representative of President Roosevelt.

Taylor had offered his services without remuneration and instead of taking up residence in the Vatican, went to live in the villa he

52. Franklin D. Roosevelt to Myron C. Taylor, Washington, D.C., December 23, 1939, NARA, DS, RG 59, 121.866A/2a.

53. Amleto Cicognani to Luigi Maglione, Washington, D.C., December 23, 1939, ADSS, vol. 1, 327–29.

54. William Phillips to Franklin D. Roosevelt, Rome, December 24, 1939, FDRPL, PDF 42; Francis Spellman to Franklin D. Roosevelt, New York, December 24, 1939, ibid., PSF 165.

55. Among the various demonstrations opposing the nomination of Taylor recorded in the Roosevelt Archives of Hyde Park, see "An Illegal Ambassador," *Christian Century*, March 13, 1940, ibid., OF 76b, box 3; see also Michael H. Carter, "Diplomacy's Detractors: American Protestant Reaction to FDR's Personal Representative at the Vatican," in Woolner and Kurial, eds., *FDR, the Vatican*, 179–208.

56. Franklin D. Roosevelt to Myron C. Taylor, Washington, D.C., January 30, 1940 (letter marked as "not sent, redrafted"), NARA, DS, RG 59, 121.866A/16A; Stanley Woodward to Tom Watson, Washington, D.C., February 10, 1940, ibid.

owned in the Fiesole hills, Florence. Assisted by Harold H. Tittmann, a young and capable official who worked in the Italian embassy, he paid periodic visits to the Vatican for various lengths of time and alternated his presence in Rome with trips to London, Madrid, Lisbon, and, after the Liberation of August 1944, Paris. Given the confidential nature of his missions and of the talks he had with the pope and European statesmen, not to mention the great heterogeneity of the topics dealt with, many of the documentary sources concerning the activities of this American diplomat can no longer be traced, and above all it is impossible to reconstruct the conversations he had with Roosevelt. However, the sources we do have show that, from the very beginning, the issue of assistance to refugees soon took second place and the diplomatic work of Taylor focused on the problem of the war in Europe, especially whenever this meant preventing Italy's entry into the conflict.[57]

Mussolini's decision to ignore the appeal of Roosevelt and Pius XII (April 24, 1940),[58] and to enter the war on the side of the Reich might seem to have reduced the usefulness of the American mission to the Holy See. But rather than interrupt contact with the Vatican, in agreement with the Department of State, Roosevelt himself considered that an American presence there was more important than ever, and he decided instead to replace Taylor temporarily with Tittmann, who had collaborated with him in previous months. He was not given the rank of chargé d'affaires until the end of December 1941, immediately after Italy's and Germany's declaration of war against the United States. In that period of time, he had occasion to collaborate in the preparations for Myron Taylor's later missions that Pius XII, in a veiled way, had wished and hoped for as early as December 1940.[59]

---

57. See George Q. Flynn, "Franklin Roosevelt and the Vatican: The Myron Taylor Appointment," *Catholic Historical Review* 58 (1972): 171–94; John S. Conway, "Myron C. Taylor's Mission to the Vatican, 1940–1950," *Church History* 44 (1975): 85–99; and George J. Gill, "The Myron Taylor Mission, the Holy See and the Parallel Endeavor for Peace, 1939–1945," *Records of the American Catholic Historical Society of Philadelphia* 98 (1987): 29–49.

58. Pius XII to Benito Mussolini, Vatican City, April 24, 1940, ADSS, vol. 1, 395.

59. Pius XII to Franklin D. Roosevelt, Vatican City, December 20, 1940, ibid., vol. 4, 300–301.

Though surrounded by Nazi-Fascist forces, the Vatican was extraordinarily important. That seemingly tiny enclave, a singular earthly expression of incomparable religious and moral strength, gave a bird's-eye view, from a privileged position, of the development of the events of the war, and above all, to operate in close contact with Eugenio Pacelli, the silent diplomatic pope who opposed the war. Roosevelt, champion of the struggle against Nazi-Fascism, was aware of all this, and he preferred a pragmatic approach to relations with the Vatican to the hard-boiled antipapism of past decades. From a formal point of view, apparently, the missions of Myron C. Taylor and the nomination of Harold H. Tittmann did not mean the setting up of diplomatic relations, neither did they cancel out all the disagreements and ideological prejudices that had scarred, and would for a long time continue to scar, the history of relations between the White House and the Holy See. They were, however, after the suspension of relations in 1867, the first signs of a thaw that would not become a reality until 1984 and which, just as during the years of World War II, would be useful in showing a united front against totalitarianism.

## AFTERWORD

Gerald P. Fogarty's foreword describes the intricate fabric of this book, focusing on the most significant aspects of Luca Castagna's research. Since I have followed its progress and am in some ways responsible for the choice of subject, I should like to underline the importance of the sources used, for they have made it possible, with a many-sided approach, to give an interpretation of the events that is in some ways innovative. The research's point of reference is certain aspects of U.S. history, and on this basis the book deals with the ways in which Vatican diplomacy operated in a context that was by no means easy: that of North America within the more general dynamic workings of international relations during a dramatic period of world history.

The author has integrated the primary sources of various provenance with an appropriate selection of Vatican documentation concerning the papacy of Pius XI and has compared this with the abundant historical studies of recent years. Among much else, he deals with the Vatican's attitude to Nazi-Fascist escalation and describes events that are familiar, so presenting us with a complete and well-articulated account. This is made possible by paying constant attention both to the internal issues and to more strictly diplomatic aspects of relations between countries. Recognition of the overall pattern of events has enabled Castagna to describe the processes that have determined the slow but evident transformation in relations between the United States of America and the Holy See, which in his opinion were due to changes brought about by the choices of positions and styles of government of the many protagonists: popes, presidents, secretaries of state, diplomatic representatives, and apostolic delegates in a mix of individual psychologies, cultural backgrounds, interests, and traditions slowly blended by the need to reach an agreement as the horizons were darkened by the crisis the European powers were experiencing, and the emergence of new ideologies and new strategic, political, and diplomatic options. Against this background, the most significant moments of change are described in the light of main international events such as the Conference of Versailles, postwar reconstruction, the 1929 crisis, the Spanish Civil War, the *Anschluss*, the Conference of Munich, and finally the outbreak of the Second World War.

Though he was not made pope until 1939, Eugenio Pacelli had reached the stage when he was able to lead Vatican policy as early as 1936–37 because of the ever-worsening condition of Pius XI's health. The convergence of the positions of the president of the United States and the Vatican secretary of state reached its height in their mutual understanding of the need for diplomatic rapprochement in the face of the deepening international crisis. The decision was made necessary by the approaching snares and threats, but was pursued with tact, circumspection, and caution not only because of Hitler's predictable and feared reactions but also because of the unrelenting anti-Catholic prejudice rooted in the United States.

This is the general picture that enables us to appreciate the wealth of references, analyses, and interpretations that Castagna has formulated with regard to personages that in some cases were not very familiar or who had been perceived differently. He does well to dwell on Amleto Giovanni Cicognani and Pietro Fumasoni Biondi, the apostolic delegates to Washington, who were expected to carry out the directions formulated in Rome, and on George Mundelein, the cardinal archbishop of Chicago, who was aware of public opinion and the views of American diplomatic and political circles.

A careful reading of the book confirms an aspect of the history of the United States that is repeatedly encountered: idealism as a force capable of orienting decisions in foreign affairs. In spite of the urgency dictated by the dangerous chain of events in Europe and the knowledge that the Vatican was a privileged observation point, uniquely strategic of its kind, the decision to send Myron C. Taylor as a personal representative to the Vatican was justified by Roosevelt by the mutual attempt to achieve peace against the forces of evil. The American president's statement on the matter finds its echo in Pacelli's words a few months earlier when, referring to the United States and the Holy See, he identified them as the two greatest "moral forces" of the world.

Luca Castagna's work throws light on a subject certainly not of minor importance in international relations in one of the most turbulent periods of the world's history. Apart from this undoubted merit, there is also the fact of the possible developments in research on the issues it raises. First and foremost, with regard to the central theme, the work serves as a point of reference for treatment of the events and relations between the United States and the Holy See in successive decades, especially because of the wealth of documentation which, it is assumed, will become available to scholars in the Vatican and in the United States. More in general, the book's subjects help us to elaborate on issues raised by the existing abundant historical studies on U.S. foreign policy, the political and cultural history of the North American Catholic Church, and the history of the pontificates of the first half of the twentieth century. Last but not least, Luca Castagna's work points to an interesting new approach to studies of the foreign policy of the Holy See, a subject that deserves to be brought to the attention of historians, particularly since it involves events that have had global impact.

Luigi Rossi
University of Salerno

# BIBLIOGRAPHY AND SOURCES

### ARCHIVES

Archivio Storico-Diplomatico del Ministero degli Affari Esteri, Rome
   Archivio Politico Ordinario e di Gabinetto, 1915–18
Affari Politici verso gli Stati Uniti d'America, 1915–30
   Affari Politici verso gli Stati Uniti d'America, 1931–45
   Affari Politici verso la Santa Sede, 1931–45

Archivio Segreto Vaticano, Vatican City
   Guerra, 1914–18
   Congregazione per i Vescovi
   Delegazione Apostolica negli Stati Uniti d'America
   Segreteria di Stato

Archive of the Catholic University of America, Washington, D.C.
   National Catholic Welfare Conference

U.S. National Archives and Records Administration, College Park, Md.
   Department of State, Record Group 59

Franklin Delano Roosevelt Presidential Library, Hyde Park, N.Y.
   President's Personal File
   President's Secretary's File
   Official File.

### PRINTED SOURCES

Blet, Pierre, Angelo Martini, Robert Graham, and Burkhart Schneider, eds. *Actes et documents du Saint Siège relatifs a La Seconde Guerre Mondiale.* Vol. 1. Vatican City: Libreria Editrice Vaticana, 1970.

Ellis, John T. *Documents of American Catholic History.* Vol. 2. Chicago: Regnery Press, 1966.

Huber, Raphael M., ed., *Our Bishops Speak: National Pastorals and Annual Statements of the Hierarchy of the United States, 1919–1951.* Milwaukee, Wis.: Bruce Publications, 1952.

Ickes, Harold. *The Secret Diary of Harold L. Ickes.* Vol. 3. New York: Simon and Schuster, 1954.

*Papers Relating to the Foreign Relations of the United States: 1867, Diplomatic Correspondence.* Washington, D.C.: U.S. Government Printing Office, 1868;

———: *The Lansing Papers, 1914–1920.* 2 vols. Washington, D.C.: U.S. Government Printing Office, 1939.

———: *The World War, 1914–1920.* Supplement 2, vol. 1. Washington, D.C.: U.S. Government Printing Office, 1933.

———: *The Paris Peace Conference.* Vol. 1. Washington, D.C.: U.S. Government Printing Office, 1942.

———: *1922.* Vol. 1. Washington, D.C.: U.S. Government Printing Office, 1938.

Rosenman, Samuel, ed., *The Public Papers and Addresses of Franklin D. Roosevelt.* Vol. 1. New York: Random House, 1938.

Stock, Francis L. *Consular Relations between the United States and the Papal States: Instructions and Dispatches.* Vol. 2. Washington, D.C.: American Catholic Historical Association, 1945.

———. *United States Ministers to the Papal States: Instructions and Dispatches.* Washington, D.C.: The Catholic University of America Press, 1933.

U.S. Department of State. *Principal Officers of the Department of State and United States Chiefs of Mission, 1778–1986.* Washington, D.C.: U.S. Government Printing Office, 1986.

## PERIODICALS CONSULTED

*America,* New York
*Americas,* Drexel University, Philadelphia
*Annuario di Politica internazionale,* Milan
*Atlantic Monthly,* Washington, D.C.
*Catholic Historical Review,* Washington, D.C.
*Catholic Messenger,* Davenport, Iowa
*Catholic Mind,* New York
*Catholic News,* Washington, D.C.
*Catholic Register,* Denver, Colo.
*Catholic World,* Mahwah, N.J.

# BIBLIOGRAPHY AND SOURCES

*Chicago Daily Tribune,* Chicago
*Christian Century,* Chicago
*Christian Observer,* Lousville, Ky.
*Church History,* Baylor University, Waco, Tex.
*Commonweal,* New York
*Crusade,* Brooklyn, N.Y.
*Evening Star,* Boston
*Extension,* Chicago
*Herald Tribune,* New York
*Il Corriere d'Italia,* Rome
*Il Corriere della Domenica,* Newark, N.J.
*Il Crociato,* Brooklyn, N.Y.
*Il Progresso Italo-Americano,* New York
*Journal of Church and State,* Baylor University, Waco, Tex.
*Jurist,* Washington, D.C.
*La Civiltà Cattolica,* Rome
*La Corrispondenza,* Vatican City
*La Voce del popolo,* Detroit
*L'Avvenire d'Italia,* Bologna
*Literary Digest,* New York and London
*L'Osservatore Romano,* Vatican City
*Menace,* Aurora, Mo.
*Monitor,* San Francisco
*Morning Post,* London
*Nation,* New York
*NCWC Bulletin,* Washington, D.C.
*New World,* Chicago
*New York Evening Journal,* New York
*New York Times,* New York
*New York Tribune,* New York
*Nuova Antologia,* Florence
*Passato e Presente,* Milan
*Pilot,* Boston
*Rassegna storica del Risorgimento,* Rome
*Revista española de derecho canónico,* Salamanca
*Theological Studies,* Marquette University, Milwaukee, Wis.
*Washington Herald,* Washington. D.C.
*Washington Post,* Washington, D.C.

## BOOKS

Adams, Charles F. *The Works of John Adams, Second President of the United States.* Vol. 7. Charleston, S.C.: Bibliolife, 2008.

Adamthwaite, Anthony P. *The Making of the Second World War.* New York: Routledge, 1989.

Ahern, Patrick H. *The Catholic University of America, 1887–1896: The Rectorship of John J. Keane.* Washington, D.C.: The Catholic University of America Press, 1949.

Alder, Selig. *The Uncertain Giant, 1921–1941: American Foreign Policy between the Wars.* New York: Collier Books, 1965.

Ambrosius, Lloyd. *Wilsonianism: Woodrow Wilson and His Legacy in American Foreign Relations.* New York: Macmillan, 2002.

Angelini, Giovanna, Arturo Colombo, and V. Paolo Gastaldi, eds., *La galassia repubblicana: Voci di minoranza nel pensiero politico italiano.* Milan: Franco Angeli, 1998.

Bagby, Wesley M. *The Road to Normalcy: The Presidential Campaign and Election of 1920.* Baltimore: Johns Hopkins University Press, 1962.

Barry, Colman J. *The Catholic Church and German-Americans.* Milwaukee, Wis.: Bruce Publishing Company, 1953.

Bennett, David H. *The Party of Fear: From Nativist Movements to the New Right in America.* Chapel Hill: University of North Carolina Press, 1988.

Billington, Ray A. *The Protestant Crusade, 1800–1860: A Study of the Origins of American Nativism.* Chicago: Quadrangle Books, 1964.

Bottum, Joseph, and David G. Dalin, eds., *The Pius War: Responses to the Critics of Pius XII.* Lanham, Md.: Rowman and Littlefield, 2004.

Broderick, Francis L. *Right Reverend New Dealer John A. Ryan: The Biography of a Priest Professor and Social Reformer Extraordinary.* New York: Macmillan, 1963.

Browder, Robert. *The Origins of Soviet-American Diplomacy.* Princeton, N.J.: Princeton University Press, 1953.

Brownlee, William C. *Letters in the Roman Catholic Controversy.* New York: Published by the Author, 1834.

———. *Popery, An Enemy to Civil and Religious Liberty; and Dangerous to Our Republic.* New York: John S. Gaylor, 1836.

Calhoun, Frederick S. *Uses of Force and Wilsonian Foreign Policy.* Kent, Ohio: Kent State University Press, 1993.

Ceci, Lucia. *Il papa non deve parlare: Chiesa, fascismo e guerra d'Etiopia.* Rome-Bari: Laterza, 2010.

Chadwick, Owen. *Britain and the Vatican during the Second World War.* New York: Cambridge University Press, 1986.

Chenaux, Philippe. *Pio XII: Diplomatico e pastore.* Cinisello Balsamo: Edizioni San Paolo, 2004.

Chiron, Yves. *Pio XI: Il papa dei Patti Lateranensi e dell'opposizione ai totalitarismi.* Cinisello Balsamo: Edizioni San Paolo, 2006.

Clements, Kendrick A. *The Presidency of Woodrow Wilson.* Lawrence: University of Kansas Press, 1992.

Confalonieri, Carlo. *Pio XI da vicino.* Turin: Editrice SAIE, 1957.

Confessore, Ornella. *L'americanismo cattolico in Italia.* Rome: Edizioni Studium, 1984.

Connelly, James F. *The Visit of Archbishop Gaetano Bedin to the United States, June 1853–February 1854.* Rome: Pontificia Università Gregoriana Editrice, 1960.

Coogan, John W. *The End of Neutrality: The United States, Britain and Maritime Rights, 1899–1915.* Ithaca, N.Y.: Cornell University Press, 1981.

Cooney, John. *The American Pope: The Life and Times of Francis Cardinal Spellman.* New York: Times Books, 1984.

Cornwell, John. *Hitler's Pope: The Secret History of Pius XII.* 2nd ed. New York: Penguin Books, 2008.

Costigliola, Frank. *Awkward Dominion: American Political, Economic and Cultural Relations with Europe, 1919–1933.* Ithaca, N.Y.: Cornell University Press, 1984.

D'Agostino, Peter. *Rome in America: Transnational Catholic Ideology from the Risorgimento to Fascism.* Chapel Hill: University of North Carolina Press, 2004.

DeConde, Alexander. *Ethnicity, Race and American Foreign Policy: A History.* Boston: Northeastern University Press, 1992.

Del Pero, Mario. *Libertà e impero: Gli Stati Uniti e il mondo, 1776–2006.* Rome-Bari: Laterza, 2008.

Devlin, Patrick. *Too Proud to Fight: Woodrow Wilson's Neutrality.* New York: Oxford University Press, 1975.

Di Nolfo, Ennio. *Vaticano e Stati Uniti, 1939–1952: Dalle carte di Myron C. Taylor.* Milan: Franco Angeli, 1978.

———. *Dagli imperi miliari agli imperi tecnologici: La politica internazionale dal XX secolo a oggi.* 3rd ed. Rome-Bari: Laterza, 2008.

Diggins, John P. *Mussolini and Fascism: The View from America.* Princeton, N.J.: Princeton University Press, 1972.

Doyle, Robert C. *The Enemy in Our Hands: America's Treatment of Prisoners of War from the Revolution to the War on Terror.* Lexington: University of Kentucky Press, 2010.

Dumenil, Lynn. *The Modern Temper: American Culture and Society in the 1920s.* New York: Hill and Wang, 1995.

Ellis, John T. *The Life of James Cardinal Gibbons.* Vol. 2. Milwaukee, Wis.: Bruce Publishing Company, 1952.

———. *American Catholicism.* Chicago: Chicago University Press, 1957.

Ernst, Eldon G. *Moment of Truth for Protestant America: Interchurch Campaigns Following World War One.* Missoula, Mont.: American Academy of Religion, 1972.

Fattorini, Emma. *Germania e Santa Sede: Le nunziature di Pacelli tra la Grande Guerra e la Repubblica di Weimar.* Bologna: il Mulino, 1992.

———. *Pio XI, Hitler e Mussolini: La solitudine di un papa.* Turin: Einaudi, 2007.

Fink, Carole. *The Genoa Conference: European Diplomacy, 1921–1922.* 2nd ed. Syracuse, N.Y.: Syracuse University Press, 1993.

Flynn, George Q. *American Catholics and the Roosevelt Presidency, 1932–1936.* Lexington: University of Kentucky Press, 1968.

———. *Roosevelt and Romanism: Catholics and American Diplomacy, 1937–1945.* Westport, Conn.: Greenwood Press, 1976.

Fogarty, Gerald P. *The Vatican and the American Hierarchy from 1870 to 1965.* Stuttgart: Hiersemann, 1982.

Ford, Nancy G. *Americans All! Foreign-Born Soldiers in World War I.* College Station: Texas A and M University Press, 2001.

Franco, Massimo. *Imperi Paralleli: Vaticano e Stati Uniti: Due secoli di alleanza e conflitto 1788–2005.* Milan: Mondadori, 2005.

Freidel, Frank B. *Franklin D. Rosevelt: The Triumph.* Vol. 3. Boston: Little, Brown, 1952.

Friedman, Max P. *Nazis and Good Neighbors: The United States Campaign against the Germans of Latin America in World War II.* New York: Cambridge University Press, 2003.

Furniss, Norman F. *The Fundamentalist Controversy, 1918–1931.* New Haven, Conn.: Yale University Press, 1954.

Gabaccia, Donna R. *Immigration and American Diversity: A Social and Cultural History.* Malden, Mass.: Blackwell, 2002.

Gaffey, James P. *Francis Clement Kelley and the American Catholic Dream.* Vol. 1. Bensenville, Ill.: Heritage Foundation, 1980.

Gannon, Robert I. *The Cardinal Spellman Story.* Garden City, N.Y.: Doubleday, 1962.

Garzia, Italo. *La questione romana durante la prima guerra mondiale.* Naples: ESI, 1981.

Gilbert, James B. *Work without Salvation: America's Intellectual and Industrial Alienation, 1880–1910.* Baltimore: Johns Hopkins University Press, 1977.

Gleason, Philip. *The Conservative Reformers: German-American Catholics and the Social Order.* Notre Dame, Ind.: University of Notre Dame Press, 1968.

Glover, Jonathan. *Humanity: A Moral History of the Twentieth Century.* New Haven, Conn.: Yale University Press, 1999.

Goldberg, David J. *Discontented America: The United States in the 1920s.* Baltimore: Johns Hopkins University Press, 1999.

Gregory, Ross. *The Origins of American Intervention in the First World War.* New York: Norton, 1971.

Hennesey, James. *American Catholics: A History of the Roman Catholic Community in the United States.* New York: Oxford University Press, 1981.

Hesemann, Michael. *Pio XII: Il papa che si oppose a Hitler.* Cinisello Balsamo: Edizioni San Paolo, 2009.

Hicks, John H. *Republican Ascendancy, 1921–1933.* New York: Read Books, 2008.

Higham, John. *Strangers in the Land: Patterns on American Nativism, 1860–1925.* 6th ed. New Brunswick, N.J.: Rutgers University Press, 2004.

Kane, Paula M. *Separatism and Subculture: Boston Catholicism, 1900–1920.* Chapel Hill: University of North Carolina Press, 1994.

Kantowicz, Edward R. *Corporation Sole: Cardinal Mundelein and Chicago Catholicism.* Notre Dame, Ind.: University of Notre Dame Press, 1983.

Kari, Camilla J. *Public Witness: The Pastoral Letters of the American Catholic Bishops.* Collegeville, Minn.: Liturgical Press, 2004.

Kauffman, Christopher. *Faith and Fraternalism: The History of the Knights of Columbus, 1882–1982.* New York: Harper and Row, 1982.

Kelley, Francis C. *The Bishop Jots It Down.* New York: Harper, 1939.

Knock, Thomas. *To End All Wars: Woodrow Wilson and the Quest for a New World Order.* New York: Oxford University Press, 1991.

LaCerra, Charles. *Franklin Delano Roosevelt and Tammany Hall of New York.* Lanham, Md.: University Press of America, 1997.

Lally, Francis J. *The Catholic Church in a Changing America.* Boston: Little, Brown and Co., 1962.

Langley, Lester D. *America and the Americas: The United States in the Western Hemisphere.* 2nd ed. Athens: University of Georgia Press, 2010.

Leffler, Melvin P. *The Elusive Quest: America's Pursuit of European Stability and French Security, 1919–1933.* Chapel Hill: University of North Carolina Press, 1977.

LeMay, Michael C. *From Open Door to Dutch Door: An Analysis of U.S. Immigration Policy since 1820.* Westport, Conn.: Greenwood Press, 1987.

Letterio, Mauro, ed., *Benedetto XV: Profeta di pace in un mondo in crisi.* Bologna: Minerva, 2008.

Leuchtenburg, William E. *Franklin D. Roosevelt and the New Deal, 1932–1940.* New York: Harper, 2009.

Lichtman, Allan J. *Prejudice and the Old Politics: The Presidential Elections of 1928.* Chapel Hill: University of North Carolina Press, 1979.

Link, Arthur S. *Wilson: The Struggle for Neutrality, 1914–1915.* Princeton, N.J.: Princeton University Press, 1960.

Lockwood, Robert P., ed. *Anti-Catholicism in American Culture.* Huntington, Ind.: Our Sunday Visitor, 2000.

Lomask, Milton. *John Carroll, Bishop and Patriot.* 4th ed. New York: Vision Books, 1962.

Lubell, Samuel. *The Future of American Politics.* 3rd ed. New York: Harper and Row, 1965.

McAvoy, Thomas T. *A History of the Catholic Church in the United States.* Notre Dame, Ind.: University of Notre Dame Press, 1969.

———. *The Great Crisis in American Catholic History: 1895–1900.* Chicago: Regnery, 1957.

McNamara, Francis. *The American College in Rome, 1855–1955.* Rochester, N.Y.: Christopher Press, 1956.

McNamara, Patrick H. *A Catholic Cold War: Edmund A. Walsh, S.J., and the Politics of American Anticommunism.* New York: Fordham University Press, 2005.

McShane, Joseph. *"Sufficiently Radical": Catholicism, Progressivism, and the Bishops' Program of 1919.* Washington, D.C.: The Catholic University of America Press, 1986.

McVeigh, Rory. *The Rise of the Ku Klux Klan: Right-Wing Movement and National Politics.* Minneapolis: University of Minnesota Press, 2009.

Miccoli, Giovanni. *I dilemmi e i silenzi di Pio XII.* Milan: Rizzoli, 2000.

Miller, Robert M. *Harry Emerson Fosdick: Preacher, Pastor, Prophet.* New York: Oxford University Press, 1985.

Morse, Samuel F. B. *Foreign Conspiracy against the Liberties of the United States.* New York: Leavitt, 1835.

Moynihan, James. *The Life of Archbishop John Ireland.* New York: Harper and Brothers, 1953.

Nicholson, Jim. *USA e Santa Sede: La lunga strada.* 2nd ed. Rome: Trenta Giorni Edizioni, 2004.

Ninkovich, Frank. *The Wilsonian Century: U.S. Foreign Policy since 1900.* Chicago: University of Chicago Press, 1999.

Nordstrom, Justin. *Danger on the Doorstep: Anti-Catholicism and American Print Culture in the Progressive Era.* Notre Dame, Ind.: University of Notre Dame Press, 2006.

O'Brien, David J. *American Catholics and Social Reform: The New Deal Years.* New York: Oxford University Press, 1968.

———. *Isaac Hecker: An American Catholic.* Mahwah, N.J.: Paulist Press, 1992.

O'Connell, Marvin R. *John Ireland and the American Catholic Church.* St. Paul: Minnesota Historical Society Press, 1988.

Orlando, Vittorio Emanuele. *Miei rapporti di governo con la Santa Sede.* Milan: Garzanti, 1944.

Pipes, Richard. *Russia under the Bolshevik Regime, 1919–1924.* New York: Alfred Knopf, 1993.

Plotke, David. *Building a Democratic Political Order: Reshaping American Liberalism in the 1930s and 1940s.* New York: Cambridge University Press, 1990.

Pollard, John F. *The Unknown Pope: Benedict XV and the Pursuit of Peace.* New York: Chapman, 1999.

Puricelli, Carlo. *Un papa brianzolo: Le radici culturali di Achille Ratti, Pio XI.* Milan: Ned Editrice, 1991.

Quirk, Robert E. *The Mexican Revolution and the Catholic Church, 1910–1929.* Bloomington: Indiana University Press, 1973.

Reeds, Rebecca. *Six Months in a Convent.* Boston: Russell, 1835.

Reilly, Daniel F. *The School Controversy, 1891–1893.* Washington, D.C.: Catholic University of America Press, 1944.

Renzi, Walter A. *In the Shadow of the Sword: Italy's Neutrality and Entrance into the Great War, 1914–1915.* New York: Peter Lang, 1987.

Rice, Elizabeth A. *The Diplomatic Relations between the United States and Mexico, as Affected by the Struggle for Religious Liberty in Mexico, 1925–1929.* Washington, D.C.: The Catholic University of America Press, 1959.

Rossi, Luigi. *L'indipendenza negata: Il Manifest Destiny di Cuba nel 1898.* Salerno: Edizioni del Paguro, 2000.

Salvatorelli, Luigi. *La politica della Santa Sede dopo la Guerra.* Milan: Istituto per gli Studi di Politica Internazionale, 1937.

Sanders, J. William. *Education of the Urban Minority: Catholics in Chicago, 1833–1965.* New York: Oxford University Press, 1977.

Sanfilippo, Matteo. *L'affermazione del cattolicesimo nel Nord America: Elite, emigranti e Chiesa cattolica negli Stati Uniti e nel Canada, 1750-1920.* Viterbo: Sette Città, 2003.

Schmitz, David F. *The United States and Fascist Italy, 1922-1940.* Chapel Hill: North Carolina University Press, 1988.

Schulzinger, Robert D. *U.S. Diplomacy since 1900.* 6th ed. New York: Oxford University Press, 2007.

Scottà, Antonio, ed., *Benedetto XV, La Chiesa, La Grande Guerra, la pace (1914-1922).* Rome: Edizioni di Storia e Letteratura, 2009.

Scroop, Daniel. *Mr. Democrat: Jim Farley, the New Deal, and the Making of Modern American Politics.* Ann Arbor: University of Michigan Press, 2006.

Seton-Watson, Christopher. *Italy from Liberalism to Fascism, 1870-1925.* London: Methuen, 1967.

Sheerin, John B. *Never Look Back: The Career and Concerns of John J. Burke.* New York: Paulist Press, 1975.

Siegel, Katherine A. *Loans and Legitimacy: The Evolution of Soviet-American Relations, 1919-1933.* Lexington: University of Kentucky Press, 1996.

Slawson, Douglas J. *The Foundation and First Decade of the National Catholic Welfare Council.* Washington, D.C.: The Catholic University of America Press, 1992.

———. *Ambition and Arrogance: Cardinal William O'Connell of Boston and the American Catholic Church.* San Diego, Calif.: Cobalt Press, 2007.

Smith, Tony. *Foreign Attachments: The Power of Ethnic Groups in the Making of American Foreign Policy.* Cambridge, Mass.: Harvard University Press, 2000.

Spadolini, Giovanni, ed. *Il Cardinale Gasparri e la questions romana: Con brani delle Memorie inedite.* Florence: Le Monnier, 1972.

Sterba, Chrisopher M. *Good Americans: Italian and Jewish Immigrants during the First World War.* New York: Oxford University Press, 2003.

Teitelbaum, Louis M. *Woodrow Wilson and the Mexican Revolution, 1913-1916.* New York: Exposition Press, 1967.

Tittmann, Harold Jr. *Inside the Vatican of Pius XII: The Memoir of an American Diplomat during World War II.* New York: Doubleday, 2004.

Traina, Richard P. *American Diplomacy and the Spanish Civil War.* Bloomington: Indiana University Press, 1968.

Trommler, Frank, and Elliott Shore. *German-American Encounter: Conflict and Cooperation between Two Cultures.* New York: Berghahn Books, 2001.

Wade, W. Craig. *The Fiery Cross: The Ku Klux Klan in America*. New York: Oxford University Press, 1987.

Wallace, Les. *The Rhetoric of Anti-Catholicism: The American Protective Association, 1887–1911*. New York: Garland Press, 1990.

Wallace, Lillian P. *Leo XIII and the Rise of Socialism*. Durham, N.C.: Duke University Press, 1966.

Walsh, James J. *Our American Cardinals: Life Stories of the Seven American Cardinals McCloskey, Gibbons, Farley, O'Connell, Dougherty, Mundelein, Hayes*. New York: Books for Libraries Press, 1969.

Wayman, Dorothy G. *Cardinal O'Connell of Boston: A Biography of William Henry O'Connell, 1859–1944*. New York: Farrar, Straus, and Young, 1955.

Wilson, Woodrow. *A History of the American People*. Vol. 5. Charleston, S.C.: Bibliolife Reprinting, 2009.

Wister, Robert J. *The Establishment of the Apostolic Delegation in the United States of America: The Satolli Mission*. Rome: Università Gregoriana Editrice, 1980.

Zivojinovic, Dragan R. *The United States and the Vatican Policies, 1914–1918*. Boulder: Colorado Associated University Press, 1978.

### ARTICLES

Bruckberger, Raymond L. "The American Catholics as a Minority." In *Roman Catholicism and the American Way of Life*, ed. Thomas T. McAvoy, 40–48. Notre Dame, Ind.: University of Notre Dame Press, 1960.

Bruti Liberati, Luigi. "Santa Sede e Stati Uniti negli anni della grande guerra." In *Benedetto XV e la pace, 1918*, ed. Giorgio Rumi, 129–50. Brescia: Morcelliana, 1990.

Carter, Michael H. "Diplomacy's Detractors: American Protestant Reaction to FDR's Personal Representative at the Vatican." In *FDR, The Vatican, and the Roman Catholic Church in America, 1933–1945*, ed. David B. Woolner, and Richard G. Kurial, 179–208. New York: Palgrave Macmillan, 2003.

Castagna, Luca. "*La Delegazione Apostolica a Washington da Fumasoni Biondi a Cicognani, 1926–38*." In *PhD. Rendiconti del Dottorato di Ricerca in Teoria e Storia delle Istituzioni*, ed. Gianfranco Macri and Antonio Scocozza, 155–74. Naples: La Città del Sole, 2010.

"Il 'modello' statunitense nel dibattito tra i democratici meridionali: Il caso de 'Il Popolo d'Italia,' 1864–65." *Nuova Antologia* 2262 (2012): 306–23.

———. "I cattolici statunitensi e il riformismo rooseveltiano: Il New Deal come occasione di riscatto." In *Studi di storia in onore di Gabriele De Rosa,* ed. Luigi Rossi, 589–604. Salerno: Plectica, 2012.

Casula, Carlo Felice. "Le segreterie di stato tra le due guerre." In *Il papato e l'Europa,* ed. by Gabriele De Rosa and Giorgio Cracco, 417–28. Soveria Mannelli: Rubbettino, 2001.

Coco, Giovanni. "Eugenio Pacelli: Cardinale Segretario di Stato, 1929–1930." In *I 'fogli di udienza' del Cardinale Eugenio Pacelli Segretario di Stato,* ed. Sergio Pagano and Michael Chappin, 39–144. Vatican City: Edizioni dell'Archivio Segreto Vaticano, 2010.

Cuddy, Edward. "Pro-Germanism and American Catholicism, 1914–1917." *Catholic Historical Review* 54, no. 3 (October 1968): 427–54.

Dalla Torre, Giuseppe. "L'appello di pace del papa e la risposta di Wilson." *Nuova Antologia,* September 1917, pp. 189–96.

Durand, Jean-Dominique. "Lo stile di governo di Pio XI." In *La sollecitudine ecclesiale di Pio XI: Alla luce delle nuove fonti archivistiche,* ed. Cosimo Semeraro, 44–60. Vatican City: Libreria Editrice Vaticana, 2010.

Ellis, John T. "James Gibbons of Baltimore." In *Patterns of Episcopal Leadership,* ed. Gerald P. Fogarty, 120–37. New York: Macmillan, 1989.

Esslinger, Dean R. "American German and Irish Attitudes toward Neutrality, 1914–1917: A Study of Catholic Minorities." *Catholic Historical Review* 53 (July 1967): 194–216.

Feliciani, Giorgio. "Tra diplomazia e pastoralità: Nunzi pontifici ed episcopato locale negli anni di Pio XI." In *La sollecitudine ecclesiale di Pio XI: Alla luce delle nuove fonti archivistiche,* ed. Cosimo Semeraro, 61–77. Vatican City: Libreria Editrice Vaticana, 2010.

Fiorentino, Daniele. "Il governo degli Stati Uniti e la Repubblica romana del 1849." In *Gli Americani e la Repubblica romana del 1849,* ed. Sara Antonelli and Giuseppe Monsagrati, 89–130. Rome: Gangemi, 2000.

Fogarty, Gerald P. "American Conciliar Legislation, Hierarchical Structure and Priest-Bishop Tension." *The Jurist* 32 (1972): 400–409.

———. "The Bishops versus Religious Orders: The Suppressed Decrees of the Third Plenary Council of Baltimore." *The Jurist* 33 (1973): 384–98.

———. "Independence: The Anomaly of the American Church." *America* 130 (June 1, 1974): 430–32.

———. "Pius XI and the Episcopate in the United States." In *Achille Ratti, Pape Pie XI,* 549–64. Rome: École francaise de Rome, 1996.

———. "La Chiesa negli Stati Uniti nella Grande Guerra e a Versailles." In *La Conferenza di pace di Parigi fra ieri e domani (1919–1920),* ed. Antonio Scottà, 211–27. Soveria Mannelli: Rubbettino, 2003.

———. "Roosevelt and the American Catholic Hierarchy." In *FDR, The Vatican, and the Roman Catholic Church in America, 1933–1945*, ed. David B. Woolner and Richard G. Kurial, 11–43. New York: Palgrave Macmillan, 2003.

Gaffey, James P. "The Changing of the Guard: The Rise of Cardinal O'Connell of Boston." *Catholic Historical Review* 59 (1973): 225–40.

Gannon, Michael V. "Before and after Modernism: The Intellectual Isolation of the American Priest." In *The Catholic Priest in the United States: Historical Investigations,* ed. John T. Ellis, 293–383. Collegeville, Minn.: St John's University Press, 1971.

Gleason, Philip. "American Catholics and Liberalism, 1789–1960." In *Catholicism and Liberalism: Contributions to American Public Philosophy,* ed. Bruce Douglass and David Hollenbach, 45–75. New York: Cambridge University Press, 1994.

Gribble, Richard. "Roman Catholicism and U.S. Foreign Policy, 1919–1935: A Clash of Policies." *Journal of Church and State* 50, no. 1 (2008): 73–99.

Guinsburg, Thomas. "The Triumph of Isolationism." In *American Foreign Relations Reconsidered, 1890–1993,* ed. Gordon Martel, 90–105. London: Routledge, 1994.

Hachey, Thomas E. "British War Propaganda and American Catholics." *Catholic Historical Review* 61 (1975): 48–66.

Hinckley, Ted C. "American Anti-Catholicism during the Mexican War." *Pacific Historical Review* 31, no. 2 (May 1962): 121–37.

Liebmann, Max. "Les Conclaves de Benoit XV et de Pie XI." *La Nouvelle Revue* 38 (July-August 1963): 46–53.

Mancini Barbieri, Alessandro. "Nuove ricerche sulla presenza straniera nell'esercito pontificio, 1850–1870." *Rassegna Storica del Risorgimento* 63 (1986): 161–86.

Manzanares, Julio. "Las conferencias episcopales en tiempos di Pio XI: Un capitulo inedito y decisive de su historia." *Revista Espanola des derecho canonico* 36 (1980): 15–56.

Margiotta Broglio, Francesco. "Marzo 1917: Uno Stato per il papa." *I Classici di Limes: Quando il papa pensa il mondo* 1 (2009): 109–12.

Martini, Angelo. "La Nota di Benedetto XV alle potenze belligeranti nell'agosto 1917." In *Benedetto XV, i cattolici e la prima guerra mondiale,* ed. Giuseppe Rossini, 361–86. Rome: Edizioni Cinque Lune, 1963.

McCormack, Richard B. "The San Patricio Deserters in the Mexican War." *The Americas* 8 (October 1951): 131–42.

McKeown, Elizabeth. "Apologia for an American Catholicism: The Petition and Report of the National Catholic Welfare Council to Pius XI, April 25, 1922." *Church History* 43 (1974): 514–28.

———. "The National Bishops' Conference: An Analysis of Its Origins." *Catholic Historical Review* 66 (1980): 565–83.

McNeal, Patricia. "Catholic Conscientious Objection during World War II." *Catholic Historical Review* 61 (1975): 222–42.

Monsagrati, Giuseppe. "Alle prese con la democrazia, Gran Bretagna e U.S.A. di fronte alla Repubblica romana." *Rassegna Storica del Risorgimento* 86 (1999): 287–306.

Petracchi, Giorgio. "La missione pontificia di soccorso alla Russia (1921–1923)." In *Santa Sede e Russia da Leone XIII a Pio XI*, ed. Massimiliano Valente, 122–80. Vatican City: Libreria Editrice Vaticana, 2002.

Pizzorusso, Giovanni. "I cattolici nordamericani e la sovranità temporale dei romani pontefici." In *Gli Stati Uniti e l'Unità d'Italia*, ed. Daniele Fiorentino and Matteo Sanfilippo, 113–24. Rome: Gangemi, 2004.

Pollard, John F. "Il Vaticano e la politica estera italiana." In *La politica estera italiana, 1860–1985*, ed. Richard J. B. Bosworth and Sergio Romano, 197–230. Bologna: il Mulino, 1991.

Reher, Margaret M. "Leo XIII and Americanism." *Theological Studies* 34 (1973): 679–89.

Ridolfi, Maurizio. "La Démocratie en Amérique di Tocqueville e la sua ricezione nell'Italia del Risorgimento." In *Gli Stati Uniti e l'Unità d'Italia*, ed. Daniele Fiorentino and Matteo Sanfilippo, 133–39. Rome: Gangemi, 2004.

Romero, Federico. "Democrazia ed egemonia: Woodrow Wilson e la concezione Americana dell'ordine internazionale nel Novecento." *Passato e Presente* 21 (2003): 17–34.

Schmitz, David F. "Speaking the Same Language: The U.S. Response to the Italo-Ethiopian War and the Origins of American Appeasement." In *Appeasement in Europe: A Reassessment of U.S. Policies*, ed. David F. Schmitz and Richard D. Challener, 75–102. Westport, Conn.: Greenwood Press, 1990.

Slawson, Douglas J. "The National Catholic Welfare Conference and the Church-State Conflict in Mexico, 1925–1929." *The Americas* 47 (July 1990): 55–93.

Slayton, Robert A. "Al and Frank: The Great Smith-Roosevelt Feud." In *FDR, the Vatican and the Roman Catholic Church in America, 1933–1945*, ed. David B. Woolner and Richard G. Kurial, 55–66. New York: Macmillan, 2003.

Spini, Giorgio. "I rapporti politici tra Italia e Stati Uniti." In *Italia e Stati Uniti nell'età del Risorgimento e della Guerra Civile*, ed. Agostino Lombardo, 121–87. Florence: La Nuova Italia, 1969.

Stock, Francis L. "The United States at the Court of Pius IX." *Catholic Historical Review* 7 (1923): 103–22.

Tokareva, Evghenia S. "Le relazioni tra l'URSS e il Vaticano: Dalle trattative alla rottura (1922–1929)." In *Santa Sede e Russia da Leone XIII a Pio XI*, ed. Massimiliano Valente, 199–261. Vatican City: Libreria Editrice Vaticana, 2002.

Veneruso, Danilo. "La Conferenza di pace di Parigi nel contesto dei tentativi di Wilson e Lenin di costruire aree ad estensione mondiale." In *La Conferenza di pace di Parigi fra ieri e domani (1919–1920)*, ed. Antonio Scottà, 45–72. Soveria Mannelli: Rubbettino, 2003.

Wangler, Thomas E. "John Ireland and the Origins of Liberal Catholicism in the United States." *Catholic Historical Review* 56 (1971): 617–29.

# INDEX OF NAMES

Adams, Charles Francis, 1n1
Adams, John, 1–2
Adamthwaite, Anthony P., 59n2
Ahern, Patrick H., 16n41
Alder, Selig, 60n5
Ambrosius, Lloyd, 57n100
Angelini, Giovanna, 6n11
Antonelli, Sara, 6n12
Armstrong, David, 3n4

Bagby, Wesley M., 61n6
Barry, Colman J., 16n42
Bedini, Gaetano, 6–7
Benedict XV, ix, xiv, 11–14, 19–25, 28–30, 32, 34, 38, 41–44, 46–47, 50, 52–53, 57–58, 66–67, 69, 72, 73, 75–76, 78, 92, 138, 159
Bennett, David H., 66n20
Benson, William, 56
Bernardini, Filippo, 80
Billington, Ray A., 64n15
Blakely, Paul L., 118n19, 125n45
Blatchford, Richard M., 7n14
Boardman, Roy, xvi
Boggiani, Tommaso Pio, 81
Bonzano, Giovanni, ix–x, 12–13, 20–21, 30–34, 36–37, 39, 43, 46–56, 73, 75, 77n45–78, 80, 85–91, 94, 101–2, 104
Borah, William, 134
Borgongini-Duca, Francesco, 136
Bosworth, Richard J.B., 23n65
Bottum, Joseph, 160n36
Bowers, Henry, 65
Brady Garvin, Genevieve, 145, 148
Brady, Nicholas, 52
Broderick, Francis L., 99n55, 104
Browder, Robert, 129n58

Brown, Charles, 146n121
Brown, Nicholas, 3n4–4
Brownlee, William C., 64
Bruckberger, Raymond L., 99n55
Bruti Liberati, Luigi, 11n29, 37n17, 43n46, 50n72
Buchanan, James, 4
Burke, John J., 70–72, 74, 80–81n61, 94, 96–99, 103–4, 133–35, 139–40, 143, 148n129–49
Busch, Joseph, 47n60
Butler, Andrew, 5

Calhoun, Frederick S., 27n77
Callahan, Patrick H., 98, 116, 125
Calles, Plutarco Elias, 101–3, 135
Campanini, Giorgio, 151n3
Cardenas, Lazaro, 134
Carmody, Martin, 134
Carranza, Venustiano, 11, 35, 101
Carroll, John, 2
Carter, Michael H., 164n55
Cass, Lewis, 4–5
Cass, Lewis Jr., 5
Castagna, Luca, ix, xi–xii, 6, 114n3, 140n97, 167–69
Casula, Carlo Felice, 91n28
Catts, Sidney J., 67
Ceci, Lucia, 143n110
Celler, Emanuel, 161
Cerretti, Bonaventura, 47, 72–73
Chadwick, Owen, 159n35
Challener, Richard D., 143n109
Chappin, Marcel, 138n94
Chenaux, Philippe, 19, 22n62, 24–25n71, 37, 160
Child, Richard, 80

187

# INDEX OF NAMES

Chiron, Yves, 92n37
Cicognani, Amleto Giovanni, xi, 128, 131–33, 136–37, 139–45, 147–49, 153–55n19, 157–59, 162, 164, 168
Cicognani, Felix, 3
Clark, Bob, xvi
Clemenceau, Georges, 54
Clements, Kendrick A., 26n76
Cleveland, Grover, 16
Coco, Giovanni, 112n101, 138n94
Colby, Bainbridge, 55
Coleman, Frederick, 127n50
Colombo, Arturo, 6n11
Confalonieri, Carlo, 77n47
Confessore, Ornella, 15
Connelly, James F., 4n7, 7n13
Conte, Alfonso, xvi
Conway, John S., 165n57
Coogan, John W., 26n75
Coolidge, Calvin, 62, 95–97, 100, 102–4
Cooney, John, 137n90
Corcoran, Thomas, 154
Cornwell, John, 152n6
Cortesi, Arnaldo, 146, 157n25
Cortesi, Filippo, 160
Cossio, Luigi, 95n41
Costigliola, Frank, 60n3
Coughlin, Charles E., xi, 146
Cox, James, 56, 86n7
Cracco, Giorgio, 91n28
Cuddy, Edward, 29n82
Curley, James M., 116
Curran, Edward L., 121
Cushman, Edwin C., 3n4

D'Agostino, Peter, x, 11, 29n83, 32n5, 34, 43, 90n23, 110–11n
Dalin, David G., 160n36
Dalla Torre, Giuseppe, 44n51
Daniels, Josephus, 135
de la Huerta, Adolfo, 101
De Lai, Gaetano, 75, 79, 81
De Lucia, Carlo, 5n10
De Martino, Giacomo, 104–5, 107, 110–11n

De Rosa, Gabriele, 91n28, 114n3
DeConde, Alexander, 27n78
Del Pero, Mario, 25n72–26n75, 61
Della Chiesa, Giacomo. *See* Benedict XV
Devlin, Patrick, 25n73
Di Nolfo, Ennio, 9n18–10, 59n1, 163n50
Diaz, Pascual, 103
Diggins, John P., 109n89
Dix, John, 4–5
Dodd, William, 152
Dougherty, Dennis, 55, 75, 77–79, 82, 102n66
Douglass, Bruce R., 100n56
Dowling, Victor, 52
Doyle, Robert C., 65n19
Duffy, Mary C., 121
Dumenil, Lynn, 61n7
Durand, Jean-Dominique, 77n47

Eagan, Maurice James, 89
Elliott, Walter, 17
Ellis, John T., 11n27, 18n50–20, 30n1, 43, 50n72, 80, 82, 99n56
Ernst, Eldon, 69
Esslinger, Dean R., 28n79
Evans, Hiram W., 97–98

Falbo, Italo, 146
Fall, Albert, 102
Farley, James, 116–17, 121, 123, 125, 142
Farley, John, 70–71, 75n42
Fattorini, Emma, 38n20, 77n47, 126n48, 138
Fay, Sigorney, 47
Feliciani, Giorgio, 83
Fenerty, Clare, 135
Ferrante, Agostino, 110–11n96
Fietta, Giuseppe, 144
Filippi, Ernesto, 101
Fink, Carole, 91n31
Fish, Hamilton, 135
Fitzgerald, James, 119
Fletcher, Henry P., 112
Flynn, Edward J., 116
Flynn, George Q., 114, 117, 119n23, 121n29, 123n39, 126n49, 165n57

# INDEX OF NAMES

Fogarty, Gerald P., x, xii, xvi, 11n25–12n30, 15n38, 17, 19, 20n56, 43n46, 50n72, 73n38, 75–76n44, 79n51–80, 82–83n67, 85n1, 154n17, 158n30, 167
Folliard, Edward T., 142
Ford, Nancy G., 66n23
Forsyth, John, 3n5
Fosdick, Harry E., 69
Franco, Francisco, 150–52
Franco, Massimo, 1n2
Franklin, Benjamin, 2
Freidel, Frank B., 116n10
Fumasoni Biondi, Pietro, x, 95–97n49, 100, 102–4, 106–8, 127–30n62, 140n97, 168
Furniss, Norman F., 66n24

Gabaccia, Donna R., 63n13
Gaffey, James P., 20n55, 76n43
Galeazzi, Enrico, 145, 156
Gannon, Michael V., 19n52
Gannon, Robert I., 136n90, 154n17
Garrett, John W., 112n102
Garzia, Italo, 22n61
Gasparri, Pietro, xi, 12–14, 21–22n59, 24n69, 32, 36, 38–39, 45, 47–51, 53–59nn87–99, 73, 75–78, 81, 86, 88n12–92, 95–96, 100, 101n62, 104, 106n76, 107n82, 112, 136, 138
Gastaldi, V. Paolo, 6n11
Gibbons, James, ix–x, 11n27, 14–17, 20, 30–31, 34, 36–40, 43, 47–55, 70, 72–76, 84
Gil, Portes, 103
Gilbert, James B., 62n9
Gill, George J., 165n57
Gillis, James, 119
Glass, Joseph, 33
Gleason, Philip, 29n82, 100n56
Glennon, John, 74
Glentworth, Horatio, 3n4
Glover, Jonathan, 26n74
Goebbels, Joseph, 153
Goldberg, David J., 61n7
Gonner, Nicholas, 32–33
Göring, Hermann, 153

Grant, Madison, 63
Greene, George W., 3n4
Gregory XVI, 3, 64
Gribble, Richard, 101n60
Guinsburg, Thomas, 57n101, 60n4

Haas, Francis J., 118, 122, 123n37
Hachey, Thomas E., 20n55
Hanna, Edward J., 43, 74, 79, 101–3n70
Harding, Warren, 56, 60–62, 68–69, 80, 86–91, 95, 100–1
Hartley, James J., 86
Haskell, William N., 93
Hayes, Carlton J.H., 111
Hayes, Patrick, 51, 52n80, 55, 71, 75, 96, 123–24, 131–32, 158
Hayes, Robert, 122
Hearn, Edward, 96
Hecker, Isaac, ix, 17
Heflin, James T., 105
Hennesey, James, 14, 37n18, 70n31, 81n60, 84n73, 99n56
Herzberger, Matthias, 23
Hesemann, Michael, 160n36
Hicks, John, 61n7
Higham, John, 31, 62n9, 63, 67n25
Hinckley, Ted C., 65n19
Hitler, Adolf, 77n47, 126, 138–39, 151–53, 158–60, 168
Hollenbach, David, 100n56
Hoover, Herbert, x, 80, 107–8, 113, 117–18, 120
House, Edward, 52, 54
Howard, Henry, 24
Howells, William D., 3n4
Huber, Raphael M., 102n68, 118n20
Hughes, Charles E., 91n32, 102
Hull, Cordell, 134, 152n8, 161–62
Hurley, Joseph, 144
Hyvernat, Henry, 78

Ickes, Harold, 122, 124n42
Ireland, John, 16–18

Jay, John, 42n41
Johnson, Herschel V., 156

# INDEX OF NAMES

Kalinin, Mikhail, 131
Kane, Paula M., 79n51
Kantowicz, Edward R., 123n40
Kari, Camilla J., 72n36
Kauffman, Christopher, 71n33
Keane, James, 74
Keane, John, 16
Keegan, Robert, 132
Kelley, Francis C., 20n55, 55
Kellogg, Frank, 96, 102
Kennedy, John Fitzgerald, xii
Kennedy, Joseph, xii, 122, 125, 149, 154, 156–57, 160, 163
Kilby, Thomas, 67
King, Rufus, 7–10
Kirk, Alexander, 142
Knock, Thomas, 46n57
Kurial, Richard G., 11n25, 115n7, 164n55

LaCerra, Charles, 115n6
Lally, Francis J., 114
Langley, Lester D., 133n80
Lansing, Robert, 24, 36, 39–43, 45, 49
Ledochowski, Vladimir, 81, 143
Leffler, Melvin P., 60n3
LeMay, Michael C., 62n9
Lenin, Nikolaij, 53n86, 91
Leo XIII, ix, 14, 16–19, 21, 119
LeRoy, Daniel, 3n4
Letterio, Mauro, 21n58
Leuchtenburg, William E., 113n1
Lichtman, Allan J., 105n75
Liebmann, Max, 77n46
Lincoln, Abraham, 8
Link, Arthur S., 25n73
Litvinov, Maxim, 132
Lloyd George, David, 92
Lockwood, Robert P., 64n14
Lomask, Milton, 2n3
Lombardo, Agostino, 28n81
Long, Breckinridge, 143, 163
Lubell, Samuel, 117n18, 125n47
Lucchesi Palli, Ferdinando, 3
Lyons, Charles W., 96

Macchi di Cellere, Vincenzo, 35, 40, 42, 45n56, 48–49
Macrì, Gianfranco, 140n97
Maglione, Luigi, 160n40–164n53
Mancini Barbieri, Alessandro, 8n16
Manzanares, Julio, 83n69
Marella, Paolo, 128–130
Margiotta Broglio, Francesco, 23n63, 24n68
Marshall, Charles G., 106
Martel, Gordon, 57n101
Martin, Jacob L., 4–6
Martini, Angelo, 38n21
Mastai Ferretti, Giovanni Maria. See Pius IX
Matteotti, Giacomo, 109
Mazzenga, Maria, xvi
McAvoy, Thomas T., 17n48, 37n19, 99n54
McCloskey, John, 75n42
McCormack, Richard B., 65n19
McCormick, Joseph, 88
McDonnell, Charles, 74
McGowan, Raymond, 125, 128
McIntyre, Marvin, 124, 135n86, 149
McKeown, Elizabeth, 72n35, 74n40, 81n58
McKinley, William, 18
McNamara, Patrick H., 93n38
McNamara, Robert F., 16n41
McNeal, Patricia, 66n21
McNicholas, Thomas J., 118n19, 158
McShane, Joseph, 71n32
McVeigh, Rory, 97n50
Menshausen, Fritz, 154n15
Mercier, Desirè, 48–49, 54–55
Merry del Val, Rafael, 19, 21, 75–77, 81, 138
Miccoli, Giovanni, 160n36
Miller, Robert M., 69n29
Mitty, John, 148
Moeller, Henry, 80
Monsagrati, Giuseppe, 6n12
Moore, Robert W., 134
Morrow, Dwight, 103
Moynihan, James, 16n41

# INDEX OF NAMES

Muench, Aloisius J., 119
Muldoon, Peter J., 71–74
Mulligan, William, 52
Mundelein, George, 20, 55–56, 74–75n42, 97, 102n66, 123–24, 135, 140, 152–55, 158–60, 168
Murphy, Charles F., 115
Murphy, Frank, 120, 122
Murphy, William C., 120
Mussolini, Benito, xi, xiii, 77n47, 109–11, 126n48, 138, 140, 143–44, 151n1, 159, 165

Nicholson, Jim, 4n8
Ninkovich, Frank, 36
Nitti, Francesco Saverio, 55
Nogara, Bernardino, 143–44
Nordstrom, Justin, 66n22

O'Brien, David J., 17n46, 120
O'Brien, Morgan, 52
O'Brien, William D., 120
O'Connell, Denis J., 16–17, 20
O'Connell, James P.E., 78
O'Connell, Marvin R., 17n47
O'Connell, William H., xi, 52, 54, 70, 75–79, 81, 103n70, 123, 136–37
O'Loughlin, J. Callan, 86
O'Mahoney, Joseph C., 134
O'Reilly, John, 65
O'Shaughnessy, Michael, 117
Obregon, Alvaro, 101, 103
Olds, Robert, 103
Orlando, Vittorio Emanuele, 13n32, 47
Orsenigo, Cesare, 152
Osborne, Francis, 161n42

Pacelli, Eugenio. See Pius XII
Pagano, Sergio, 138n94
Page, Thomas N., 24, 41–42nn35–39, 54n89
Palmer, Mitchell, 55
Parker, Alton, 115
Parrella, Roberto, xvi
Parsons, Wilfred, 111, 119
Perkins, Frances, 122n32

Petracchi, Giorgio, 92n36
Phelps, Wilbur F., 67
Phillips, William, 152, 156, 158–60, 164
Pierce, Franklin, 7
Pignatti, Bonifacio, 149, 151
Pinto, Carmine, xvi
Pipes, Richard, 92
Pius VI, 2
Pius IX, xiv, 3–8, 10, 65, 77
Pius X, 14, 18–19, 21, 75
Pius XI, x–xv, 69, 77–81, 83–84, 91–95, 103n70–104, 112, 114, 116, 119, 121, 126, 128, 132, 136–38, 144–45, 151–52, 157–59, 167
Pius XII, xi–xiii, xv, 25, 38, 84, 112, 126–33, 136–40, 142–49, 151–61, 159–161, 163–66, 168–69
Pizzardo, Giuseppe, 91–92, 128, 129n56, 144, 149
Pizzorusso, Giovanni, 28n81
Plotke, David, 113n2
Polin, Joseph, 125n47
Polk, James, 4
Pollard, John F., 22n60–23n65
Pompilj, Basilio, 75
Puricelli, Carlo, 77n47

Quirk, Robert E., 101n61

Rampolla, Mariano, 138
Randall, Alexander W., 7n14
Raskob, John J., 105
Ratti, Achille. See Pius XI
Reading, Rufus, 48
Reeds, Rebecca, 65n18
Reher, Margaret M., 18n51
Reilly, Daniel F., 17n47
Renzi, Walter A., 22n61
Ridolfi, Maurizio, 6n11
Rolandi Ricci, Vittorio, 91n32
Romano, Sergio, 23n65
Romero, Federico, 36n15
Roosevelt, Franklin Delano, xi–xvi, 11n25, 56, 86, 112–18, 120–26, 129, 131–36, 139–44, 146–51, 154–66, 169
Roosevelt, James Jr., 154–55

# INDEX OF NAMES

Roosevelt, Theodore, 115
Rosenman, Samuel I., 115–16nn8–13, 135n85
Rossi Longhi, Alberto, 146
Rossi, Luigi, xvi, 18n49, 114n3, 169
Rossini, Giuseppe, 39n21
Ruiz, Leopold, 103
Rumi, Giorgio, 12n29
Russell, William, 71, 73
Ryan, John A., 99n53, 111, 117, 119, 122–23, 125
Ryane, John D., 52

Salandra, Antonio, 13
Salvatorelli, Luigi, 22n61
Salvemini, Gaetano, xiii
Sanders, James W., 99n54
Sanders, William C., 3n4
Sanfilippo, Matteo, 6n11, 28–29nn80–81
Sarto, Giuseppe Melchiorre. *See* Pius X
Sartori, Giovanni, 2–3
Satolli, Francesco, 16
Sbarretti, Donato, 103n70
Schmitz, David F., 109n89, 143n109
Schrembs, Joseph, 71, 73, 79–81, 103n69
Schulzinger, Robert D., 60n4
Scottà, Antonio, 12n30, 22n60, 39n21, 44, 53n86
Scroop, Daniel, 116n12
Semeraro, Cosimo, 77n47, 83n68
Sepiacci, Luigi, 15
Seton-Watson, Christopher, 44n48
Seward, William, 8–9
Shannon, William V., 121
Sharp, William, 42n40
Sheehy, Maurice, 122
Sheerin, John B., 81n61
Shepherd, John, xvi
Shore, Elliott, 16n42
Siegel, Katherine A., 129n58
Skinner, Richard, 117n14
Slawson, Douglas J., 71n34, 76n43, 103n71
Slayton, Robert A., 115n7
Smith, Alfred E., x–xi, 52, 105–8, 115–17
Smith, Thomas, 52

Smith, Tony, 27n78
Sonnino, Sidney, 13n32, 23, 35, 40n27, 42, 44, 45n53, 48–49
Spadolini, Giovanni, 22n59
Spellman, Francis J., xi–xii, 112, 136–37, 145, 147, 149, 154–56, 158, 160n38, 162–64
Spini, Giorgio, 28n81
Spring Rice, Cecil, 40n26
Sterba, Christopher M., 29n82
Stillman, W.J., 3n4
Stock, Francis Leo, 3n4, 7n14, 141
Stoeffler, Jane, xvi
Sturzo, Luigi, 109
Surratt, John, 8
Sweeney, Charles P., 67n26

Tacchi Venturi, Pietro, 143
Tardini, Domenico, 144–45, 159
Taylor, Myron C., xii–xiv, 9n18, 163–65, 169
Tedeschini, Federico, 153n13
Teitelbaum, Louis M., 11n27
Thompson, Charles W., 116n11
Tierney, Richard, 33
Tittmann, Harold H. Jr., xiv, 160n37, 162n46, 165–66
Tocqueville, Alexis de, 6n11
Tokareva, Evghenia S., 94n39
Traina, Richard P., 150n1
Traynor, William J.H., 66
Trohan, Walter, 135n88
Trommler, Frank, 16n42
Tumulty, Joseph, 53

Vagnozzi, Egidio, 137
Van Buren, Martin, 3n6
van Heuvel, Jules, 24
Van Rossum, William, 75
Veneruso, Danilo, 53n86
von Bergen, Diego, 153
von Bulow, Bernhard, 23
von Faulhaber, Michael, 152
von Ritter, Otto, 25
Vorovskij, Vaclav, 92

# INDEX OF NAMES

Wade, Wyn C., 68n28
Walker, Frank, 149
Wallace, Henry, 117
Wallace, Les, 66n20
Wallace, Lillian P., 17n45
Walsh, David I., 52, 124
Walsh, Edmund A., 93–94, 118, 129, 131–32
Walsh, Frank, 119, 125
Walsh, James J., 75n42
Walsh, Louis, 79
Walsh, Thomas J., 116, 121
Wangler, Thomas E., 17n47
Watson, Tom, 67
Wayman, Dorothy G., 78n48

Welles, Sumner, 161–62n45
Wilkes Booth, John, 8
Wilson, Woodrow, ix–x, xiv, 11–12, 20–21, 25–27, 29–31, 33–37, 39–45, 47–57, 59–60n4, 66–68, 73, 75, 85–86, 90, 98, 101
Wister, Robert J., 16n43
Wood, Percy, 154n18
Woodring, Harry H., 163
Woodward, Stanley, 164
Woolner, David B., 11n25, 115n7, 164n55
Wynne, John, 46, 47n59

Zivojinovic, Dragan R., 24n67, 40n30

*A Bridge across the Ocean: The United States and the Holy See between the Two World Wars* was designed in Frutiger Serif with Ostrich Sans and Meta display type and composed by Kachergis Book Design of Pittsboro, North Carolina. It was printed on 55-pound Natures recycled and bound by Sheridan Books of Ann Arbor, Michigan.

www.ingramcontent.com/pod-product-compliance
Lightning Source LLC
Chambersburg PA
CBHW070253010526
44107CB00056B/2442